We have been Christians for many years. One of the most common concerns in Christian marriages is praying together with your spouse. *A Cord of Three* has been most helpful in our marriage. We try to set aside sometime each day, read the message for that day and pray together. We found this time together brings us closer to God and, even after 50 years of marriage, brings us closer to each other. We would consider this book as a wonderful tool for marriage enrichment.

Arthur Lee, M.D. and Carol

As a couple, and individually, we have made *A Cord of Three* our daily devotional book for the past three years. Through these devotions, we have had God confirm His word to us, confirm His direction for our lives, brought us to tears of repentance, and given us reason to hope. Reading this devotional book along with the Bible has strengthened our marriage and our relationship with Jesus. Without a doubt Sheryl Sanderson has truly been *inspired* by the Holy Spirit in writing this devotional book. We highly recommend *A Cord of Three*.

Pastor Gord & Jeanne Demchuk

Sheryl is not only a gracious woman of God, but she is also a model wife and mom to her sons. When I first read the manuscript of, *A Cord of Three: Christ Centered Marriage*, I was not surprised by her insight and writing ability. As a teacher for many years, Sheryl has developed a notable strength in communication.

What I loved most was the depth of spiritual wisdom she generously shows in her writing. Every devotion seemed to hit its bulls-eye. To me, her book is akin to Chamber's *My Utmost for His Highest*—it explodes with colour and supernatural application.

I recommend both Sheryl and her writings with enthusiasm.

Dr. Barry Buzza
Lead Pastor, Northside Church
Author

a CORD of THREE

Devotional for couples to strengthen their relationships with each other and God

Sheryl Sanderson

A CORD OF THREE: CHRIST-CENTRED MARRIAGE

Copyright © 2014 by Sheryl Sanderson

All rights reserved. Neither this publication nor any part of this publication may be reproduced or transmitted in any form or by any means, electronic or mechanical, including photocopying, recording or any information storage and retrieval system, without permission in writing from the author.

Unless other indicated, all scriptures taken from the Holy Bible, New International Version®, NIV®. Copyright © 1973, 1978, 1984, 2011 by Biblica, Inc.™ Used by permission of Zondervan. All rights reserved worldwide. www.zondervan.com. The "NIV" and "New International Version" are trademarks registered in the United States Patent and Trademark Office by Biblica, Inc.™ Scripture quotations marked (NLT) are taken from the Holy Bible, New Living Translation, copyright © 1996, 2004, 2007 by Tyndale House Foundation. Used by permission of Tyndale House Publishers, Inc., Carol Stream, Illinois 60188. All rights reserved. Scripture quotations marked (NKJV) are taken from the New King James Version®. Copyright © 1982 by Thomas Nelson, Inc. Used by permission. All rights reserved. Scripture quotations marked (NASB) are taken from the New American Standard Bible®, Copyright © 1960, 1962, 1963, 1968, 1971, 1972, 1973, 1975, 1977, 1995 by The Lockman Foundation. Used by permission.

Printed in Canada

ISBN: 978-1-4866-0190-5

Word Alive Press
131 Cordite Road, Winnipeg, MB R3W 1S1
www.wordalivepress.ca

Cataloguing in Publication information may be obtained through Library and Archives Canada

Acknowledgements

Firstly, I am forever grateful to the other two members of my "cord of three"—my Saviour Jesus Christ and my loving husband, Russell. Without them, this book would never have been created. This is my first book, and I wrote it in response to what I believe the Lord has been saying to me. My husband encouraged me from the original concept through the entire project. He also patiently edited my work and gave valuable feedback.

I would like to express my appreciation to my parents, all my Sunday School teachers, pastors, Bible study leaders, and others who have contributed to my spiritual development. Many of them will see the influence of their teachings within these pages.

Thank you to many friends who have encouraged me from the beginning of this project. Someone always seemed to be sent to me with encouragement or insight at just the right time. Thank you all for your faithfulness.

Thank you to Pastor Barry Buzza, for sharing your wisdom and experience in publishing. Thank you, Jennifer Roberts, for offering your graphic arts advice, and Derrick Sanderson for creating the cover design.

INTRODUCTION

United with God

Though one may be overpowered, two can defend themselves. A cord of three strands is not quickly broken.
(Ecclesiastes 4:12)

The picture on the cover of this book is of a three-stranded cord. The red strand symbolizes the blood of Jesus Christ, the blue strand the husband, and the pink strand the wife.

It is so true that when you're going through a difficult time or circumstance, having someone else with you gives you strength. No matter the battle you face, or the type of support available, there is strength in sharing your burden with someone else. When you invite Jesus to be the centre strand of your relationship, He will give you stability and strengthen your marriage.

This is not a one-time, "we said it in our wedding vows" thing. You must endeavour to keep your marriage Christ-centred at all times—in the good times and the bad.

Picture the cord again. Now imagine that one of the strands is too loose, too tight, or torn. What happens to that cord? The centre strand, Jesus, always remains strong. It's up to each of you to maintain your role in relationship to Him, and to each other. If even one of you chooses to disregard your relationship with Jesus, or with the other spouse, strain and tension will result.

Fortunately, Jesus will always be there when you turn back to Him. He remains strong, but it will be up to you to reconnect or repair your relationship with Him. However, we're only human. We may not always have the opportunity to reconnect or repair our relationship with our spouse once it's compromised.

I would encourage you to invite Jesus to be the centre of your relationship—and head of your home—at all times.

Spend time together daily in prayer.

JANUARY 1

The Power of a Praying Spouse

Beloved, I pray that in all respects you may prosper and be in good health, just as your soul prospers.
(3 John 2, NASB)

One of the most loving things you can do is pray for one another. No matter how much you love your spouse, God loves him/her more. You simply need to continually lift your spouse to the Lord in prayer. In addition, as much as you would want everything to go well and be perfect for your spouse, there are some things you cannot control. With God, all things are possible. We need to trust Him to know what's best for us and the ones we love.

Spend time right now, and on a regular basis, checking in with each other, asking, "What things would you like me to be praying for in your life? Would you please pray for me regarding *(fill-in-the-blank)*?" Remember to check back to see how these prayers are answered.

Your prayers may start by thanking the Lord for blessing you with the spouse He has given you. Thank God for some of the qualities you see in your spouse. Ask the Lord to show you how you can be a blessing to your spouse. Thank Him for the prayers He has already answered for you and your spouse.

Furthermore, talk to God about what plans He has for your lives as individuals, and as a couple.

JANUARY 2

This Is Beyond Me!

Carry each other's burdens, and in this way you will fulfill the law of Christ.
(Galatians 6:2)

We all have those days when we feel the weight of the world on our shoulders. How fortunate this is for those who have a loving spouse with whom to share their burdens.

To be able to go to another person whom we trust as much as our own consciences is indeed a blessing. Many times when I go to my husband in distress, all I really need him to do is listen. Knowing I can throw at him all my confused thoughts and sort them out later is very comforting. Over the years, my husband has developed the knack of distinguishing between those times when I'm just venting or thinking out loud and when I truly need intervention and active assistance.

There have been times, however, when my spouse has had to lovingly and gently point out that my attitude needs to be adjusted. He has an amazing ability to make me re-evaluate a situation when necessary, without making me feel judged or condemned. I can always trust that His input comes from a loving concern for what's right and best for me.

There are also times when nothing can be humanly done to change what has happened or to fix a problem—for example, the death of a loved one, a physical injury, or an illness. With these burdens, a spouse's only possible response is to assist us with our limitations and nurture. These are the times when we should join together in prayer. Fortunately, all things are possible for God, and He desires what is good for us.

I'm so grateful to have a spouse who's willing to stand beside me and lift me up in times of difficulty. I'm also grateful that in all things we can join together and go to our Father in heaven.

Now is the time to hold tightly to the cord of three.

JANUARY 3

Weather-Proofing Your Marriage

Therefore everyone who hears these words of mine and puts them into practice is like a wise man who built his house on the rock. The rain came down, the streams rose, and the winds blew and beat against that house; yet it did not fall, because it had its foundation on the rock. (Matthew 7:24–25)

Those of us who know Jesus know that He is always with us. However, in the good times we tend to "go it alone." It is when times are tough that we call out to Him. He's there, but can you hear what He's saying or where He's directing you to go? Do you know His voice?

God shouldn't be an emergency doctor that you only call in times of trouble. Each of you needs to spend time investing in the word of God and hearing what He has to say about your relationship with Him and with each other. If you each have a deep relationship with Jesus, and are committed to your marriage, you will be able to stand on a solid foundation when the storms of life arrive.

We cannot always control the happenings around us, but we can choose how we react. A lifeguard cannot control the water conditions or the behaviour of others, but she can study and practise rescue skills to be prepared to take action if necessary. When a problem arises, that's not the time for her to dig out the books and training videos. Take preventive action in your life and marriage. Be prepared, avoiding difficulties when possible and handling the storms of life when necessary. Spend time regularly reading the Bible and being familiar with the word. Spend time in prayer and develop a relationship with Jesus. Spend time nurturing your marriage relationship.

Jesus is always with you, especially in times of trouble. He is all-knowing and all-powerful. Allow Him to work in your lives and your marriage.

JANUARY 4

God Knows Best

He has made everything beautiful in its time. He has also set eternity in the hearts of men; yet they cannot fathom what God has done from beginning to end.
(Ecclesiastes 3:11)

I was feeling rather discouraged one day, doubting that God hears and responds to my prayers. My young son was sick with a high fever, so I prayed for His healing. I expected immediate results, and that just didn't happen. Was it that I didn't pray with the right words? Maybe I didn't have enough faith?

As I read through Acts 9, I was struck by how obedient and faithful the disciple Ananias was. He fully trusted that God knew all things—past, present, and future. He knew also that God watched over him and was in control. When told by God, Ananias went to the very man who was out to kill all Christians (Saul), laid hands on him, and prayed for healing. Ananias' prayer was short and simple, but inspired by God Himself.

Then there is Peter. Peter had the faith to step out of a boat and walk on water when Jesus told him to. Peter went on to do many miraculous things as directed by Jesus. He went with strangers not knowing where or why they were going, because God told him to. Peter was obedient to God rather than to his own imagination, whims, and fears.

Well, the truth is I don't know why my son wasn't healed instantly. Only God knows, and He knows the bigger plans. The fact is, my son did get better in time. In God's time, not mine. My job is to allow God to work in my life. I will trust God to do what is best.

Is there something God is telling you to do? Have you asked? Pray with your spouse that you would both hear and obey the calling God has given to each of you.

JANUARY 5

Fruits of the Spirit

> *But the fruit of the Spirit is love, joy, peace, patience, kindness, goodness, faithfulness, gentleness and self-control.*
> (Galatians 5:22–23)

It sounds wonderful, doesn't it? Why do we experience such conflict then? Of course we desire to experience love, joy, peace, patience, kindness, goodness, faithfulness, gentleness, and self-control. How wonderful it would be for these aspects to always permeate our lives. It is a goal worthy of our best effort!

What do we need to do to attain these attributes? Is it just a matter of willpower? Maybe we need to avoid or ignore the negative things happening around us. If I don't see or hear the bad, it doesn't exist and can't hurt me, right? Perhaps I should spend my energy looking for the silver lining and practise saying kind things to myself and others.

God's word tells us that it isn't possible for us to attain this wondrous state in our own willpower. To experience inner transformation, one must receive freedom from the laws of nature, a freedom which Jesus Christ gave us through His death and resurrection. He sent the Holy Spirit to live within us.

> *For the sinful nature desires what is contrary to the Spirit, and the Spirit what is contrary to the sinful nature… But if you are led by the Spirit, you are not under law.* (Galatians 5:17–18)

The answer lies in allowing the Holy Spirit to work in your life. If you walk by the Spirit, you will receive all of these fruits.

Encourage one another and lift each other up in prayer so that you can both seek to walk in the Spirit and not allow the burdens of this world to sidetrack you, robbing you of experiencing these fruits.

JANUARY 6

Children Are a Gift from God

Behold, children are a gift of the Lord, the fruit of the womb is a reward. (Psalm 127:3, NASB)

We have been blessed with two very special sons. When they were born, I remember gazing at them in marvellous wonder. Looking at the miracle of our newborns, I was reassured of the reality of God.

One day when our children were a toddler and an infant, respectively, I thought about the responsibility of raising them. I felt a little overwhelmed. Then the Lord spoke, reminding me that these precious children didn't really *belong* to my husband and me. In fact, they belonged to *Him.* He had just entrusted my husband and I to help raise them in this world. The Lord oversees our family and is always with us to guide our ways.

We have done our best to raise them in God's grace and instruct them in the ways of the Lord. Thankfully, they both accepted Christ at an early age. Did we make any mistakes along the way? Of course. Did our children ever rebel or spurn our authority? Yes, there were times of conflict. However, God is a big God, and He has guided our children along their pathways to becoming the godly men they are today.

There may be times when you find that your children, in spite of your best efforts, make choices you know are in discord with what's in their best interest and what God would have for them. Remember that God is all-knowing and all-powerful. Lift your children to the Lord in good times and bad. Pray for them and trust in *Him.*

Thank You, Lord, for giving us the privilege of partnering with you in raising Your children.

Do you consult God in how to raise your children? Teach your children the word of God and provide them with the opportunities for spiritual development. Leave the rest to God.

JANUARY 7

Spread the Word

I am not ashamed of the gospel, because it is the power of God for the salvation of everyone who believes... For in the gospel a righteousness from God is revealed, a righteousness that is by faith...
(Romans 1:16–17)

Praise God for His mercy and grace, for who in his own right is worthy of salvation and eternal life? Thankfully, even though we are sinners, we can be saved by the grace of God through faith in Jesus Christ. Oh, that the entire world would know Jesus and receive His gift of salvation! Would we not then have peace and harmony?

Are you ashamed of the Gospel? Do you desire that many would know Jesus and receive His gift of salvation? Have you ever stood by, saying nothing while others mocked Christianity or the existence of Jesus? Have you ever found yourself listening to a non-Christian's misery and not offered to pray for them? When someone has marvelled at your strength in times of trouble, have you given the glory to God?

As Christians, through our faith, we have received righteousness from God. Righteousness means being right with God. What could be more righteous than offering others an opportunity to receive salvation? How are you putting aside your shame and proclaiming salvation others?

Spend some time discussing with your spouse how others might see God working in your life. Talk about how you might be willing to reach out to others and offer them what God has given you.

Remember that this gift is to be received; you cannot force someone to accept it.

JANUARY 8

Power of the Holy Spirit

But you will receive power when the Holy Spirit comes on you. (Acts 1:8)

A baby cannot make himself worthy to receive care and food. Neither can we make ourselves good enough, smart enough, or worthy enough to receive the gift of the Holy Spirit. Only God can enable our spiritual growth.

Some people think that when you're baptised in the Holy Spirit, you become an all-powerful spiritual giant. There is this misconception that we will become all-knowing and wise. The only being who can meet these attributes always has been, and always will be, God Himself.

Baptism in the Holy Spirit is actually designed to reduce us so that more of God's presence and power can dwell in us and flow through us. The glory is not ours, but His. In Acts 2:4, we read, *"All of them were filled with the Holy Spirit and began to speak in other tongues as the Spirit enabled them."* Christ Himself reported,

> *I tell you the truth, the Son can do nothing by himself; he can do only what he sees his Father doing, because whatever the Father does the Son also does.* (John 5:19)

If Jesus was unable to attain all knowledge and power on His own in human form, certainly no other man will ever be able to.

Do miracles happen then? Does man ever receive wisdom? Of course. Many of us have received wisdom from the Holy Spirit and witnessed the power of the Holy Spirit working through man. The point is, the more we try to accomplish wisdom and power on our own, the less we will have. When we totally submit to God and His work through us, we can attain wisdom and witness miracles in His name.

Pray for one another that you would empty yourselves of your own agendas, allowing the power of the Holy Spirit to work in your lives today.

JANUARY 9

Let Your Light Shine

And surely I am with you always, to the very end of the age.
(Matthew 28:20)

We all have those times in our lives when the road gets a little rough. Sometimes life seems *very* challenging. I often wonder how people who don't know Jesus make it through. I am grateful that I can rest in the knowledge that Jesus is, and always will be, there for me. His word has promised that.

As a Christian, I'm aware that how I handle difficult times speaks to those around me. What great opportunities they are to witness to others. Today's verse promises God's presence; it doesn't say anything about never encountering difficulties here on earth. In fact, going through difficult times helps us grow spiritually. If everything were to be perfect all the time, we would likely begin to believe we didn't need God and could handle things on our own.

My prayer during one such difficult period in my life went something like this: "Lord, I thank You that through this time of many changes and challenges You are always with me to comfort and guide me. Help me to be Your light and a comfort to those around me. Thank You for Your never-ending faithfulness. Amen."

How we handle the good times also speaks to those around us. We must take care not to take all the credit for experiencing good things. Rather, we must remember to thank God for His blessings and give Him the glory.

It is so important to keep our eyes on Jesus and take the time to listen for His direction. When life throws challenges your way, are you ready? Is there a situation in your lives, or in the life of a person in your circle of influence, for which you need God's comfort right now? Pray for the Lord's comfort and wisdom and let His light shine through you both.

JANUARY 10

Gratitude for God's Faithfulness

And he passed in front of Moses, proclaiming, "The Lord, the Lord, the compassionate and gracious God, slow to anger, abounding in love and faithfulness…"
(Exodus 34:6)

This verse was spoken to Moses after he returned from Mount Sinai with the stone tablets on which God wrote the Ten Commandments. In great distress over the sin of his people, Moses threw the stone tablets to the ground and broke them. God, in His faithfulness and mercy, did not turn His back on the people. Instead He instructed Moses to chisel out two more stone tablets and start the process over again.

Moses repented for himself and his people. He bowed down in worship to the Lord. Moses pleaded with God to forgive them and begged God not to leave them. Thankfully, God complied with Moses' request.

I'm so grateful that God continues to show compassion and forgiveness to all His children to this day. I have definitely made mistakes in my walk, as have the people I'm responsible for leading. At such times, it is good to remember God's mercy and take note of the things we are grateful for in the life He has given us. I would encourage each of you to write a list of all the things for which you are grateful. Secondly, write a list of all the things for which you hope. Include things that apply to yourself and those whose Christian walks you may be guiding.

Conclude your time with a prayer that goes something like this: "Lord, I thank You that through this time of many changes and challenges You are with me and always will be. Thank You for your comfort and guidance. Help me to be Your light and a comfort to those around me. Thank You for your never-ending faithfulness. Amen.

JANUARY 11

This is the Day!

This is the day the Lord has made; let us rejoice and be glad in it. (Psalm 118:24)

It is a fact that each day comes from the Lord. As Christians, we believe God created the world. He has assigned to you each and every day of your life on this earth. Embrace that fact and allow the Lord to have charge of your day. It's not up to you to solve the problems of the world. Merely listen to God and do the part He gives you as best as you can. Let Him orchestrate the details.

The psalmist also said, *"Let us rejoice and be glad in it."* This is the part you can control. It's a choice. Regardless of what's happening in the world around you, you can choose to be positive or negative. I was reminded of this today when I received an email in response to a short message I had sent. I sent the original message with the intent of expressing concern and love. The response, it seemed to me, expressed annoyance. I was hurt. The receiver had misunderstood! However, when I paused to consider the email, I realized that *I* had read the annoyance in it. My defensive attitude affected how I received the message. I could now choose to be hurt, or receive the message for what it was.

What attitude have you put on today? Give special consideration to your attitude towards your spouse. Are you open to receiving encouragement and blessings, or are you defensive and bitter? As for me, I will choose to rejoice. I'll need to make this choice each and every day, again and again. Remember, today is the day that spills over into eternity.

> Yesterday is history, tomorrow is a mystery, today is a gift of God, which is why we call it the present.[1]

[1] Bil Keane, "Quotes About Present," *Goodreads.com*, September 23, 2013 (http://www.goodreads.com/quotes/tag/present).

JANUARY 12

Time

But seek first his kingdom and his righteousness, and all these things will be given to you as well.
(Matthew 6:33)

Jesus spoke these words to His disciples when He was teaching on the anxieties of this world. Yes, we all have responsibilities. We need to responsibly take care of all that God has provided us and purposed for us to do. But where are our priorities?

How many of us get up in the morning thinking of all the things we have to accomplish that day? Work has to be done, the daily chores need to be tended to, there are people we need to contact. It's so easy to charge headlong into the day in a frantic rush.

Where do you think God was while you were sleeping? Do you think He's just waking up and clearing His head as well? Of course not! He knew from the beginning of time what this day has in store for you. He hasn't forgotten the responsibilities you have.

There are many days when I awake and become disconcerted with all I think I need to accomplish. However, I've learned that cutting out—or shortening—my devotional time isn't helpful. On the contrary, when I set aside time to be with God, my day ends up going much smoother. I seem to be able to accomplish the things that really matter. I often even have time left over, or I'm able to address something I hadn't even considered! Furthermore, I have much more inner peace. If you seek God first, lining yourselves up with His will, He will guide you in getting done the things that really need to be accomplished today.

Don't forget to also spend quality time with your spouse. You may think you're saving time, but where do you think your marriage relationship will end up in the long run?

JANUARY 13

Just for You

While they were eating, Jesus took bread, gave thanks and broke it, and gave it to his disciples, saying, "Take it; this is my body." Then he took the cup, gave thanks and offered it to them, and they all drank from it. (Mark 14:22–23)

Imagine Jesus' disciples sitting in a meadow by some beautiful trees, having a picnic. Now imagine Jesus standing off to the side under a big, leafy shade tree. He holds out to you bread and wine. He's smiling and glowing with love and joy. He's personally offering you the symbols of His life! The disciples continue their picnic with much joy and laughter. Jesus then returns amongst His disciples and joins in the picnic as if He had never left.

Yes, each of us is but one of many Christians. Thankfully, God isn't limited as we are. He can oversee the entire world and yet be present with each of us. Just as He has personally offered us the gift of salvation, He also offers us communion with Him.

Communion is a sacred event. In Luke 22:19, Jesus instructed His disciples to take the bread and wine as symbols in remembrance of Him. Christian churches today have communion in various forms. The procedure may vary, but the point is always the remembrance of Jesus. There is something very intimate in taking communion in a personal relationship with Jesus, and at the same time joining together with other Christians.

I would suggest that you take time with just Jesus and your spouse to partake in this very special practice of remembrance. Take time to join together in focussing on Jesus and all that His ultimate sacrifice means to you. Share your thoughts with one another. How much more intimate does it get?

JANUARY 14

It's Who You Know

Once the owner of the house gets up and closes the door, you will stand outside knocking and pleading, "Sir, open the door for us." But he will answer, "I don't know you or where you come from."
(Luke 13:25)

I received a call today from a dear Christian friend. She knew somebody whose child was going through a serious illness, and who was also going through some medical difficulties of his own. My friend asked me to pray for their situation. When I asked her if this person had a relationship with Jesus, she assured me that her friend was a Christian; he and his family just hadn't gone to church in a long time. She wasn't sure where he stood as far as reading the Bible or spending time in devotions. She informed me that his mother worked for a Christian, his good friend was a pastor, and his cousin went to a church in the community. You can see where I'm going with this, can't you?

In this world, we sometimes take advantage of our connections. You might be able to get preferential treatment from someone you know when it comes to getting tickets or appointments. Based on the personal reference of a friend or family member, you might get a job interview, or even the job itself. However, Jesus has clearly warned us that if we don't choose to develop a personal relationship with Him, when the time comes, He won't be able to honestly say that He knows us.

Do you have a relationship with Jesus? Do you know Him or do you only know *of* Him? Chances are, if you're reading these devotionals, you're in an ongoing relationship with Jesus. Therefore, you don't run the risk of standing outside the door knocking. Never take the risk of allowing that relationship drift away.

Thank the Lord for your friend in Jesus.

JANUARY 15

How Big of a Sin Counts?

But if Christ is in you, your body is dead because of sin, yet your spirit is alive because of righteousness.
(Romans 8:10)

We are all sinners. In God's eyes, if we break even one law a little bit, we are as much a sinner as someone who breaks a lot of laws, or a more important law. Think about this for a minute. If the maximum speed limit is fifty km/h and you drive at eighty km/h, are you breaking the law? What about if you drive at sixty kilometres per hour? How about fifty-one kilometres per hour?

Okay, now think of a sin. Let's pick a big one—murder. If you murder lots of people face-to-face in cold blood, is that a sin? What about if you kill one person unintentionally by your carelessness; is that a sin? What if in your anger, you wish someone else to die; is that a sin? What if you think angry thoughts about someone else?

It's impossible for us to live free from sin in our flesh. Why should we then try to obey the Biblical laws? The reason is that God's love is never-ending. His is the gift of life. We must strive to be in His will, to be obedient to Him.

Likewise, we aren't always pleasing to our spouses. Hopefully, we always desire to be in unity with them, but being in the flesh, we will sometimes fail. Does that mean you should stop attempting to please them, or not care how your words or behaviours affect them? I hope not! Set your hearts on what is right with God. Also set your hearts on what is pleasing to your spouse.

Pray that God would reveal to you any area of your life for which you need to seek forgiveness and repentance with Him, or with your spouse. Thank God again for the relationship you have with Him and with the spouse He has blessed you with.

JANUARY 16

Why Do I Do the Things I Do?

Each one should test his own actions. Then he can take pride in himself, without comparing himself to somebody else, for each one should carry his own load.
(Galatians 6:4–5)

What do these verses tell us? How does one test one's own actions? The Apostle Paul is referring to our heart's intent. Are you doing what you're doing only because everybody else is, or are you motivated by what you believe is right according to your understanding of what the Lord is telling you? Is "fitting in" more important than doing what you believe to be right?

When my children were young, they often argued with me when I told them they couldn't do something. They would say, "Everybody else's parents let them!" We would both realize how weak that argument was, so I'd respond with, "Well, I guess their parents don't love them as much as I love you."

There were also times when my children and I role-played difficult social situations they might find themselves in. In their early years, I told them that they were welcome to use me as an excuse. If they felt they were being asked to be in a situation that was inappropriate, they could say they weren't allowed, that they had to be home by a certain time, or that Mom just said no. As they grew older, they were better able to make decisions and take a stand based on their own beliefs.

So, when everybody else is running down their spouses, telling coarse jokes, or doing other things that make you feel uncomfortable, what do you do? Do you compromise and join in? Do you remove yourself from the situation? Do you openly state your belief? What's right for you? Test your own actions, and unless you receive a word from the Lord instructing you to do otherwise, let others test theirs.

JANUARY 17

Forgive One Another

Be kind and compassionate to one another, forgiving each other, just as in Christ God forgave you.
(Ephesians 4:32)

It is not possible to go through life here on earth without feeling wronged at some point. Sometimes we're able to recover from the sting of feeling wronged quicker than other times. In fact, some people seem more adept at releasing the sting. We know from the word of God that we are commanded to be forgiving.

You might say, "I'm okay with that. I've forgiven everyone I need to." Or perhaps, "Forgive them for what? I don't know what I've done wrong! They're the one who needs to change." But are you still upset or angry about a past event? Do you continue to rehash old happenings? Are you trying to use denial or your own willpower to overcome hurt or anger? What is it you can't quite let go of?

Our God is all-powerful. Allow Him to work His peace in your situation. Seek Him to help you set your heart right. Ask your spouse to join you in prayer. Turn to God and pray something like this: "Lord, please reveal to me what I need to forgive and help me to let go. Help me to release You to do any work You need to do in this situation. Amen." If you don't feel the release, turn to God again. You can't fool Him into thinking you're fine when you're not. He is a patient and forgiving God.

Now, do you feel the need to seek forgiveness from God and/or the other person for a wrong attitude or misunderstanding? Are you at peace? Feel the weight of the burden lift from your shoulders and the joy of the Lord return to you in all things.

God forgives us so much. Although the situation may be great in human terms, we have so little to forgive in comparison to what we have been forgiven for.

JANUARY 18

Life Goals

With this in mind, we constantly pray for you, that our God may count you worthy of his calling, and that by his power he may fulfill every good purpose of yours and every act prompted by your faith.
(2 Thessalonians 1:11)

The Apostle Paul wrote these words as an encouragement to the church of Thessalonica. I would also use them to encourage you. Paul commended this church for their growing faith and the love they had for one another. He assured them that God was watching over them. Paul encouraged them to keep their eyes on Jesus in anticipation of Jesus' return to earth. That's exactly what I desire to do, and I would encourage you to do the same.

What are your goals? Are your goals strictly for earthly recognition and personal gain? Be assured that God desires good for us. If you are successful in earthly terms, that's not necessarily a bad thing, as some would judge. God is pleased to prosper us. Just keep your focus on Jesus. Do not allow the evil one to deceive you with pride.

The essence of this verse is that Paul was pleased with the heart intent of the people in the Thessalonica church. Their motivations for what they did were based on love and the glorification of the Lord. If you keep your heart intent in alignment with God's will, *"by his power he [will] fulfill every good purpose of yours and every act prompted by your faith."*

This might be a good time to talk over your own goals with your spouse. Are they motivated by your focus on Jesus and desire to glorify the Lord? Are they in alignment with God's word? Are there any goals you may need to amend or adjust in light of this word?

Let us use Paul as an example. Lift up others in prayer, especially your spouse. Pray for God's power to be fulfilled in them. Look for opportunities to encourage them in their faith and spiritual goals. Give all glory to God!

JANUARY 19

By What Name Are You Known?

However, if you suffer as a Christian, do not be ashamed, but praise God that you bear that name.
(1 Peter 4:16)

In our North American culture, women usually take on their husband's last name when they get married. I was given the name Sheryl Charlton at birth, but I am now known as Sheryl Sanderson. Other wives may choose to keep their birth name, add their husband's last name to their maiden name, or use the title "Ms." In other cultures, such as in Latin America, it's more common for the woman to take on her husband's last name *in addition* to her birth name—which would make me Sheryl Sanderson Charlton.

I would suggest that it's not important what name one chooses to use. Wives, what is the motive for the name you chose? Is it out of tradition, to be identified with your husband; for your career, to demonstrate your independence; or because you don't have brothers or male cousins to carry on your family name? We need to consider our names, and why we have chosen them.

As for me, I want to first, and most importantly, be known as a Christian. I recognize that I'm not fully like Christ. I know that I'll never attain that perfection this side of heaven. However, my desire is to be identified with Christ. I want to see with His eyes, hear with His ears, and speak His words in love. I desire for others to see, seek, and glorify God because of my example. Secondly, I choose to be identified with my husband. I desire to love and respect him, and be a blessing to him. My desire is for other couples around us to see our relationship and be encouraged to focus on their own marriages.

May those marriages, and especially yours, be strengthened as you seek the righteousness of the Lord.

JANUARY 20

It's All Good

And we know that in all things God works for the good of those who love him, who have been called according to his purpose.
(Romans 8:28)

This is a well-known verse of hope and encouragement. Unfortunately, it is often misused. This verse doesn't mean that God is a fairy Godfather who grants you any wish you desire. Nor does it mean God is obliged to you in any way if you recite this verse.

Let's take a closer look. The verse starts with *"And we know…"* How do you know? By faith. Today's verse says *"that in all things God works for the good of those who love him."* Does this say He makes everything perfect for Christians? No. We are not of this world, but we live in this world. Sometimes God permits things to happen for His divine purpose. Bad things sometimes happen because we do things our own way, and God won't force His will on us. Sometimes bad things happen as a consequence of our poor choices, or those of another person. Bad things happen for a variety of reasons.

Some take this verse to mean that God will make things work for our comfort, wealth, or ease of life. In fact, it is to conform us to the image of Jesus. What could be better than that?

The verse continues: *"…who have been called…"* You have a part to play, too. This verse refers to Christians who walk out their faith with Him. And finally, the verse ends with, *"according to his purpose."* What is God's purpose? His purpose is to conform us into the image of Jesus. God can, and will, guide you in finding the "good." He may use a situation to grow your faith, reveal His glory, and give you understanding and compassion for those He leads to you now or in the future. Only God knows.

You may not understand the "good" right now. Trust in Him. He wants to breathe hope in you and through you.

JANUARY 21

Who Is Righteous?

For it is not those who hear the law who are righteous in God's sight, but it is those who obey the law who will be declared righteous.
(Romans 2:13)

"I go to church every Sunday! Sometimes I even go there during the week. I've memorized 'x' number of verses by heart!" So you have it all covered, right? Obviously not.

Jesus presented a parable in Matthew 21:28–31. A father of two sons asked each of them to go work in the vineyard. The first son said he wouldn't go, but reconsidered and ended up going. The second son said he would, but then didn't follow through. Jesus asked, *"Which of the two did what his father wanted?"* (Matthew 21:31) Jesus' point was that it doesn't matter what has gone on before. Anyone who believes in Him, and obeys God's word now, will be declared righteous.

Have there been times when you believed God was directing you to do something, but you ignored Him or made excuses? "I'm not worthy enough. I'm not smart enough yet. I haven't been a Christian long enough. Someone else could do it better than me. I don't have time." Have there been times when you knew what God's word said, but chose to do otherwise because it suited you better?

Fortunately, our God is a God of second chances. He will not turn His back on you, but wait for you to turn your face back towards Him. That doesn't mean there might not be consequences for your choices, but God will not ignore your repented heart.

Pray together with your spouse. Ask God to reveal to you any areas in which you have known His word but have not been obedient. Ask for His forgiveness, and receive it. Choose today to be obedient to God's word and will for your lives.

JANUARY 22

Condemnation or Reconciliation

You who preach against stealing, do you steal? You who say that people should not commit adultery, do you commit adultery? You who abhor idols, do you rob temples? You who brag about the law, do you dishonor God by breaking the law? As it is written: "God's name is blasphemed among the Gentiles because of you."
(Romans 2:21–24)

The Apostle Paul scribed these words to the Jewish Christians in Rome. The Jewish leaders presented themselves as having a superior relationship to God. They supposedly had the authority to teach the law. Paul challenged this authority, which they based solely on their birth as Jews. Paul emphasized that they should look at their own heart motivation. Taking on the superior role carries great responsibility.

I have heard more than once, "If he/she is such a good Christian, and they behave like that, then I'm not interested." Our claim to be Christian carries the responsibility of always striving to be Christ-like.

Are you reflecting God's glory to the world around you? Do you steal (take something without permission, or more of something than you should)? Do you commit adultery (lust after someone other than your spouse)? Do you rob temples (withhold some or your entire tithe to spend on other things)? Do you brag about the law ("I'm a good and perfect Christian")?

Do not allow God's name to be blasphemed because of you. Encourage those who have been offended to take responsibility for their own relationship with God, and to bring peace and unity among God's people. Help them to know which behaviours are of God and which are of the flesh.

Pray with your spouse and ask God to reveal to you any wrong attitudes either of you may be carrying. Ask God to free you from wrong attitudes and create in you a right spirit.

JANUARY 23

Assumptions

Aren't you the Egyptian who started a revolt and led four thousand terrorists out into the desert some time ago?
(Acts 21:38)

Assumption. What a dangerous word. The Winston Dictionary of Canadian English defines assume as: "to take upon oneself, especially without authority; to take for granted."[2] Can you begin to imagine the position the Apostle Paul found himself in merely because someone else "assumed" something about him? Earlier, some people had made another assumption in regards to Paul: *"They had previously seen Trophimus the Ephesian in the city with Paul and assumed that Paul had brought him into the temple area"* (Acts 21:29). This would have been a very serious offense! However, neither assumption was true.

Hopefully, the assumptions made about you, or the assumptions you make about others, don't leave anyone in such a dangerous place. Our assumptions tend to be based on our previous knowledge (e.g. if I turn the key in the ignition, the car will start) or on our attitudes (e.g. all police officers, teachers, and preachers are good/bad).

Is your attitude that all people are good until proven otherwise, or that all people are out to do harm until they earn your trust? How about your attitude towards each day? Do you wake up in the morning dreading the challenges God or others will present to you, or do you have an attitude of gratitude for all the opportunities and blessings that await you?

Of course, there are times when we need to be cautious of dangerous situations. However, be careful what you assume. Be slow to believe evil of others. Be careful of what you repeat about others when you don't have the authority. Pray that God will give you wisdom each and every day, that He will create a right attitude in you.

---

[2] *The Winston Dictionary of Canadian English* (Toronto, ON: Holt, Rinehart and Winston of Canada, 1969), 33.

JANUARY 24

Stay Tuned

Through the Spirit they urged Paul not to go on to Jerusalem. But when our time was up, we left and continued on our way.
(Acts 21:4–5)

The Apostle Paul received gifts from various churches for the church in Jerusalem. Naturally, he made plans to deliver the gifts. In Paul's own words, the Holy Spirit had warned him several times that he would soon face prison and hardships (Acts 20:23). A prophet named Agabus then came from Judea to warn Paul also: *"The Holy Spirit says, 'In this way the Jews of Jerusalem will bind the owner of this belt and will hand him over to the Gentiles'"* (Acts 21:11). Paul insisted on going anyway. He declared that he was willing to suffer what lay ahead, to fulfill what he believed God wanted of him. The prophecies were fulfilled, and Paul indeed ended up arrested and imprisoned.

Did Paul get it right? Indeed, God did give Paul *"the task of testifying to the gospel of God's grace"* (Acts 20:24). However, would God have sent the Holy Spirit several times to warn Paul about Jerusalem if His intent was for Paul to go there? Could Paul have found another way to have the gifts delivered? God did continue to use Paul and gave him opportunities to witness for Him, but there were consequences for Paul's determination to complete the job using his own plans.

I believe we can learn from Paul's mistakes. Listen not only for God's direction in your life, but continue to listen to how He would have you reach His goals. I also encourage you to take heart. Even the Apostle Paul didn't always get it right, but our gracious God continued to work through him. He will use you, too, even if you make mistakes.

JANUARY 25

Be Positive

Finally, brothers, whatever is true, whatever is noble, whatever is right, whatever is pure, whatever is lovely, whatever is admirable—if anything is excellent or praiseworthy—think about such things.
(Philippians 4:8)

I recently spoke to someone who had made big changes in her life. When noticing how negative someone always seemed to be, she recognized her own life going down that road. This realization was life-changing. She decided at that point to rid herself of negativism and look for the good. With her change in attitude, she made tremendous improvement to her physical, emotional, and spiritual life.

I happened to speak to another woman two days later with a family member who had made some poor choices. She, too, committed to not hearing or seeing the bad, but focusing on the good, deciding not to say anything negative about this person (or anyone else). She wouldn't even allow others to make negative comments about them, even if they were well-meaning. This woman took it one step further and encouraged her family member every chance she got. She told him that she enjoyed his presence, that she loved him, and that she would be waiting for him when he wanted to come to her. She put aside judgement and condemnation. Instead she chose to love and encourage.

Now, she wasn't living in denial. If you have a car accident, you need to deal with the repairs. You do have a choice, though: you can continue to be angry and judgemental of the person who hit you, or you can thank God for His protection. After all, you're alive to deal with the repairs.

I have great admiration for both of these women. What a wonderful world we would live in if everyone could grasp this. I, for one, desire to follow the instructions Paul sent the church in Philippi. I want to think about the "praiseworthy" things. How about you?

JANUARY 26

Anxiety

Do not be anxious about anything, but in everything, by prayer and petition, with thanksgiving, present your requests to God. And the peace of God, which transcends all understanding, will guard your hearts and your minds in Christ Jesus.
(Philippians 4:6–7)

A mother's parting words to her child might be, "Drive carefully!" Well, that seems like obvious advice. Are they going to purposely drive recklessly into a ditch? Probably not. She might better say, "I love you. I thank God for you. I'm grateful that God will watch over you." Then there's the retort: "Don't worry!" This suggests that worry can be turned off just because someone told you to. It's like saying to the snow, "Don't land on my driveway."

It's not wrong to care or be concerned about people or things. The important thing is what you do with that concern. Concern that motivates you to action is good. A friend is ill and you offer to take them a meal or do a chore for them. You see poverty and choose to donate to a food bank.

However, a constant state of anxiety about everyone and everything isn't healthy—and it's not godly, either. Do you really believe God is in control? *"Be still, and know that I am God"* (Psalm 46:10). If you desire *"the peace of God, which transcends all understanding,"* ask for it. You may know this peace instantly, or you may need to practise it like any other discipline. God's grace is present; you will receive according to your faith.

Does this mean that once you receive this peace, you'll be free to go for all times and all things? No. Notice the condition: *"but in everything by prayer and petition, with thanksgiving, present your requests to God."*

What do you need to prayerfully thank God for today? Present your request and receive His peace.

JANUARY 27

Civil Obedience

Remind the people to be subject to rulers and authorities, to be obedient, to be ready to do whatever is good...
(Titus 3:1)

We are very fortunate here in Canada to have democratic governing systems. Democracy gives us direct input into whom and how our country, provinces, and municipalities are run. Although your vote may not always be for the person or party that's ultimately elected, you have the opportunity to participate in the selection. However, we are not immune to the same political squabbling and mudslinging visible all around the world.

The word of God instructs Christians to be subject to their governing bodies. We are to be obedient to the rules (laws). Furthermore, in Exodus 22:28, we are instructed: *"Do not blaspheme God or curse the ruler of your people."* Yes, as Christians, we are citizens of a heavenly kingdom, but Jesus would have us get along with our governments. After all, *"Everyone must submit himself to the governing authorities, for there is no authority except that which God has established"* (Romans 13:1). If there are laws (or potential laws) that you believe are in opposition to our Lord, there are processes through which we can make our opinions and concerns known. In the meantime, are you *"ready to do whatever is good"*?

Do you keep your talk free from bad-mouthing our government representatives? Do you pray for your governing bodies—not just for your parties or candidates of choice to win at election time, but for ongoing wisdom and discernment? Do you take opportunities to encourage civil employees and express your appreciation for what they do? Are you involved in supporting efforts to make our communities and world a better place?

JANUARY 28

The Greatest Commandment

Jesus replied: "'Love the Lord your God with all your heart and with all your soul and with all your mind.' This is the first and greatest commandment."
(Matthew 22:37–38)

Many of us can quote this verse by memory. It was, in fact, used by all Jews in their daily prayers, even during Old Testament times. It is a worthy goal and was emphasized by Jesus as *"the first and greatest commandment."* It's easy to understand that if all people were to obey this one commandment, we would be living in a very great world indeed!

Well, you cannot impose your will on others. In fact, even our Lord won't impose upon those who do not wish Him to be a part of their lives. What you choose is your own focus. Our heart refers to our emotions, how we feel; our soul refers to who we are, our personalities; and our mind refers to our thoughts. Jesus tells us to have all these components focused on loving God at all times.

I would encourage you to pray this verse every day. As you spend time with Jesus and pour out your love to Him, may your walk draw closer and closer to Him. May you recognize the love and blessings of Jesus in all you see and do. If you accomplish this, then even when you make mistakes, Jesus will forgive you, and likely so will those you have inadvertently offended.

As a side-effect of this focus on loving the Lord your God with all your being, you'll have an influence on those around you, recognizing in them a deeper love of God. When this happens, give thanks to God for His graciousness in allowing you to be His representative, bringing His goodness to others who will in turn give their love and all the glory to God.

JANUARY 29

Faithfulness

Now faith is being sure of what we hope for and certain of what we do not see.
(Hebrews 11:1)

Do you have those moments when you feel weak in your faith? Are there times when you just don't feel your faith is strong enough to do all that you believe the Lord is asking of you? You're not the only one. Don't entertain such thoughts and give the enemy a foothold.

Read Hebrews 11. The author gives a quick summary of some of the Biblical examples of people who met huge challenges and yet chose their faith and weren't found lacking. Relating to those situations and responses is very encouraging.

"Yes," you say, "But those were Bible characters." Let me tell you a quick modern-day story. A friend of mine recounted an experience in which she set the kettle on the stovetop to heat water for tea. As she waited for it to boil, she busied herself with tidying up the kitchen counters. As she reached over the kettle for something, she bumped it. The kettle tipped over and spilled boiling water over one of her arms and down the counter. She immediately raised her in arms in praise and prayer. After she finished praying, she stopped and looked. Her arm was fine! There wasn't even any redness! Then she looked at the counter her arm had been leaning on. The heat of the boiling water had curled up the laminate top. She then ran out to share the news with her husband. He returned to the kitchen and witnessed the kettle and countertop. Being a carpenter, he offered to repair the counter right away. She asked him not to. When her faith was weak, she wanted to be able to look at the damaged counter again. Praise God!

What reminders can you create to help you in your times of weakness?

JANUARY 30

Be True

Above all, my brothers, do not swear—not by heaven or by earth or by anything else. Let your "Yes" be yes, and your "No," no, or you will be condemned.
(James 5:12)

James was encouraging all Christians to be honest. It was a reminder of what Jesus had taught in Matthew 5. In essence, we should simply say what we mean, without deception. As Christians, our words should be counted on.

This verse doesn't forbid solemn oaths, however. In Exodus 22, Moses refers to oaths being used to validate the truth in settling property disputes. In Romans 1, Paul claims God as a witness to His faithfulness and honesty in preaching the Gospel. Then, in Matthew 26, when the high priest charged Jesus *"under oath by the living God"* (Matthew 26:63), Jesus responded in truth. We swear an oath of faithfulness in our wedding vows and other legal matters.

James was referring to flippant, profane, or blasphemous oaths. Yes, I believe it's okay to avoid telling someone about a surprise gift planned for a later date. I also believe it's okay to avoid hurting someone's feelings over matters of no eternal importance, such as how their new hairstyle or piece of clothing looks. However, we should also not attempt to deceive or manipulate with words.

As Christians, hopefully we are known to be honest people. I would suggest that you pray for the Lord to reveal to you any remaining area of your attitude that needs to be more honest. Give Him permission to bring to mind those situations where you have been less than honest. Are there any areas you need to correct or bring into alignment with God's will? We are to be a reflection of Jesus Himself.

JANUARY 31

No Condemnation

My prayer is not that you take them out of the world but that you protect them from the evil one.
(John 17:15)

A friend of mine recently took a public step of faith. It was a very good thing, but she was concerned about what the reaction of some of her not-yet Christian family and friends might be. Her desire was to keep her focus on Jesus, but the reality was that she felt the pull of distraction.

How many of us have found ourselves in similar situations? We may be in front of a wide range of people, or in a small circle of friends and family. I was raised in a loving family and I tried very hard to be a "good" daughter, for which I received condemnation. I also tried very hard to be "good" during those difficult teen and young adult years. In fact, to this day I try to do what is "good" and "right" in the eyes of Jesus. Notice, however, that I said I "received condemnation." I had a choice. In fact, the very words "she's the good one" may not have even been intended as condemnation, but rather an acknowledgement.

It is good to be "the good one." My prayer for my friend was not that she would feel condemned, or thought of as weird, but that her public step of faith would be an attraction for others towards Jesus. I prayed that others would realize how important Jesus was in her life, and actually give Him some consideration themselves. Perhaps they would be drawn to the light they saw shining through her. If they didn't choose to receive Jesus today, then hopefully they would in the days to come, as they watched her example.

Keep your eyes on Jesus and let Him do the work in the hearts of those around you.

FEBRUARY 1

Companionship

The Lord God said, "It is not good for the man to be alone. I will make a helper suitable for him."
(Genesis 2:18)

God's good plan was for husband and wife to be companions and helpers for each other.

When you are first married, this seems obvious. You desire to spend as many waking moments with each other as possible. Then life crowds in. Things start happening in each of your lives; these may even be positive, such as personal growth, job promotions, children, or new hobbies. Gradually, you may find yourselves going in separate directions.

It's not wrong to grow and develop, or even to have separate interests and experiences. The point is to purposely continue to look for opportunities to work and play together. Companionship doesn't just happen. Some friendships we have for a time, while others are lifelong. Friends may move away, no longer interact with us in the same way (e.g. work together), or change the focus of their relationship energies. It is a choice to invest in a relationship. With your spouse, the commitment is to be a lifelong relationship. You are to invest much more in a marriage relationship than into a casual friendship. Furthermore, God has commanded that your marriage relationship be lifelong.

It is important that you continue to develop interests you enjoy together. What interests and activities do you currently share? What are some things your spouse is interested in? Is there some way you could be a part of them? What things are you involved in? Is there a component in which you could include your spouse?

FEBRUARY 2

Tithes[3] (Part One)

Give, and it will be given to you. A good measure, pressed down, shaken together and running over, will be poured into your lap. For with the measure you use, it will be measured to you.
(Luke 6:38)

Finances are one of those areas that can create tension within a relationship. Not only can money create tension between husband and wife, but also between man and God.

It is hoped that within your marriage relationship you have come to an understanding of how your income will be attained, and generally how it will be spent.

Have you given this same consultation between yourselves and God? Have you asked for His direction on how you earn or spend your family income? Whose money is it, anyway? In most situations, you've worked hard for your income. Who has provided those opportunities for you? The honest answer is, obviously, God.

As you sit down with your spouse to discuss your financial contributions to whichever congregation or fellowship you belong, consider these verses:

Now the law requires the descendants of Levi who become priests to collect a tenth from the people… (Hebrews 7:5)

Each man should give what he has decided in his heart to give, not reluctantly or under compulsion, for God loves a cheerful giver. (2 Corinthians 9:7)

[3] The word "tithe" comes from the Old English word *teogoba*, meaning "one-tenth."

FEBRUARY 3

Tithes (Part Two)

A tithe of everything from the land, whether grain from the soil or fruit from the trees, belongs to the Lord; it is holy to the Lord.
(Leviticus 27:30)

We previously discussed the meaning of the word "tithe." It is hoped that the three of you (God included) have come to an agreement on your financial contributions. However, have you considered aspects beyond money?

How much of your time do you devote specifically to ministry? This does not necessarily need to be done entirely within the limits of your congregation's ministry. Perhaps there are ways you could demonstrate the love of Jesus in your neighbourhood, community, or the world at large. Is there an area of ministry you could do as a couple? I invite you to explore the possibilities together.

The next question is *what* time you give to God. I know we are to always walk with Him, but what time do you specifically set aside for God? For example, when do you do your devotions? First thing in the morning, last thing before you go to sleep, maybe after dinner? Is that the best time of your day? If you're at your best in the morning, and you're trying to stay awake long enough to do your devotions at night, are you giving God the best part of your day? If you believe God is asking you to get up early on a Saturday and care for the needy, are you obedient or do you make excuses? If you believe God is asking you to take your vacation time and spend it on a particular missions trip, are you obedient or do you create more excuses? Do you think God needs you to complete His work? No, rather He is providing you with an opportunity for your benefit. Keep in mind that Jesus told us, *"For my yoke is easy and my burden is light"* (Matthew 11:30). He is not asking too much.

In conclusion, *"Give to Caesar what is Caesar's, and to God what is God's"* (Matthew 22:21).

FEBRUARY 4

Tithes (Part Three)

For where your treasure is, there your heart will be also.
(Matthew 6:21)

Have you ever heard or thought, "But we don't have any money left after paying all our bills!" or "We're busy people. We don't have any time left to take on a ministry."

Stop to meditate on today's verse for a moment. If you are truly putting God first and are in alignment with His will, how do the above statements apply? Take the time to discuss how well you're doing with your tithes at this time. Are you meeting or exceeding what the word of God instructs? Malachi 3:8 asks, *"'How do we rob you?' In tithes and offerings."* Are there areas in your lives where you're spending time or money that may not be appropriate?

Take heart! It's not all bad news! There are also great promises for us. The Lord also said:

> *"Bring the whole tithe into the storehouse, that there may be food in my house. Test me in this," says the Lord Almighty, "and see if I will not throw open the floodgates of heaven and pour out so much blessing that you will not have room enough for it."* (Malachi 3:10)

The Lord knows your needs and desires. He's not unaware of your income and expenses. He's not ignorant of your time commitments. He's not surprised by the crises that present themselves to you.

Go ahead: test God by bringing your whole tithe into His storehouse. Present to Him your "first fruits." Then watch for the blessings that will flow into your lives.

FEBRUARY 5

God's Children

Train a child in the way he should go, and when he is old he will not turn from it.
(Proverbs 22:6)

Raising children touches all of our lives. There are many joys in raising children, and many trials. Today I will address the trials, particularly around the teen years when kids are developing their own identities.

Take heart if your child is going through a particularly challenging time. I've heard that the closer children are to their parents, the more they may initially struggle to separate themselves in an attempt to determine exactly who they are in themselves. Unfortunately, this may be as extreme as trying drugs or alcohol, questioning their sexuality, tattooing or piercing their body, stealing, or lying. Whatever aspect they choose, it is a test as much for themselves as for their parents.

What do you do? Start with preventive measures. Anchor your marriage in Christ, teach your children the word of God and how it applies to their lives. Model for them what it looks like to be in the word (e.g. reading and studying the Bible, attending church), spend time in prayer, and turn to God in prayer at all times. If faced with a child's poor choice first, determine to *"not be overcome by evil, but overcome evil with good"* (Romans 12:21). Spend time looking to your Father in heaven for guidance. Present your wisdom at a non-confrontational time in as loving and caring way as possible.

If you're currently in the battlefield, I pray you find these verses and words helpful. If you are not yet there, I pray that your preventive training will save you, and your child, many struggles. If you have come through the other side, thank God. If you don't have children, my hope is that this will help you be understanding towards those friends or family in their time of challenge raising their children.

FEBRUARY 6

His Peace

Peace I leave with you; my peace I give you. I do not give to you as the world gives. Do not let your hearts be troubled and do not be afraid. (John 14:27)

There are many disappointments in life. There are also many reasons to rejoice. Just because we are Christians, we are not exempt from earthly life. There is a well-known expression that says you can look at life as a cup half-full, or a cup half-empty. I would encourage you not to be disappointed in what is not, but rejoice in what is. It may not change the actual event, but it lightens your load immensely.

I received a phone call the other day from someone who felt overwhelmed with all he had to do. He was discouraged and didn't think he could do it all. He didn't feel like those around him were being very understanding. We talked a bit about what he thought his major problems were and what areas he could do something about. We talked about how his stress level may be tainting his perspective of reality. I then asked if I could pray with him over the phone. We asked Jesus for His peace and calmness to help clarify his mind and set priorities. When I finished praying, I suggested he take a few moments after we hung up and sit quietly, allowing the Lord to answer. You can't hear if you don't listen. It seems contradictory to take more time aside when you're feeling the pressures of time, but it saves so much in the end.

We all live in a world of relationships and events. Take a few moments now and bask in the peace of our Lord Jesus Christ. Allow all your burdens to roll off your shoulders. That's not to say you don't need to do something to deal with your issues, but they're better handled in a peaceful manner than in a state of high anxiety. Both the experience and the result will benefit.

FEBRUARY 7

Effective Living

For if you possess these qualities in increasing measure, they will keep you from being ineffective and unproductive in your knowledge of our Lord Jesus Christ.
(2 Peter 1:8)

This verse grabs my attention! Who wouldn't want to avoid being *"ineffective and unproductive"* in their *"knowledge of our Lord Jesus Christ"*? So what is the key Peter gives us? The previous verses were directed to a church, that they were to

> *make every effort to add to your faith goodness; and to goodness, knowledge; and to knowledge, self-control; and to self-control, perseverance; and to perseverance, godliness; and to godliness, brotherly kindness; and to brotherly kindness, love.* (2 Peter 1:5–7)

Think of a person you know really well, perhaps your spouse. You know, the type of person with whom you can finish each other's sentences, or repeatedly start to say the same thing at the same time. Suppose someone reports to you something that person has said or done. You would know immediately if it was out of character. Either the person making the report was out-and-out lying or there was a huge misunderstanding.

Peter was encouraging the Christians to *"make every effort"* to know Jesus Christ and His teachings. That way, when false teachers came along, the Christians would immediately recognize them as false. Then the Christians in that church wouldn't be fooled and led astray.

The same holds true for us today. If you put into action the instructions our heavenly Father has provided us through this letter of Peter's, you too will know Jesus Christ. Your life will not be "ineffective and unproductive" for His kingdom, but fruitful. The better we know Jesus, the less able the evil one is to fool and distract us from all that Jesus would have for us.

FEBRUARY 8

Witnessing

But in your hearts set apart Christ as Lord. Always be prepared to give an answer to everyone who asks you to give the reason for the hope that you have. But do this with gentleness and respect.
(1 Peter 3:15)

When preparing for a missions trip to a country which was not English-speaking, I was told to have my testimony ready and be prepared to lead others in the sinner's prayer. What!? I wasn't sure I could do that, especially since I didn't speak the language! Could you? I thought that meant I had to have a prearranged script, that I had to be ready to spout off with set words, like a recording.

Originally, it was way out of my comfort zone! But then I spent some time thinking about it. We would have access to interpreters, eliminating the language excuse. Then I realized I have already given my testimony many times. I may not have stood up in front of a crowd and recapped my entire life, but I've shared from my experiences when speaking with others. What I shared depended on what I was trying to relate. Was it what God had done for me in family relations, work environments, personal growth, or miraculous healings? My daily life—and my words—should be an ongoing testimony.

What about the sinner's prayer? There are many scripted versions of this already in existence. However, my style is not "religious"; rather it's "relational." It's important for me to be able to share spontaneously as the Lord leads. Yes, it's important to cover the basics—belief that Jesus, the son of God, died for one's sins; Jesus' resurrection and power over death; confession of one's sins; asking Jesus for forgiveness; and inviting Jesus to rule one's life now.

We are called to be ready from our hearts to witness to others. We are also called to do so with gentleness and respect.

FEBRUARY 9

Jesus Only!

This is how you can recognize the Spirit of God: Every spirit that acknowledges that Jesus Christ has come in the flesh is from God, but every spirit that does not acknowledge Jesus is not from God. This is the spirit of the antichrist, which you have heard is coming and even now is already in the world.
(1 John 4:2–3)

We live in a society that includes many different cultures and religions. We've tried to be very tolerant and accommodating. That's all very nice, but as a result, there is great confusion as to what is true. Who is right? If someone does "good" things, does that make them authorities on what is right? If someone says they are "spiritual," does that mean they know Jesus? Will we see them in heaven in eternity? No!

The Bible is very clear on this. Only those who acknowledge *"that Jesus Christ has come in the flesh"* are from God. Remember, Satan is a fallen angel. He knows how to appear as light. So no, we're not all heading to the same place along different paths.

Jesus answered, "I am the way and the truth and the life. No one comes to the Father except though me." (John 14:6)

What about different cultures? Can someone from any culture be a Christian and therefore have the spirit of God? Yes! God's desire is that we all come to Him through His son Jesus Christ. Of course you can celebrate and remain in your own culture and still know Jesus. The caution here, as with any area in life, is to make sure you're not trying to serve two Gods. You must separate worship of other gods and spirits from the Spirit of God. You must turn from the first, and seek the latter.

When you are uncertain of a spiritual aspect, test it out. Does it line up with the word of God? Pray about it. To borrow a saying, "What would Jesus do?"

FEBRUARY 10

The Lure of the Evil One

And lead us not into temptation, but deliver us from the evil one. (Matthew 6:13)

Jesus knew no sin (2 Corinthians 5:21), yet He was persecuted and ultimately crucified. The Bible is full of examples of Christians who were persecuted for their faith. There are those who not only faced verbal abuse, but paid for their faith with their very lives. The same is true today. In many parts of the world, it is illegal to be a Christian. These Christians must meet in secret, have limited access to Bibles and spiritual teachings, and risk their freedom—maybe even their lives—for their faith.

Here in Canada, persecution is much more subtle. We think we are free to meet together and formulate our own beliefs without risk. After all, our country was founded on Christian values. However, we are no longer allowed to teach the Lord's Prayer or any other Christian aspect in our public schools. We now experience discrimination in many public areas. If someone of another faith wishes to abstain or modify a public or work practise for their belief, adjustments are made. However, if a Christian makes a similar request they are often met with ridicule or condemnation. How about the lure of sexual sins in our advertisements, movies, and dress? What about the love of bigger and better, or the love of money?

These struggles are not new. Read about the Apostle Paul's struggles in Romans 7. Like Paul, we find it difficult to do what we know is right and not do what we know is wrong. We tend to get confused by the lure of the enemy. He attacks our very souls.

So, as Jesus taught us, let us pray, *"Lead us not into temptation, but deliver us from the evil one."* Be on guard and ask the one true God for help. These are not rote words like an incantation, but a heartfelt plea.

FEBRUARY 11

You Are a Priest

As you come to him, the living Stone—rejected by men but chosen by God and precious to him—you also, like living stones, are being built into a spiritual house to be a holy priesthood, offering spiritual sacrifices acceptable to God through Jesus Christ.
(1 Peter 2:4–5)

Jesus Christ is the *"living Stone."* He is the solid foundation to life, the one who was *"rejected by men but chosen by God."* God did not just choose Him; He considers Him *"precious."* As Christians, God also considers us like Jesus! We are chosen and precious in His sight, spiritual beings in the process of continual spiritual development. It's like the slogan goes: "Please be patient. God hasn't finished with me yet." God has called us to be *"a holy priesthood."* We are to continually offer *"spiritual sacrifices acceptable to God through Jesus Christ."*

You are good enough! You are holy enough! You are spiritual enough! You have been made so through Jesus. You don't need the pastor, minister, or elder—or anyone else with a religious title—to go to God for you. He is always there for you to talk to Him. You don't have to act as if He is in some other room or far-off place.

That being said, it's good to continue studying under, and learning from, those who have progressed further down their spiritual walks and Biblical studies. We can also learn from those who are working their way alongside us.

Our sacrifices need not be animal blood, as in Old Testament times. Jesus Christ has shed His blood for us once and for all. Neither do we need to offer incense or other physical substances at the altar. Our sacrifices are to be of a spiritual nature. Worship the Lord. Minister to others. In all we do and in all we say, we should be doing so as if it were for God Himself. You are a priest in God's eyes.

FEBRUARY 12

Freedom in Forgiveness

Do not repay evil with evil or insult with insult, but with blessing, because to this you were called so that you may inherit a blessing.
(1 Peter 3:9)

We are called to love one another and live in harmony. Sometimes this is much easier said than done. If we rely on our flesh, we will fail. However, if we strive to stay in a right relationship with Jesus in these difficult times, we'll have His strength and wisdom. What is happening when we contemplate repaying *"evil with evil or insult with insult"*? It's our defensive reaction to hurt feelings. Why has the other person struck out at us? Only Jesus knows the real reason. Let's not allow Satan to plant assumptions and false ideas.

In Luke 6, Jesus tells us to always go one step further. We are to love our enemies, to bless them and pray for them. When He tells us to pray for them, I don't think He means, "Dear Jesus, make this idiot smarten up!" It's okay to tell God that you're upset. He already knows. Ask for His help in being forgiving. Ask Him to reveal any of your attitudes or behaviours that need repentance. Pray for those who mean evil against you. Nothing anyone can do to you is worth interfering with their—or your—relationship with our Father.

In John 20:23, Jesus tells us, *"If you forgive anyone his sins, they are forgiven; if you do not forgive them, they are not forgiven."* On judgment day, do you really want to be responsible for someone else's separation from God? Then, in Matthew 6:14–15, Jesus said,

For if you forgive men when they sin against you, your heavenly Father will also forgive you. But if you do not forgive men their sins, your Father will not forgive your sins.

Is it worth separation from our Father?

The added blessing to forgiveness is the burden that is lifted from you right now. Enjoy your freedom in Jesus Christ!

FEBRUARY 13

Way to Go!

And let us consider how we may spur one another on toward love and good deeds.
(Hebrews 10:24)

Oh, what fun! Take your eyes off of yourself and everything you think you need to accomplish today. Yes, I know there are some things we must do to exist in this life on earth. However, try going through your day with your eyes on how you can encourage others, rather than trudging through the work you need to perform.

Smile at the people you pass in the hall. Smiling is highly contagious! Will you really be that much later if you let that car merge in front of you? Or will you be that much earlier if you cut off another car? Have you noticed how carefully your spouse may have dressed today? Tell them how nice they look. Is someone a few minutes late for your appointment? As they rush in, a smile and reassurance that you aren't angry with them can melt away a lot of stress. Your meeting will likely go much smoother. Are those dishes that need washing really more urgent than a phone call to a friend who may be going through a difficult time? Before you hang up, remember to wish them a good day. Do you have children or an employee struggling to learn a new concept? Tell them that you've noticed how hard they're trying. Encourage them to keep going.

Aren't you glad God doesn't keep throwing back at us all the mistakes we've made in the past? He has forgiven us and forgotten all about those failures. Jesus already wiped our slates clean. Our Father in heaven only wants what is good for us. He is cheering us onwards. Let's try to do the same for those around us.

Not only will you be a blessing to others throughout your day, you may find that all the "work" you have to do is a lighter load than you thought. Be blessed, and pass it on.

FEBRUARY 14

How Do I Love Thee?

Love is patient, love is kind. It does not envy, it does not boast, it is not proud. It is not rude, it is not self-seeking, it is not easily angered, it keeps no record of wrongs. Love does not delight in evil but rejoices with the truth. It always protects, always trusts, always hopes, always perseveres. Love never fails.
(1 Corinthians 13:4–8)

Well, as you read the above verses, how are you doing? Are these verses a fair measuring rod for the way you love your spouse? This side of heaven, none of us are perfect; however, these verses are a great reminder of what our goals should be.

Share with your spouse how you see them fulfilling the above goals in your relationship. Give each other examples of the God-like love you experience. Keep up the good work! Is there a younger or struggling couple in your circle of influence? Ask God to provide an opportunity for you to offer to be their mentors in creating a stronger, God-like marriage.

Considering the attributes generated from the above discussion, can you think of any areas in which you could improve? Does your spouse agree with your perspective? What can you do specifically to develop that goal? Look around you. Are there couples in your life who you witness doing a good job of loving each other? You may observe different aspects of some very loving actions from various couples in your life. If you and your spouse identify a Christian couple you believe are doing a particularly good job of loving one another, I would suggest you approach that couple and ask them if they would be willing to mentor you in your marriage relationship.

FEBRUARY 15

Why Church?

Let us not give up meeting together, as some are in the habit of doing, but let us encourage one another—and all the more as you see the Day approaching.
(Hebrews 10:25)

I have known people who have said to me that they don't believe they have to attend a church to be a Christian. They are correct. Attending church does not make you a Christian. Nor does sitting in the cockpit of an airplane make you a pilot. Believing that Jesus came to earth and died for your sins, and asking Jesus into your life, makes you a Christian. However, there are many good reasons for *"meeting together"* with other Christians.

The focus is not the building, but rather unity in Christ. Attending some form of church is a wonderful opportunity to join together with others in worshipping the Lord. It is an opportunity to set time aside to enter into His presence. It provides us a chance to further our understanding of God's word, to pray together, and to give and receive encouragement and support. It is an opportunity to work together with other like-minded Christians in developing our spiritual walks. Attending a church and developing relationships with other Christians helps keep us accountable and assists in preventing us from slipping away from all God would desire for us.

Why should you attend church? To be obedient to God's word. God does not direct us to do useless things for His amusement. He doesn't ask us to worship Him to build Himself up. He is already complete. Worshiping God is for our benefit. Attending church will assist you in fulfilling God's purposes for your life. It will help keep your life God-centred rather than egocentric.

Don't worry about the elaborateness of the building. Find a church that believes in Jesus Christ and join in!

FEBRUARY 16

Are You Ready? (Part One)

Therefore put on the full armor of God, so that when the day of evil comes, you may be able to stand your ground, and after you have done everything, to stand. Stand firm then, with the belt of truth buckled around your waist, with the breastplate of righteousness in place, and with your feet fitted with the readiness that comes from the gospel of peace.
(Ephesians 6:13–15)

This is one of my favourite illustrations in the Bible. The metaphor the Apostle Paul uses here is of a soldier. Most of us have no idea what it would be like to be in a physical war, where our lives are on the line at all times. To never know how, or from where, the enemy may attack. To never know if this will be the day when your life on earth will end. However, the reality is that everyone is constantly in a spiritual battle. The battle is for eternal life. The question is, are you prepared, or are you just going to give yourself over to the enemy?

The belt is what keeps us pulled together. The Apostle Paul uses the belt to illustrate "truth." This is truthful living and sharing the truth of the Gospel. Jesus is the truth! The breastplate of righteousness covers our hearts. Are you motivated by what you know to be right in the eyes of Jesus? Is your heart protected by righteousness? Next, the footwear symbolizes the Gospel of Peace. This is the peace that surpasses all human understanding, the peace you have in knowing Jesus and trusting that He's always there for you, the peace of trusting that you're in His hands and that He desires good for you, the peace you have in knowing God's word.

Knowledge is the first step. Knowledge without action is worth nothing. If we take action to attain truth, righteousness, and knowledge of the Gospel of Peace, we will have a firm foundation. Consider it life's training camp.

FEBRUARY 17

Are You Ready? (Part Two)

In addition to all this, take up the shield of faith, with which you can extinguish all the flaming arrows of the evil one. Take the helmet of salvation and the sword of the Spirit, which is the word of God.
(Ephesians 6:16–17)

Today we will look at verses that address battle readiness. We first address the soldier's shield. The Apostle Paul ascribes "faith" to this item. Are you protected from the evil one and his harm by strong faith?

The sword accompanies the shield. This is the only offensive weapon mentioned. The sword is symbolic of the spirit, or word of God. Do you continually study God's word and spend time in prayer with Him so that you'll have a good understanding of what He's saying to you? Are you ready to use God's word to go on the offence for your life and to save others? Do you share your faith with others so that they also may be saved? Let us gain ground in deflecting all of Satan's attacks and bring glory to God.

The head covering (helmet) is a representation of your salvation. Our head is where we store all our knowledge, both conscious and unconscious. We owe our very lives to our brains telling us to breathe without us consciously thinking about it. Do you have secure knowledge in your salvation through the blood of Jesus Christ?

Every piece of armour is necessary. If we leave one area exposed, we risk fatal injury—in this case, our eternal life! Ignoring the constantly raging spiritual battle, or simply doing nothing at all, gives Satan the victory. We have the power in Jesus Christ to win our war and gain ground for God's glory. Are you ready?

How will you gain ground for God today?

FEBRUARY 18

Are You Ready! (Part Three)

Pray also for me, that whenever I open my mouth, words may be given me so that I will fearlessly make known the mystery of the gospel...
(Ephesians 6:19)

Many times, when we quote the "armour of God" section of Ephesians, we stop at verse 17 or 18. However, verses 18–20 give us vital life application. The great Apostle Paul asked for prayer support from the Christians he was teaching. He didn't request a general "dear God watch over and protect me" prayer. Paul asked for very specific prayer to overcome his human fears, enabling him to teach others about our Lord. He sought to boldly bring God's word to others in such a way that they would understand. Paul travelled far in his missions, facing unknown dangers, direct attacks, and difficulties with language and culture.

I have recently been the recipient of this type of prayer from my husband and friends. I stepped out into a culture and language not familiar to me. I was thrilled with the boldness I experienced when reaching out to others in a foreign country with an unfamiliar language. I know it was by the grace of God! It was so exciting to see the fruit of my team's efforts in bringing to the people the knowledge and love of Jesus.

Do you desire to overcome the fear of condemnation and persecution from others as you make Jesus Christ known to others? Then ask for it! The armour of God is something we need to put on daily, but also remember prayer! Ask your spouse and other prayer partners for specific prayer support when you know you're headed into battle. Pray that God will give you His words, in His timing, in all situations. Then open your mouth in confidence.

Ask God to show you the fruit of your labour, whether your battleground is close to home or in a foreign land. Charge with the love of Jesus!

FEBRUARY 19

Keep Your Eyes on Jesus

"Lord, if it's you," Peter replied, "tell me to come to you on the water." (Matthew 14:28)

The disciples were in a boat during stormy weather. Jesus walked out on the water towards them. When the disciples saw Jesus, in their fear, they mistook Him for a ghost. Jesus called out, *"Take courage! It is I. Don't be afraid"* (Matthew 14:27). Peter then tested his faith with the above verse. When Jesus commanded him, Peter stepped out of the boat and began to walk towards Jesus. What faith! Then Peter took his eyes off Jesus and noticed the waves. He began to sink. He called out to Jesus for help. Jesus put out His hand, and Peter looked back to Jesus and took His hand. They both climbed safely into the boat.

How many times do we start out in faith, in obedience to Jesus, only to be distracted? We allow the worries of this world, the lies of the enemy, or a return to self-reliance to capture our attention. Are things going a little rough? Are you struggling? Where are you looking? As Peter cried out for help, Jesus held out His hand. Peter would have had to look back towards Jesus to see His outstretched hand and take it. Jesus is holding out His hand to each of us. Look to Him and take it.

Notice that Jesus took Peter back to the boat where Peter would feel safe. It makes one wonder what would have happened if Peter had kept his focus on Jesus in the first place. Jesus is always ready to meet us where we are. It is our faith that limits how much He can use us to further His kingdom. Our God is a God of second chances. Don't focus on where you have failed or what you have done wrong. Keep your eyes on Jesus. If you lose your focus, you *can* turn back. He'll still be there.

Pray for each other that you would hear God's command and be able to remain focused on Him, no matter what storms of life surround you.

FEBRUARY 20

Giving God a Hand

...so she said to Abram, "The Lord has kept me from having children. Go, sleep with my maidservant; perhaps I can build a family through her." (Genesis 16:2)

God promised Abram that he would have a biological son as an heir. God told Abram that he would have more offspring than he would be able to count. This promise was given when Sarai and Abram were already in their eighties and nineties, well beyond childbearing age. I definitely give Abram credit for his faith in believing that God would bring this about.

However, time passed. Ten years later, Sarai still was not pregnant, so she decided that maybe she should help God out. She sent Abram to her maid in hopes that her maid would bear a child for Abram as an heir. Abram listened to Sarai and went along with the plan. Guess what? The maid did get pregnant. Sarai got her wish. However, when the maid knew she was pregnant by Abram, trouble started between her and Sarai. Sarai resented and mistreated the maid, blaming Abram for all the troubles.

Amazingly, God was merciful. He took care of the maid and her son, but He still fulfilled the promise that Sarai (now called Sarah), the wife of Abram (now called Abraham), would conceive and have a son. There were consequences to Sarah and Abraham's actions, and also for the maid, her son, and generations to come.

God does not work in our timing. It may be difficult to be patient when we pray for something or hear the word of God. Keep in mind that God sees and knows all things. He doesn't need our advice or help.

God wants us to be in unity with our spouse, but first we must be in unity with Him. Give your spouse permission to remind you of God's will. He would never ask us to sin.

FEBRUARY 21

Being Cheerleaders

Do not let any unwholesome talk come out of your mouths, but only what is helpful for building others up according to their needs, that it may benefit those who listen.
(Ephesians 4:29)

What a great verse to start your day! I would even suggest you write it out and put in on your bathroom mirror, by your coffee pot, or anywhere you know your eyes will fall on it early in the day.

One command in this verse is to stop the unwholesome talk. Why mention what you don't like? Is it just to voice your negative thoughts, or is it really to lovingly bring change where needed? Is it important? To be truly successful in this endeavour, you will need to stop your unwholesome thoughts. Intentionally avoid focusing on what is not pleasing. If you continue to feel negative but try to restrain your thoughts by your own willpower, you will always struggle to be positive. Controlling your talk may make things very quiet for a while.

The second aspect of this verse is to build others up and benefit your listeners. What could you say today to encourage others? Seek out ways to compliment the people around you. Compliment their appearance, efforts, and successes. Don't start each encounter with remembrance of negative past experiences. Build upon positive history and start each encounter with a desire to move forward. Like most things, practice will make it easier day by day until it is the natural outpouring of your heart.

You don't have to do this on your own. Ask for God's help. Take time to pray with your spouse that you would both be encouragers. Point out your spouse's positive attitude.

The intent is to encourage your spouse and those around you. The bonus is how positive you will end up feeling. Joy can be contagious!

FEBRUARY 22

Joy in the Lord

The kingdom of heaven is like treasure hidden in a field. When a man found it, he hid it again, and then in his joy went and sold all he had and bought that field.
(Matthew 13:44)

The ultimate treasure is the kingdom of heaven, salvation, and eternal life with Jesus. Those who find it have great joy! Why hide it? This man did not have access to banks or safety deposit boxes. He went out and sold everything (gave up all he had) in order to buy the field where he found it. He held back nothing because he knew this treasure (the Gospel) was far more valuable than anything he had previously owned.

Are you willing to give all you have, and all you are, for the kingdom *with joy*? We aren't just talking about money here. What else might you be holding onto that you cannot joyfully give up for Jesus and His kingdom? Is it status, family, friends, time, or worldly possessions? Are you willing to pray to God and give Him permission to convict you of any areas you're trying to hide from Him or hold back?

The question is, are you joyfully willing? Do you completely trust God to lead you? Our God is a loving God. He wants what is good for us. He won't necessarily ask you to give away everything. We are to be good stewards of what we have been blessed with. Instead, *"put [your] hope in God, who richly provides us with everything for our enjoyment"* (1 Timothy 6:17).

Are you excited by all that Jesus has in store for you? Are you willing to step out in faith to receive more of Him? Joyfully offer everything to Jesus and listen intently for His direction. There's nothing worth more than the privileges and hopes of the kingdom.

FEBRUARY 23

God's Gift

Then the Lord God made a woman from the rib he had taken out of the man, and he brought her to the man.
(Genesis 2:22)

God noticed that all the animals had mates, but that Adam did not have a companion. Therefore, He created woman from Adam's rib. Eve was created from a part of Adam to become one with Adam. God specifically chose Eve for Adam.

Human beings have various ways of selecting their spouse. Various cultures influence our selection process. However it may happen, God's intent is for man and his wife to live together as companions until death of their earthly bodies separates them.

When you are given a gift, you can receive it joyfully, ignore it, or toss it aside. You may have asked for a specific gift or you may have been surprised by what was given to you. What you do with the gift of the companion you have been given is up to you. You can treasure your spouse and put them in a place of honour in your life, take them for granted, or toss them aside.

My husband and I had the privilege of choosing one another. Even so, we have discovered many things about each other along the way. We have joined together to embrace life and encourage each other along the path on which God is leading us.

I am thankful to the Lord for the man He gave me. I pray that He helps me to be that matching piece I am meant to be. How do you respond to the gift (spouse) that was given to you? May you continue to discover how much better you fit together as you give yourselves to each other in Jesus' name.

FEBRUARY 24

Life's Challenges

Consider him who endured such opposition from sinful men, so that you will not grow weary and lose heart.
(Hebrews 12:3)

At times in your Christian walk, you will feel challenged in your faith. Ultimately, this need not be a bad thing. Challenges make you really think about why you believe what you believe. They can be times of great spiritual growth, of drawing even closer to Jesus.

Consider that Jesus Himself was denied and opposed many times. Jesus didn't always oppose the uninformed, either. Even the people from Jesus' own town didn't believe in Him. There were places where Jesus performed miracles and still the people didn't believe in Him. His disciples would forget the miracles Jesus had performed when they were faced with challenges (for example, in Matthew 14, and again in Matthew 15, when Jesus fed the thousands). Nothing you will encounter can come close to that which Jesus bore for you.

The verse for February 19 encourages us to keep our eyes on Jesus. Jesus persevered with joy when He was opposed. Ask Jesus for His guidance and direction. He knows the way—and after all, He wins! He empowers you to win, too! As you come into a deeper relationship with Jesus, imagine all you will accomplish for His kingdom.

So, how should you face those challenges? Continue to read and study the Bible. Spend time in prayer. Spend time listening for His words. Jesus has given you a spouse as a companion. Ask your spouse for their prayer support. Focus not on the challenge, but on Jesus. The situation may not always melt away, but its hold on you will.

Stay in the word and encourage one another.

FEBRUARY 25

Why Do My Prayers Matter?

And when he had taken it, the four living creatures and the twenty-four elders fell down before the Lamb. Each one had a harp and they were holding golden bowls full of incense, which are the prayers of the saints. (Revelation 5:8)

Why pray? It's not that God won't know about an issue or event if you don't tell Him. It's not that God will only pay attention if you're concerned about something. It's not even that God will let the world will fall apart if you don't do your part. It is your privilege to pray.

Today's verse is written by the Apostle John, who wrote down that which he saw in a vision, or revelation, that the Lord gave him. As John sees into the heavenlies, he is witness to the worship of the Lamb (Jesus). In the Old Testament, the priests would burn incense as a pleasing aroma and sacrifice to God. God said He would meet with the priests if they were to do so (Exodus 30:36). It is clear from today's verse that our prayers are seen as sacrifices to Jesus Himself. The elders sing our prayers in a song of worship to Him.

What a privilege we have now, in New Testament times, to pray directly to Jesus. As we join our hearts to Jesus, He meets us and receives our prayers. Ours are the prayers of *"a kingdom and priests to serve our God"* (Revelation 5:10).

As you respond in prayer to what God puts on your heart, you join with Jesus to release the work of the Holy Spirit here on earth. Amazing, isn't it? Your prayers really matter! Take this moment to pray with your spouse, and remember that Jesus hears every word from your hearts.

FEBRUARY 26

What Did You Say?

But my covenant I will establish with Isaac, whom Sarah will bear to you by this time next year.
(Genesis 17:21)

I don't know about you, but I wish God was always so specific when He speaks to us. There doesn't appear to be room in this verse for confusion or doubt. God clearly stated what would happen, and in what timing. God was very specific in this case.

I can understand that Sarah might have found this hard to absorb, as she was well past her childbearing years. *"After I am worn out and my master is old, will I now have this pleasure?"* (Genesis 18:12) God knew her attitude even though Sarah tried to deny her disbelief. I wonder what was harder for Sarah to accept. Was it that she would have a child in her old age, or that God would choose her and her husband for such a great honour as to parent the one with whom God had chosen to establish His covenant?

We so easily judge Sarah for her unbelief in the face of such a clear word from God. However, remember that we have the book that tells of Sarah's future and how things end. Fortunately, Sarah didn't have to wait long to experience the truth of God's promise.

When God speaks to you, no matter what the venue, I would encourage you to write down what He declares. Don't allow the enemy to plant doubt or confusion. "Is that what God said? Did I hear Him right? Maybe He didn't word it the way I remember. Did He say when it would happen?"

Be assured that God is not fickle. He will not change His mind or make amendments to what He has declared. For our own reassurance, it is good to revisit what exactly was declared. Be patient! God knows the whole story, and nothing is *"too hard for the Lord"* (Genesis 18:14). Do not doubt what God has declared, but accept that His timing is perfect.

FEBRUARY 27

Where Can I Run?

The word of the Lord came to Jonah son of Amittai.
(Jonah 1:1)

Remember the story of Jonah and the big fish? God told Jonah to go to Nineveh and tell the people about God. Jonah didn't want to go. He thought the people there were too wicked to deserve knowing God. Jonah actually tried to run away and hide from God. He went down to the seashore and bought a ticket for passage overseas, in the opposite direction of Nineveh.

Well, as the story goes, a terrible storm came up. The sailors feared that their boat would be overturned and they would all die. When the captain of the ship called Jonah to pray to his God to stop the storm, Jonah confessed. He told the captain that the storm was his fault and that to save themselves, the sailors must throw Jonah overboard, which they did.

It would seem that the story should end there, but it didn't. The storm did stop. In addition, God sent a big fish to swallow Jonah whole. Jonah sat in the belly of that fish for three whole days before he finally prayed to God. Jonah cried out to God. He turned back to the Lord and admitted, *"Salvation comes from the Lord"* (Jonah 2:9). Jonah vowed to keep his promise and obey the Lord.

God gave Jonah a second chance. The Lord had the fish spit Jonah up on land. God again directed Jonah to go to Nineveh, and Jonah obeyed. Jonah took God's message to Nineveh and all the people believed him. They repented of their evil ways and God had compassion and spared them. Thank God that He saw past the people's evil ways and sent a messenger to them. We serve a just and merciful God.

So, what is God telling you? Are you willing to obey? Pray and ask for His direction. He will prepare the way. Trust in the Lord always.

FEBRUARY 28

Consecrate Yourself

Consecrate yourselves, for tomorrow the Lord will do amazing things among you.
(Joshua 3:5)

The word consecrate means "to set apart or dedicate as sacred; or to devote to some worthy purpose."[4] This is the Lord's call to set yourselves apart for Him to do His work in and through you. When He says "tomorrow," He may not mean the very next day; more likely, it means any time in the future.

The Lord was directing Joshua, and I believe us, to purposefully prepare ourselves to fulfill our destiny in Jesus Christ. What does that mean to you? Perhaps you are to devote more time to reading the word, praying, fasting, or taking Bible study courses. Perhaps He will lead you in some other way. The point is, His desire is that we work on developing our spiritual walk and intimacy with Him. If we are faithful to do so, we allow the Lord to *"do amazing things"* in and through our lives.

Notice it is not you, but the Lord who *"will do amazing things."* All we need to do is respond to His direction. He doesn't want us to plan ahead what we will do for His work to happen. By doing so, we just get in the way. Don't limit His work by telling Him what to do.

This call is not just for a day, but for each and every day. Yes, life goes on and we need to take care of our physical needs. However, just as we are to *"pray without ceasing"* (1 Thessalonians 5:17, NASB), we should strive to be God-centred every minute. Be willing to follow His commands, trusting in His power and wisdom.

I would encourage you to take some time now by yourself, and then with your spouse, to ask God what He would have you to do in order to consecrate your life for His purposes. Whether your assignment is to be done alone, with your spouse, or with others, be prepared to be amazed!

---

[4] *The Winston Dictionary of Canadian English* (Toronto, ON: Holt, Rinehart and Winston of Canada, 1969), 131.

MARCH 1

Motivational Gifts

We have different gifts, according to the grace given us. If a man's gift is prophesying, let him use it in proportion to his faith. If it is serving, let him serve; if it is teaching, let him teach; if it is encouraging, let him encourage; if it is contributing to the needs of others, let him give generously; if it is leadership, let him govern diligently; if it is showing mercy, let him do it cheerfully.
(Romans 12:6–8)

Motivational gifts are foundational, but different than the gifts of the Holy Spirit. (The gifts of the Holy Spirit are explored elsewhere in this book.) These gifts are what inspire you to do what you do. They are: perceiver, server, teacher, exhorter (encourager), giver, administrator, and compassion (mercy). There are numerous sources for motivational gifts surveys. I would encourage you to find one and complete it for yourself. It is helpful to be aware of what motivates you.

When I first completed a survey, I was very surprised at the outcome! I have a degree in education. I was certain that teaching would be my strongest gifting. It was not; in fact, teaching was rated as my third gift. Upon reflection, I realized that I chose to train as a teacher with an emphasis on children with special needs. Out of my motive to help those I felt were more vulnerable (compassion), I took training (methodology) to help them receive an education.

It is also helpful to seek out what the strengths and weaknesses of each gifting are. For example, someone with a compassionate gifting has a great capacity to show love, but is easily hurt by others and has difficulty making decisions.

It will be interesting to share what your giftings are with your spouse and discuss how you complement each other. It may also be helpful to be aware of what strengths and weaknesses you each have. Discuss how you might best use each other's strengths and support each other's weaknesses.

MARCH 2

Marriage Responsibility

Therefore what God has joined together, let man not separate.
(Matthew 19:6, Mark 10:9)

Many marriage ceremonies include this verse. It sounds so good and permanent as we stand together, perhaps in front of friends and family, and rejoice. God is talking to you!

It is your responsibility as a married person to see to it that you don't let anyone come between you and your spouse. There may be times when another relationship requires more time (e.g. young children, a sick family member, or friend), but they should not take priority over your spouse. Do not entertain romantic thoughts of others. Do not allow others to poison your thoughts towards your spouse in any way. Do not think or say derogatory things about your spouse, even as a joke. Do not allow others to do so in your presence.

Instead, focus your thoughts and comments on the positive qualities you see in your spouse. Never assume they know how much you admire them. Compliment their appearance, their accomplishments, and their kind intentions. Take the time to express your appreciation for everyday things, such as, "Thank you for making dinner. It is great!" or "I really appreciate it when you help me with…" or "You are so thoughtful of me when you…"

We all have different ways of expressing and receiving love. Ask your spouse what things are most important to them. Likewise, tell them what expressions of love mean the most to you. I challenge you to devote yourself to concentrating on what you can do to bless your spouse rather than focussing on what they can do for you. If you both set your hearts on blessing each other, it can only be a win-win situation.

MARCH 3

Do I Have a Gift? (Part One)

There are different kinds of gifts, but the same Spirit. There are different kinds of service, but the same Lord.
(1 Corinthians 12:4–5)

Every person who has accepted Jesus Christ as their Lord and Saviour has received the gift of eternal life. In addition, Jesus has fulfilled His promise to send the Holy Spirit to us who are believers. Through the Holy Spirit, we have all been given gifts *"just as he determines"* (1 Corinthians 12:11). Those gifts are: wisdom, knowledge, faith, healing, miraculous powers, prophecy, distinguishing between spirits, speaking in different kinds of tongues, and the interpretation of tongues.

So, which gift do you have? The Bible tells us you have them all! *"God works all of them in all men"* (1 Corinthians 12:6). However, you may find that you use one gift more than another at various times in your life. The question may more aptly be, what gift are you using predominantly right now? I would suggest that you both read through 1 Corinthians 12. Then ask yourself what gift(s) you think you are using now. Consult with your spouse as to where they see your gifting. Most importantly, ask God to help you determine which gift(s) He has chosen for you to use.

The Holy Spirit has offered you these gifts. Have you received them? Have you opened any of them and used them? These gifts were not meant to be kept under wrap, to look pretty for some day in the future. Go for it! Open them up!

Like learning to play the piano or learning a new language, one must practice using one's gifts to become more proficient with them. God will show you what to do with them. They are of God, not of you. Ask your spouse to continue to walk with you as you discover and use your spiritual gifts.

May all the glory be to God!

MARCH 4

Do I Have a Gift? (Part Two)

Speaking in Tongues

When the day of Pentecost came, they were all together in one place… All of them were filled with the Holy Spirit and began to speak in other tongues as the Spirit enabled them.
(Acts 2:1, 4)

The Bible refers to speaking in tongues as early as the books of Isaiah 28:11–12. In the above verses, we are told how the followers of Jesus *"were filled with the Holy Spirit and began to speak in other tongues as the Spirit enabled them."*

Speaking in tongues refers to the God-given ability to speak in one or more languages you have not previously learned. It is God-inspired, with you doing the speaking. Why then are we so intimidated by the thought of people, particularly ourselves, speaking in tongues? Imagine the scene in Acts 2:6–13, where the people all heard the followers of Jesus speaking in the listeners' own languages. What was their response? From the hardness of their own hearts, they accused the Christians of being drunk!

I would suggest that right now you both stop and turn your hearts towards Jesus. Freely give your will to Him. Ask Him to enable you to open your mouths and speak in tongues, by the power of the Holy Spirit within you. Go ahead and do it out loud. Remember, like choosing when to pray, you have the ability to determine when to speak in tongues and when to stop. Continue to practise this gift regularly in your private prayers. You will find that you are drawn closer and closer to God. Often when I run out of my own words, or I'm uncertain how to pray for a situation, I allow the Holy Spirit to move within me and give me the words (speak in tongues) to pray to the Father.

Don't let pride steal this precious gift from you. This is the only gift that is for your personal edification. (In addition to all other eight gifts, speaking in tongues can also be used for the building up of others.)

MARCH 5

Do I Have a Gift? (Part Three)

Interpretation of Tongues

> *If there is no interpreter, the speaker should keep quiet in the church and speak to himself and God.*
> (1 Corinthians 14:28)

When speaking in tongues in your private prayers, you will receive various fruits of the spirit. It may be peace, joy, wisdom, knowledge, or whatever God determines you need. When speaking in tongues for the edification of others, however, there must be an interpretation. As Paul writes,

> *Now, brothers, if I come to you and speak in tongues, what good will I be to you, unless I bring you some revelation or knowledge or prophecy or word of instruction?* (1 Corinthians 14:6)

Interpretation is the God-given ability to speak in your mother tongue the substance of what has just been spoken in tongues. So then, who does the interpretation? Well, sometimes the Holy Spirit will enable the person who spoke in tongues to also interpret. Other times, the Holy Spirit will work in unity in the body and give the interpretation to someone else. Like practising speaking in tongues, you need to be willing to take the step of faith and give the interpretation when it is given to you. Thirdly, as on the day of Pentecost, I have heard of occasions when the person speaking in tongues speaks in another earthly language he has not previously learned. In that same gathering, there was a person with knowledge of that language who was able to give the interpretation.

We must remember that *"God is not a God of disorder but of peace"* (1 Corinthians 14:33). Therefore, if there is no interpreter, the speaker must be quiet. The gifts are for edification of others in the gathering. If there is no understanding of the tongues, disorder is created and others may be driven away from God.

MARCH 6

Do I Have a Gift? (Part Four)

Word of Knowledge

...then you will understand the fear of the Lord and find the knowledge of God.
(Proverbs 2:5)

The word of knowledge is one of three revelation gifts. We will look at the word of wisdom and the discerning of spirits another day.

The word of knowledge is that which is made known to you by God. It is not mind-reading, or digging for gossip or random facts. A word of knowledge comes when God reveals facts to you that you would not possibly be able to know otherwise, to bring glory to God.

We can find many examples of this gift in use in the Bible. Notice that the knowledge is always given for a purpose and is motivated by love. Its purpose is to be in alignment with God's will and may be used to lead others to Christ, build up faith in others, restore a believer, or enlighten us for our protection. God may give you a word of knowledge by intruding directly on your consciousness or by using any one of your senses—smell, hearing (audible), seeing (vision or dream), touch (feeling), or taste. These are not for you to create your own interpretation; allow God to reveal the meaning to you.

As a young Christian, I received a vision concerning two of my family members. These two people, to my knowledge, were not yet Christians. I didn't have any experience with visions and I told God I didn't understand. He then impressed on my mind that these two people would become Christians. It took eighteen and a half years to come to fruition, but the word provided me with much hope in times of despair.

I would encourage you to apply your heart to instruction and your ears to words of knowledge. If God gives a word of knowledge, He means for you to do something about it.

MARCH 7

Do I Have a Gift? (Part Five)

Word of Wisdom

If any of you lacks wisdom, he should ask God, who gives generously to all without finding fault, and it will be given to him.
(James 1:5)

The word of wisdom works with the word of knowledge and the discerning of spirits. The word of wisdom knows what to do with the knowledge you have, whether received by obvious means or as a revelation by a word of knowledge. It is God's instructions of what to do. It is not your own wisdom, not always practical, nor an action you would have thought of on your own.

For the Lord gives wisdom, and from his mouth come knowledge and understanding. (Proverbs 2:6)

As we look to Jesus for an example, notice that He did not always heal the blind in the same routine or ritualistic manner. In each instance, He followed the directions the Father gave for that instance. The word of wisdom is not a set of rules you can learn. It is the ability to take on to yourself a revelation of what to do about a situation, once you know the facts concerning the case.

How do you know it is of God and not your own thoughts? A word of wisdom will be natural. It will be immediate, not studied or researched. You will recognize the word of wisdom by its good fruition: *"But wisdom is proved right by her actions"* (Matthew 11:19).

Have you ever had a "where did that thought come from" moment? Whether it's what to say or do, or not to say or do, will the results be for good? Like any gift, you need to receive the word of wisdom and then practise using it. However, when in doubt, don't do it!

MARCH 8

Do I Have a Gift? (Part Six)

Discerning of Spirits

Dear friends, do not believe every spirit, but test the spirits to see whether they are from God, because many false prophets have gone out into the world.
(1 John 4:1)

The discerning of spirits means being aware of spiritual existence, and being able to distinguish between good and evil spirits. Satan loves to use any means of deception he can, including appearing as a spirit of light.

And no wonder, for Satan himself masquerades as an angel of light. It is not surprising, then, if his servants masquerade as servants of righteousness.
(2 Corinthians 11:14–15)

Be aware of the manifestations of the spirits. Evil spirits will come in various forms, including infirmities, negative emotions, sorcery, seducing spirits, divination, and particular animal forms. Watch for the fruit of the spirit. Satan seeks to steal, kill, and destroy. God desires good things for us.

But the fruit of the Spirit is love, joy, peace, patience, kindness, goodness, faithfulness, gentleness and self-control. (Galatians 5:22–23)

Once one has discerned an evil spirit, the gifts of faith and the performing of miracles may be used to take dominion over, bind up, or cast out evil spirits so they can't do any more harm. Do not be afraid of the discerning of spirits. Do you recognize where that fear would come from? Remember that through the Holy Spirit we have been given authority to take dominion over evil spirits. God is mightier than Satan!

Confess your faith, confess any previous involvement in occult practises, renounce Satan/evil spirits, and command them to leave in the name of Jesus. Continue to keep your eyes on Jesus and invite the Holy Spirit to work in you.

MARCH 9

Do I Have a Gift? (Part Seven)

Faith

Does God give you his Spirit and work miracles among you because you observe the law, or because you believe what you heard?
(Galatians 3:5)

The gift of faith is one of three power gifts of the Spirit. The gift of faith is different from the faith you have in Christianity itself: *"Now faith is being sure of what we hope for and certain of what we do not see"* (Hebrews 11:1). The gift of faith is your response to God's ability. It is knowing in your heart that something *is*, yet having no outside reason to base it on. Faith is not a matter of your own desire or willpower. The gift of faith expects to receive that which is prayed for, takes risks based on revelation, and comes by hearing God.

Consequently, faith comes from hearing the message, and the message is heard through the word of Christ. (Romans 10:17)

The gift of faith requires the use of other gifts to reveal its power. An example from my own life is a healing I received many years ago. Someone used their gift of knowledge to reveal that there was someone present who had a specific type of recurring headache. When I identified myself, someone else prayed in tongues over me and used the power of their gift of faith to believe for my healing. I returned to my seat. About fifteen minutes later, I felt and heard a crack in my neck area. I have never experienced that type of headache again.

Are you being asked to use your gift of faith? There are many examples of the gift of faith throughout the Bible, and I would encourage you to investigate them. Notice in the example above that you will not always be directed to perform all the gifts, but we must each do our part as God determines.

Remember: faith untested is powerless.

MARCH 10

Do I Have a Gift? (Part Eight)

Performing of Miracles

I have given you authority to trample on snakes and scorpions and to overcome all the power of the enemy; nothing will harm you.
(Luke 10:19)

The performing of miracles is another power gift of the Spirit. This gift is God demonstrating His miracles through you. The results will appear to be contrary to nature.

There are many examples throughout the Bible of the gift of performing miracles. When directed by God, Jesus turned water into wine, walked on water, fed the thousands, and raised the dead. Elisha obeyed God's direction when he multiplied the widow's oil. Joshua stopped time, and on it goes.

Today, God continues to use His people to perform miracles. We have previously mentioned this gift working in relation to the discerning of spirits to free people from evil spirits when God so directs. There are miraculous healings that cannot be explained by human understanding.

During a missions trip I took part in, we experienced the multiplying of clothing. We had taken a few suitcases of children's clothing with us to give away to needy families. As we moved from house to house, we gave a few items to each child. At the end of the morning, our suitcases were still mostly full! God more than provided for their needs and we were able to leave extra clothing for families we weren't able to see that day.

The focus again is to keep your eyes on God. This gift is not of your making. You don't have to be physically strong or have a super intellect. It is not meant to entertain or amuse others.

The gift of performing miracles is to glorify God and bring souls to Christ.

MARCH 11

Do I Have a Gift? (Part Nine)

Healing

When Jesus had called the Twelve together, he gave them power and authority to drive out all demons and to cure diseases, and he sent them out to preach the kingdom of God and to heal the sick.
(Luke 9:1–2)

The gift of healing is one of three power gifts of the Spirit. The Bible records numerous examples of the healings Jesus performed during His three years of ministry here on earth. In the above verse, Jesus clearly directed and empowered His disciples to use the gift of healing. Later, Jesus sent out seventy-two others.

After this the Lord appointed seventy-two others... Heal the sick who are there and tell them, "The kingdom of God is near you." (Luke 10:1, 9)

That mandate continues to those of us who are Christians and have received the baptism of the Holy Spirit.

Healing, like joy, should be an everyday experience of Spirit-filled believers, not something reserved for special meetings.

God's desire is to alleviate the sickness and disease for all mankind. There are many reasons why someone may not be healed, but only God is all-knowing of each individual case. The gift of healing is our response to God's ability and direction. However, you will notice that Jesus says that the purpose for healing is to preach the kingdom of God and bring glory to God. It is not us doing, hoping, or wishing for healings. This gift must be accompanied by the workings of other spiritual gifts, particularly the gift of faith. It's not just a matter of *wanting* to be healed, or *hoping* to be healed, but having the faith to *expect* to be healed.

Is the Holy Spirit prompting you to use your gift of healing? If using this gift is the desire of your heart, ask for it. Be ready to hear God speak through you.

Note: Not all healings are instantaneous; that would be the gift of performing miracles.

MARCH 12

Do I Have a Gift? (Part Ten)

Prophecy

But everyone who prophesies speaks to men for their strengthening, encouragement and comfort.
(1 Corinthians 14:3)

The gift of prophecy must be inspired, have an effect, and serve a purpose. The purpose of prophecy is clear in the above verse.

Above all, you must understand that no prophecy of Scripture came about by the prophet's own interpretation. For prophecy never had its origin in the will of man, but men spoke from God as they were carried along by the Holy Spirit. (2 Peter 1:20–21)

Thus, a prophecy will be given and should be spoken at the time. You may receive the prophecy as a word of knowledge, a picture or vision, or a given understanding of the word. The gift of prophecy is neither fortune-telling nor your own predetermined thoughts or interpretation of what you think God is saying.

How do you trust a prophecy? If it was a prophecy God gave you to speak, you will have received it directly, not after meditating on a subject and working it through yourself. If it's from someone else, then God's word tells us: *"Do not put out the Spirit's fire; do not treat prophecies with contempt. Test everything. Hold on to the good. Avoid every kind of evil"* (1 Thessalonians 5:19–22). Is the prophecy for *"strengthening, encouragement and comfort"*? Does the prophet bare good fruit? Is there any other confirmation from God? The prophecy may not be understood immediately, and if so, it should be stored up for later.

I received a word of knowledge that I was to write this devotional book. As I looked back over my journals and notes from over the years, I came across a prophecy from twelve years previous. The prophet hadn't known me, but she prophesised that I was "storing up for another day" and then asked if I was writing something. That made no sense to me at the time and seemed totally unlikely. Well, here I am today! May this work bless many others in Jesus' name!

MARCH 13

Do I Have a Gift? (Part Eleven)

Conclusion

Each one should use whatever gift he has received to serve others, faithfully administering God's grace in its various forms.
(1 Peter 4:10)

I think that you can see by now that the gifts of the Holy Spirit are interrelated. Sometimes one person may use several gifts, and other times God will enable several people to work in unity to complete His work.

It is good to desire all the gifts in order to build up your faith, the faith of others, and to bring glory to God. Share with others the gifts you have been given. Jesus is the only hope for every nation, and we are His messengers. The Holy Spirit will lead, guide, and give you whatever gift is needed, but you need to be willing to be empowered and use them for His kingdom here on earth. Don't seek specific gifts; seek Jesus. The Holy Spirit will provide the right gift for you at the right time to fully meet God's purpose.

This devotional is not the place to provide a complete teaching on the gifts of the Holy Spirit. If this topic has spoken to your heart in the last few days, I would encourage you to search out further teaching specifically on the gifts of the Holy Spirit.

It is my hope that this short study has provided opportunities for you and your spouse to explore God's purpose in your lives. I pray that it draws you both closer to God, and in sharing your experience, closer to each other. May your cord of three be in perfect harmony.

MARCH 14

The Husband's Role

Husbands, love your wives and do not be harsh with them.
(Colossians 3:19)

What is a Christian husband's main role? Did anyone answer "leadership"? In the passage which today's verse is taken from, the Apostle Paul doesn't mention leadership, but love. The Greek word for "love" used here is the word *agapao*. This word is used to mean a love by choice, or a covenant kind of love. This is not sexual love or passionate love. Nor is this word used when we strongly like something, such as "I love chocolate!" This word is the purposeful nurturing love that provides a woman with the security she needs. It is the love where a husband respects, values, and honours his wife.

The rest of the verse implores husbands to *"not be harsh"* with their wives. Well, for the most part it would seem obvious that you would not be harsh if you purposefully choose to love your wife. However, the Apostle Paul felt that it was important enough to express it again. I have heard that it takes seven positive expressions to emotionally overcome one negative expression. Snapping at your wife even one time could take seven other times of affirmation to balance out. This isn't to say that all you need to do is keep a balance. Your goal is to encourage and nurture her. Choose to love her in all circumstances and tip the scale.

With this in mind, if a husband does a good job of loving his wife (*agapao*), and doesn't treat her harshly, she will most likely take joy in submitting to his leadership willingly and respectfully. What better way to honour the marriage God has blessed you with and avoid the cultural pitfalls of today's disposable relationships?

Thank God for the spouse He has provided you with. Husbands, ask Jesus to show you how to choose to love your wife. Wives, thank Jesus for blessing you with your husband's *agapao*.

MARCH 15

Submission

Submit to one another out of reverence for Christ.
(Ephesians 5:21)

There's that word again! This word leans towards two main directions. The first group of definitions we tend to cringe at are: "to give way or field to the power or authority of another; surrender."[5] This looks like the giving over of control of your life to another. However, the other group of definitions goes like this: "to refer or present for criticism, judgment, or decision."[6] In a loving, Christ-centred marriage, submission should be desirable, mainly because the Bible tells us that is the way it should be.

The second group of definitions is not so difficult. This definition suggests cooperative decision-making and loving consideration of one another. Let's look at the first group again, keeping in mind the type of marriage relationship Jesus intended. If my spouse truly loves me and puts me first, should it be threatening to refer or present myself for criticism, judgment, or decision? It seems that it's not so much giving over control of our lives as it is accepting their nurturing and protection.

As we grow from childhood into adulthood, it is healthy to develop a sense of independence from our parents. We spend a lot of energy determining who we are as separate beings from the parents who raise us, and learning how to take responsibility for ourselves. Now we are being told to submit to someone else? We need to understand that this submission emerges from our care and love for one another. Learn to appreciate, not resent, submission.

When you choose to submit to your spouse as Christ intended, you will find it is not so much a suppression of self as it is the acceptance of their love. Submit to one another out of respect for Christ and each other.

[5] Ibid., 714.
[6] Ibid.

MARCH 16

How Can I Witness for God?

Then Philip began with that very passage of Scripture and told him the good news about Jesus.
(Acts 8:35)

In this chapter, Philip responds to the Lord's command and goes where he is directed. He ends up right where he's supposed to be when he's supposed to be there. So far, this sounds pretty simple. All Philip did was initiate a conversation. It was the other person that asked Philip for instruction. Philip simply answered the man's questions about the Scripture the man was already reading. As more questions were asked, Philip was able to present the *"good news about Jesus."*

As the two continued, they came to a place where there happened to be a body of water. The man asked Philip to baptise him. When Philip's work was done, *"the Spirit of the Lord suddenly took Philip away"* (Acts 8:39). The man went away rejoicing. Philip didn't force anything upon the man; the man sought Philip's help. As a result, the man received Jesus and eternal life.

Philip heard the Lord's command because he knew Him. He spent time building a relationship with the Lord, and reading the Torah. The closer we are to someone, the better we are able to hear and understand them. Some people we know so well; we know what they are thinking and can finish their sentences for them.

Is there something you're trying to accomplish for the kingdom of God? Is there someone you're struggling to make understand their need for Jesus? I would suggest you lift up the person of concern to Jesus. Then let the Lord do His work. The spiritual wellbeing of each person is a matter between them and the Lord. God knows what is needed and when. Our job is to be prepared to listen to the Lord and allow Him to determine the who, what, where, when and hows. What are you doing to be prepared?

MARCH 17

Faith

Immediately the boy's father exclaimed, "I do believe; help me overcome my unbelief!"
(Mark 9:24)

Here is a story of a man who had been seeking help for his sick son. His son had been sick from birth and was at risk of dying from each new attack. I'm sure this loving father tried any number of different cures, but finally he came to Jesus' disciples for help. However, even Jesus' disciples seemed unable to help the boy.

Jesus could have received the information necessary from Father God, but chose to question the sick boy's father. In so doing, He established a verbal witness for those around them. It also gave Jesus an opportunity to hear the man's true belief. The man said, *"But if you can do anything..."* (Mark 9:22) Jesus pointed out the man's doubt. Suddenly, the man recognised his own attitude and weakness to change on his own. Not only did the son need healing, but so did the father. Today's verse is the man's response. Jesus then answered the man. The Bible doesn't spell it out, but I trust that the man's faith was strengthened and he believed Jesus could heal his son. Jesus then healed the boy, using the situation to continue instructing His disciples.

Many times when we hear this story, we focus on the healing, or on the lesson of prayer in which Jesus instructs His disciples. However, the lesson Jesus was teaching through the boy's father is also very important. All of us struggle with our faith at some point. We can try to hide our imperfection from others, and even ourselves, but Jesus knows our hearts. Those are the times to confess our lack of faith and cry out to Jesus, *"I do believe; help me overcome my unbelief!"* In Jesus' own words, *"Everything is possible for him who believes"* (Mark 9:23).

In what areas do you lack faith? Ask Jesus to reveal to you, as He did the boy's father, any areas in which you might lack faith. Then ask Jesus to help you overcome your unbelief.

MARCH 18

Persecution

But Joseph said to them, "Don't be afraid. Am I in the place of God? You intended to harm me, but God intended it for good to accomplish what is now being done, the saving of many lives."
(Genesis 50:19–20)

The story of Joseph is heart-breaking from a human perspective. Here is a person who suffers at the hands of others all his life through no apparent wrongdoing of his own. Joseph's father favoured Joseph and promoted an atmosphere of jealousy from the other siblings. The siblings went so far as to try to kill Joseph to get rid of him for good. It seemed all was lost, but God watched over Joseph and he ended up in a favourable position in Pharaoh's household.

Joseph always chose to stay God-centred and make the best of his situation. However, once again Joseph was to suffer because of someone else's ego. He ended up in prison. Joseph continued to focus on God, and God blessed him. Joseph then found himself as the right-hand man of Pharaoh. At this point, Joseph's family came back into his life. Joseph held the very lives of his brothers in his hand. He did make them squirm a bit to learn a lesson, but ultimately Joseph loved his family and forgave them.

Although your problems may seem insurmountable at times, not too many of us can really claim to be wronged more than Joseph was. I am in no way saying that what you're going through isn't very real or painful. What I am suggesting is that you learn from Joseph's horrible story of persecution and keep your eyes on Jesus. You can't even imagine what God has in store for you. God always intends good for those who know Jesus and love Him.

Pray that Jesus would help you keep your eyes on Him through all things. Look for opportunities for Jesus to allow you to turn your troubles into blessings for others.

MARCH 19

Level Ground

Every valley shall be raised up, every mountain and hill made low; the rough ground shall become level, the rugged places a plain.
(Isaiah 40:4)

Our lives can be described in terms of mountains, hills, and valleys. At times, we feel like everything is going great and life is just moving along as it should. At other times, we go through struggles. It may seem that no matter where we turn, or what we try to do, something is in the way to prevent us. That would be the mountains. Sometimes it's hard to see past these obstacles. Then there are times when we seem to be mired down, unable to get a hold to pull ourselves out of our difficult circumstances. It is God's will that through Him we make our paths smooth as a plain.

You can get focused on the little things in your daily living—the traffic jam, finding money on the ground, or having your alarm go off only to realize it's your day off. It's a more interesting exercise to draw your life out in a timeline. Mark the significant events that have happened in your life so far. You might record things such as deaths, your marriage, important changes in where you live or in your jobs. Can you see the hills and valleys? The good times would be on the line, the obstacles you encountered would be the mountains, and the times you felt mired down are the valleys. Where was Jesus during those times? Did you know He was there? Did you call on Him and the power He has given you through the Holy Spirit?

How do you think the rest of your life here on earth might look? What might you do in the valleys? What might you do when faced with mountains? What can you do to make that rough ground level? Think of the person who believes they are about to drown. They thrash around and panic rather than reaching out for the hand that's extended to pull them to safety. Take the hand of Jesus.

MARCH 20

Lovingly Forgiving

Be kind to one another, tender-hearted, forgiving each other, just as God in Christ also has forgiven you.
(Ephesians 4:32, NASB)

Although this verse was written to the church in Ephesus as instruction for their attitudes towards other Christians, we're going to apply it closer to home today. Think of your spouse as you read this verse again.

Firstly, the Apostle Paul writes that you are to be *"kind to one another, tender-hearted."* Each of you must read this verse in the first person, not as judgement on how well your spouse is doing. Do you always try to be kind to your spouse? Are you always tender-hearted towards them, forgiving them? Before you take offense at something, consider whether it was intended as such or if you might have misunderstood. In a gentle, loving manner, seek clarification. If you still feel offended, you need to address the offence itself—the behaviour, not your spouse's character. Forgiveness requires a conscious choice to soften yourself towards the offender and let go of the offence. Initiate the words and actions to bring about peace and harmony. When you forgive, you must give up all rights to punish the offender for the offence now and in the future.

Why should you be so forgiving? Consider that Paul wrote this letter from prison. His crime was nothing more than spreading the good news to others. What about Jesus Christ? He was without sin, but He died for your sins, as well as for those who were mistreating Him. Matthew 6:14 tells us, *"For if you forgive men when they sin against you, your heavenly Father will also forgive you."* Now that's a good reason! However, I would suggest that your motive should be based on the fact that Jesus would want it of you, and because you care about your spouse. I'm sure you wish your spouse well. Pray for them and their welfare. Seek to bless their day.

MARCH 21

Taking a Bath

And now what are you waiting for? Get up, be baptized and wash your sins away, calling on his name.
(Acts 22:16)

You've taken a bath, scrubbed away all the dirt and grime, and are all cleaned up. Would you ever consider that to be enough for the rest of your life? Of course not! We get dirty again just going about our daily lives and need to wash ourselves clean again and again. Does that mean you weren't thoroughly cleaned the first time?

When we repented and accepted Christ into our lives, He *completely* cleansed us of all our sins. Many of us will have been baptized as a symbol of the washing away of our sins. Are we completely free of sin forever now? No. We live in a sinful world. Satan has been given rule over this world for the time being. There is sin and temptations all around us. We are all sinners.

That doesn't mean we accept sin as inevitable and continue to purposefully wallow in it. You wouldn't stop washing yourself just because you're going to get dirty again. In the same way, we must continually return to Jesus, repent of our sins, ask for His forgiveness, and allow Him to cleanse us anew.

I had an opportunity to watch a film being made. The film wasn't created in one continuous take. To aid in the appearance of a continuous story, photographs were taken at the end of each clip. When the characters returned to record the following scene, someone would look at the photographs and smear dirt back on the characters in the same place as before. Fortunately, we serve a merciful God. When we come back to Him to repent of our new sins, He doesn't smear all our old sins back on us. You don't need to remind Jesus of the things He has already washed away, nor do you need to be cleansed of those sins again. Wash often.

MARCH 22

Purification

For seven days no yeast is to be found in your houses. And whoever eats anything with yeast in it must be cut off from the community of Israel, whether he is an alien or native-born.
(Exodus 12:19)

Exodus 12 tells the story of the institution of the Passover. Take the time to read over the event. Remember that yeast symbolized sin. A lamb without blemish was assigned as an atonement sacrifice for sin.

The people were commanded to abstain from yeast for seven days. Now, I've had to avoid all yeast products for a time due to a health issue. Yeast is in a lot of things you might not think of. It is possible to avoid yeast for several days, but it's not easy! To make sure nobody slipped up and ate a yeast product without thinking or realizing it, the Israelites were directed to take a sweep through their house and get rid of yeast and yeast products. In a society that didn't grab dinner on the way home from the office, they would probably be fairly successful in their "no yeast" diet. That helps us understand the severity of the punishment a little better—being cut off from the community. It would have to be a fairly intentional act to eat yeast under those conditions.

If the command is, "No sin is to be found in your lives for seven days," there is no hope of success. It's not possible to remove all temptation from our lives, intentional or not. What is the punishment? To be completely cut off from the Lord!

I'm so grateful that once again the Lord provided a way. Jesus Christ was assigned as an atonement sacrifice for all Christians, Israelites, and others! Jesus was, and is, without sin or blemish. Thankfully, we can go to Jesus each and every time we find sin in our lives. Through His blood, we are allowed to remain a Christian, a child of God.

MARCH 23

The Heart of Jesus

Filled with compassion, Jesus reached out his hand and touched the man. (Mark 1:41)

I love to read the Gospels—Matthew, Mark, Luke, and John! I love to read about Jesus' life here on earth. It is amazing that He would leave the Father in heaven and be willing to come to earth for me, you, and mankind in general. Jesus demonstrated wisdom, miracles, and power during His days here on earth. He came to experience life as we experience it and teach us how to live. He came to ultimately be crucified in our place.

It is interesting to read about Jesus' attitude. Time and again, we read about His compassion. No matter what His plan for the day was, no matter how tired He was, Jesus always had compassion for others. It was because of His compassion that He healed people, performed miracles, and taught the people beyond a reasonable length of time. He didn't stop when He had put in His forty hours for the week.

We can never claim to be Jesus, but we can always seek to be like Him. We will never be able to witness to all people for Jesus on our own. He hasn't asked us to. We will never be able to meet the needs of every person we have compassion for. That's not our job, either. What we need to do is be compassionate like Jesus. Allow the Holy Spirit to work through your life in the situations you are called to. Allow the love of Jesus to shine through your very being.

The better you get to know Jesus, the better you'll be able to experience His compassion and share His love. Discuss with your spouse what it is you do now to attain that compassion. What do you do to express the love of Jesus? Is there any way you can think of together to promote an even deeper understanding of that compassion?

Thank Jesus for the compassion He has for you. Then go out and share that compassion in His name.

MARCH 24

It's All for Jesus

Peter went with them, and when he arrived he was taken upstairs to the room. All the widows stood around him, crying and showing him the robes and other clothing that Dorcas had made while she was still with them. (Acts 9:39)

I will never forget the fear and challenges of going on my first overseas mission trip. I knew God was calling me to go, but many problems arose and tried to get in the way. One particularly difficult circumstance was the terminal diagnosis my very dear aunt received. She lived some distance from me, and I began to feel uncertain about whether I should continue with my plans to go on the missions trip, or use the money and time to visit my aunt one more time.

I began to telephone my aunt more often. On one of those calls, I broke down and shared my uncertainty with her. I so wanted to be by her side. My aunt loved Jesus and me dearly. It was because of that love that she urged me to go on the missions trip. She also assured me she knew I loved her. She shared with me that she was sorry she hadn't done something like a missions trip herself. She felt she hadn't done anything for Jesus with her life. You can't imagine my surprise. Here was my aunt, whom I looked up to as a spiritual leader, saying she didn't think she had ever done anything useful with her life for Jesus! I expressed my shock and told her that I had always thought of her as a Dorcas. "Who is Dorcas?" she asked. I reminded her of Dorcas, from the book of Acts.

My aunt was the one whose heart went out to everyone going through difficulties. She was the one who would visit someone in the hospital and massage their feet. She would bring baking to those who were laid up. She witnessed to others by her very life.

What do you do for Jesus? What will you be remembered for?

MARCH 25

Where Is Your Investment?

Be sure you know the condition of your flocks, give careful attention to your herds; for riches do not endure forever, and a crown is not secure for all generations.
(Proverbs 27:23–24)

Many people in our society put a lot of time, money, and energy into storing up for their retirement. Then the focus seems to move from retirement to leaving an inheritance for their children. Being responsible with what you have been blessed with, and planning for the future, are good qualities. The question is the focus.

Do you know the condition of the people in your care or circle of influence? Are you watchful that they are where they should be and not wandering off into harmful areas? How much time, energy, and even money do you invest in making sure your family is learning and developing their spiritual walk? If you don't invest in the spiritual health of this generation, who will lead and teach the next generation?

Your money or material things will not endure forever. The "things" you acquire will not be around for future generations. What can last is faith in Jesus Christ. Not only will it affect the eternal lives of those directly under your care now, but also those in generations to come.

I am very blessed. It really is not important that I receive great financial wealth when my loved ones leave this world heaven-bound. I know I come from a Christian family background. I don't know how many generations back that might go. I guess I'll find that out when I meet Jesus face to face. Some of you might not have had that advantage. However it has come about, you can influence your future generations right now.

With your spouse, contemplate each person under your influence. What is their condition? What are you doing right now, today, to invest in the security of your future generations?

MARCH 26

Why Does God Allow Sickness?

He said, "If you listen carefully to the voice of the Lord your God and do what is right in his eyes, if you pay attention to his commands and keep all his decrees, I will not bring on you any of the diseases I brought on the Egyptians, for I am the Lord, who heals you."
(Exodus 15:26)

I have heard many different possibilities suggested for why we have disease and illness in our lives. Some would attribute it to the sin in our world and the consequences of that sin. Some say it's because God allows illness or disease to teach us. Then there's the theory that we all have to die somehow if we are to get to heaven.

In today's verse, God clearly laid out the law for His people. Although this was spoken to the Israelites after they were brought out of Egypt, I believe it also applies to Christians today. First we need to *"listen carefully"* to Him, and then obey His word. Notice that He has required us to take action. We are to *"do what is right,"* not just sit and read or listen to it. His promise is that if we obey His commands, He won't bring any of the diseases on His people (us) that He brought on the Egyptians. God goes on to assure us that should we become ill, no matter the reason, He is the Lord who heals us.

Why do some good people get horrible illnesses? It is unknown why some people are miraculously healed, or receive treatment that their body responds to, while others don't. Only God knows. There are no right words to pray, no right amount of faith, no right formula for every person to be healed of every illness, every time. As you read through the Gospels, notice that Jesus performed miraculous healings differently from one situation to another. I do believe that the Lord continues to protect and heal today here on earth. I trust that when we meet in heaven, we will be free of disease.

MARCH 27

United We Stand

When Moses' hands grew tired, they took a stone and put it under him and he sat on it. Aaron and Hur held his hands up—one on one side, one on the other—so that his hands remained steady till sunset.
(Exodus 17:12)

What a beautiful example of how to support someone in a time of need. First, Moses the leader gave direction to and supported his men. Then, Aaron and Hur supported their leader in carrying out his role. What I love about this illustration is that neither Aaron nor Hur came in and started telling Moses what he was doing wrong or how they would approach the situation differently. After all, Moses was the one who heard directly from God.

Moses had sent Joshua and his men out to do battle. He assured them that he would be lifting them to the Lord (with his staff) as they fought. Now, as Moses was lifting Joshua and his men to the Lord, he became weary. He began to weaken and his hands began to fall. This is when Aaron and Hur went into action. They didn't badger Moses about why he was having trouble carrying out God's plan. They saw Moses' purpose, assessed what they were able to do to help, and then did it!

Fortunately for us, we live in New Testament times. Each of us can be a Moses. Every Christian has direct access to God through Jesus Christ. He will direct us and always be there for us. It's not up to us to come running in and tell God how to do things better or easier. Trust Him! The Lord knows what is best!

There are times when someone you know is in a battle of their own. We are to remember that *"our struggle is not against flesh and blood, but… against the spiritual forces of evil"* (Ephesians 6:12). We are to do our part and be willing to step into action to support our fellow Christians when they step out in obedience to God. How can you help?

MARCH 28

The Permanent Caregiver

...he will watch over your life; the Lord will watch over your coming and going both now and forevermore.
(Psalm 121:7–8)

I love my children dearly. I will always remember giving birth to each of them. I marvelled at the miracle God created within me. I remember bringing each precious bundle home from the hospital. I specifically remember holding our firstborn son in my arms and wondering what I was supposed to do. I had younger siblings and had babysat other infants and children many times, but here I was with our very own baby. What if I made a mistake? What if I didn't have all the answers on how to take care of him and raise him the right away? What would happen when I had to sleep? If our baby needed me, would I wake up? Could I keep him from harm and sickness? What if he did get hurt or ill? Would I do the right thing to restore him to health?

Thankfully, we managed. We didn't have all the answers, and we didn't always do things the right way the first time. However, with God's help, and that of the people He provided to help us along the way, we have two godly, healthy, well-adjusted young adult sons.

I am comforted by the knowledge that God is watching over my life. He knows what choices I have made and those I have yet to make. He is always with me and will guide me if I choose to listen and obey. I find it comforting to know God also knows my husband and each of our children personally. God has been watching over each of them from their very conception to now, and forevermore.

Take comfort in knowing He is watching over you, your spouse, and your loved ones *"both now and forevermore."*

He will not let your [or their] foot slip—he who watches over you [and them] will not slumber. (Psalm 121:3)

Thankfully, He has the answers. Our job is to listen and obey.

MARCH 29

Don't Waste God's Blessings

They all ate and were satisfied, and the disciples picked up twelve basketfuls of broken pieces that were left over.
(Matthew 14:20)

Remember the story of the feeding of the thousands? The people had followed Jesus and were listening to His teaching. By night time, there were about five thousand men plus their wives and children. The disciples wanted to send them away so that the people could go and find food for themselves. Jesus had compassion on them and said, *"They do not need to go away. You give them something to eat"* (Matthew 14:16). All that was available was five loaves of bread and two fish. Jesus gave thanks and broke the pieces. The disciples handed it all out to the people. They all *"ate and were satisfied."*

Did you notice what happened next? Jesus had the disciples pick up all the leftover broken pieces! Twelve baskets full! (Perhaps that was one basketful for each disciple.) I don't think it was because Jesus was afraid He might be hungry later and wouldn't have enough to eat. Jesus didn't want even the leftover crumbs to be wasted.

Can you think of a blessing you have received from the Lord? Did you give thanks? Did it satisfy your need? Have you made use of every little bit of that blessing? Have you respectfully saved the leftovers? In what way might you be able to use your blessing to bless others and further God's kingdom? Brainstorm with your spouse what the Lord has blessed you with and in what ways you could use the extras. What about your marriage? God has blessed you with a Christian spouse. Do you continue to give thanks to God for your spouse? Do you appreciate your spouse? In what ways can you use the overflow of your relationship for Jesus?

MARCH 30

Great Leadership Advice

Moses' father-in-law replied, "What you are doing is not good." (Exodus 18:17)

Moses was appointed by God to lead the Israelites. It seemed right and good that he should pronounce judgement over the people's conflicts. Why then is Jethro, his father-in-law, also a man of God, telling Moses that what he is *"doing is not good"*?

Jethro actually gave Moses very good advice. Jethro could see that the people were coming to Moses more and more and Moses was becoming overworked and bogged down with all the little disputes of the people. This didn't leave him with the time or energy for the things he should have been focusing on. Jethro advised Moses to delegate! He didn't suggest Moses just pass the buck to the next person like a hot potato.

Jethro's advice was to take the time to train the people in the laws of God and how they should live. This process would provide everyone with the tools to make better decisions on their own. Secondly, Jethro advised that Moses select capable men. This would suggest careful consideration. These men would be assigned to judge over smaller groups of people. They would then bring to Moses only the few cases they were unable to resolve themselves. Jethro finished by saying, *"If you do this and God so commands, you will be able to stand the strain, and all these people will go home satisfied"* (Exodus 18:23). Moses was advised to provide good training, make careful selection, and then release those he had trained to do their work. Notice that everyone benefited, not just Moses.

What great advice for anyone in leadership! This can apply to ministry, employment, or family life. If you're feeling overwhelmed in your circumstance, take the time to study Exodus 18. Ask Jesus to help you apply it to your situation.

MARCH 31

Let Me Do That

When they came to the threshing floor of Kidon, Uzzah reached out his hand to steady the ark, because the oxen stumbled. The Lord's anger burned against Uzzah, and he struck him down because he had put his hand on the ark. So he died there before God.
(1 Chronicles 13:9–10)

When we read this story in 1 Chronicles 13, the Lord seems so unfair! After all, the oxen had stumbled and the ark may have fallen to the ground and even been damaged if Uzzah hadn't steadied it! Why was the Lord angry?

Well, let's go back to Exodus. God gave very specific instructions on how the ark was to be built, and how it was to be carried. Nobody was to touch this very holy ark! Only priests were allowed to carry the ark using the poles created specifically for that purpose.

Someone came up with the bright idea of helping God out. Instead of the priests having to carry the weight of the ark on poles, they would put the ark on a cart and have oxen carry it. Touching the ark itself was a sin which was punishable by death.

How many times do we try to help God out? "Hey God, I have a better idea! This way would be better, easier, more efficient." Do you see the danger? Can you relate?

Thankfully, Jesus has already paid the price for our arrogance and resulting sin. Through Jesus, our sins have been forgiven. He has died in our place. Our part is to die to ourselves. We must recognise the authority, power, and wisdom of the Lord. Listen carefully and be obedient.

Yes, the Lord is to be feared, but do not allow that fear to bring separation from the Lord, as it initially did to David. Later, in 1 Chronicles 15, David recognized their error and reinstated the Lord's original specifications for carrying the ark. This was an attitude of respect that prompted realignment with the Lord's will. David was forgiven, but the consequence had already taken place.

APRIL 1

Two in One

"...and the two will become one flesh." So they are no longer two, but one. (Mark 10:8)

Today's verse is part of Jesus' response to the question of divorce. Jesus tells us that God's intent from the beginning of creation was for man and woman to be united together for as long as they live on this earth together.

A dramatic illustration of this concept was shown to me using paper doll cut-outs. Imagine a blue paper doll and a corresponding pink paper doll. Glue them together and let the glue set for a while. Now, try pulling the two apart. They do not separate to their original condition intact. There will be tears; some pink left on the blue, and some blue left on the pink. This happens even after only a short time of being glued together.

In the Gospels, Jesus explained that Moses permitted divorce only because the people's hearts had become hard. This doesn't happen overnight, although it may sometimes appear to. The gradual deterioration and neglect of the relationship allows one's heart to harden towards the other.

Remember also that marriage is about more than man's paperwork. Some couples stay married only because they think that's what they should do. God is concerned about the heart. When you allow yourselves to cease being companions, you allow the seeds of divorce to enter your lives.

The best way to avoid the pain of divorce is to keep your hearts from becoming hard. Keep your lives and marriage Christ-centred. Honour your marriage, respect your spouse, and express your love daily.

APRIL 2

Superwoman (Part One)

She speaks with wisdom, and faithful instruction is on her tongue. She watches over the affairs of her household and does not eat the bread of idleness. Her children arise and call her blessed; her husband also, and he praises her…
(Proverbs 31:26–28)

Ah! The Proverbs 31 woman! She's got it all together! When you read of all the things she does, she appears to be a "superwoman." Many strive to be like her Frankly, just reading about her made me tired. Then I realized that this woman didn't just appear out of thin air, get married, and have it all together instantaneously. If that were the case, I'm sure there would be even more written about her.

This is a woman whose heart was in the right place. Being human, she must have made some mistakes along the way. As she grew, learned, and developed into the woman of God we read about, her eyes were not on herself. It wasn't about when she would get a break, what others could do for her, or what credit she was given.

She embraced the role she was in. She obviously loved her husband, her children, and her life. She didn't just gather things up for herself. Notice that she "*speaks with wisdom, and faithful instruction is on her tongue.*" She was willing to reach beyond herself and speak into the lives of others that which she had learned. This woman was God-centred!

The bonus is the favourable light in which her children, husband, and others saw her. What better position could one be in to point others towards the Lord?

Wife, continue to seek to be in the Lord's will always. Husband, pray for your wife, that she may not stumble, but continue to keep her eyes on Jesus.

APRIL 3

Superwoman (Part Two)

Husbands, love your wives, just as Christ loved the church and gave himself up for her to make her holy, cleansing her by the washing with water through the word, and to present her to himself as a radiant church, without stain or wrinkle or any other blemish, but holy and blameless. (Ephesians 5:25–27)

You knew it was coming, didn't you? Husbands, if you want a Proverbs 31 wife, you need to be an Ephesians 5 husband. I love my husband deeply, and I know he loves me. However, it's a big calling to love someone *"just as Christ loved the church."* As the Proverb 31 woman didn't appear instantaneously, neither did the Ephesians 5 husband.

Let's look at the intent of these verses. They give us the goal for which husbands are to continuously strive. It's not the position you suddenly attain; it's the process. The point is not to make your wife look good so that you look better. Jesus wants you to invest in your wife for her wellbeing and spiritual development. Help her to study and understand the word of God. Encourage her in her walk with the Lord. Lovingly help her to be cleansed by the Holy Spirit so that her faults or mistakes (*"stain or wrinkle or any other blemish"*) will be washed away.

What areas in your life do you need to address in order to better be able to love your wife? What things might you do to help keep her on the path Jesus has planned for her? What encouragement or support could you provide? Are there stumbling blocks you could help her overcome?

How much time do you spend in prayer for, and with, your wife?

APRIL 4

He Wants to Live With Me?!

They will know that I am the Lord their God, who brought them out of Egypt so that I might dwell among them. I am the Lord their God. (Exodus 29:46)

It's hard to imagine that God would want to dwell amongst us. We, like the Israelites, fail again and again, but His love endures. God loves every person. Now, I know I've messed up at times, but I also know that there are people in this world who have messed up even more. Some people have even been given the opportunity to know Jesus personally, and turned Him down! God continues to love even them. He wants everyone to receive Jesus and spend eternity with Him. It grieves Him when we turn our backs on Him and decline a proper relationship with Him.

A few things come to mind as I contemplate this. One is my relationship with Jesus. I would desire to have Jesus live in my heart and guide all my attitudes, thoughts, and behaviours. Secondly, I think of my relationships with other people. I may not condone all the choices other people make, I may even get angry or hurt, but can I be compassionate, forgiving, and merciful towards them with the love of Jesus?

Lastly, I consider the relationship between spouses. God desires to dwell with us in our marriages. He wants to walk with us, talk with us, and guide us through all times. He's there to help us resolve and forgive disagreements. Jesus is there to help you live each day in a loving, respectful relationship with your spouse. Sometimes one or the other in the relationship will mess up. It happens because of our humanity. Choose to love one another with the love of Jesus. Be compassionate, merciful, and forgiving in times of conflict. Enjoy the companionship. Rejoice in the love. Thank the Lord for His unimaginable great love for each of us.

APRIL 5

Well Done Good and Faithful Servant?

For everyone who has will be given more, and he will have an abundance. Whoever does not have, even what he has will be taken from him.
(Matthew 25:29)

Today's verse comes from the parable of the talents. One servant was given five talents from his master, a second servant was given two talents, and yet a third servant was given one talent. The master went away for a while. When he returned, he called the servants in to ask for an account of what they had done with what they had been given charge of. The first two servants had doubled their investments. The last had not used the talent, but had hidden it to keep it safe.

The first two, who had done the best they could with what the master had given them, both received the same reward. The master responded, *"Well done, good and faithful servant! You have been faithful with a few things; I will put you in charge of many things. Come and share your master's happiness!"* (Matthew 25:21, 23) The last servant was only accountable for one talent. He did not think well of his master and was afraid of him. He therefore didn't even try to manage the talent, merely hiding it. The result was that even that small blessing was taken from him and given to those whose hearts were favourable towards their master.

Those who truly know Jesus will desire to do His work with joy. *"Whatever you do, work at it with all your heart, as working for the Lord, not for men"* (Colossians 3:23). Their desire is to please Jesus and honour Him. Those who only know of Jesus will not have a right attitude towards the work of God.

Don't worry about how little you might feel you can do, or how many results you see. Jesus knows what you have been given and your heart attitude.

Be prepared to *"share your master's happiness"* with your spouse and all those around you.

APRIL 6

Be Strong!

Watch and pray so that you will not fall into temptation. The spirit is willing, but the body is weak.
(Matthew 26:41)

Jesus had invited three of His disciples to accompany Him when He went to the garden of Gethsemane to pray. Jesus told them that His *"soul [was] overwhelmed with sorrow"* (Matthew 26:38). Jesus then instructed the disciples to keep watch with Him. Jesus moved off by Himself and prayed fervently to the Father. When Jesus returned to the place where He had left the disciples, He found them sleeping. He woke them and spoke today's verse. He went away again to pray, and twice more, when He returned, the disciples were asleep.

Notice that Jesus didn't implore the disciples to pray for Him. It wasn't that Jesus needed their prayers. Later, in Matthew 26:53, Jesus says, *"Do you think I cannot call on my Father, and he will at once put at my disposal more than twelve legions of angels?"* Jesus knew His time had come and that He would soon be leaving earth to return to the Father. He would be leaving His followers to do that for which they had been trained. Jesus said, *"Watch and pray so that you will not fall into temptation."* Jesus' concern was for Peter. He knew what Peter would face when He was gone, and Jesus wanted Peter to be prepared.

Now, if Jesus was concerned for the faith of Peter, on whom He had promised to build His church, where does that put you and me? I believe, like Peter, Jesus would urge us to watch and pray. Be on alert! Watch for pitfalls. Be aware of the enemy's schemes. Set aside time in your daily life for prayer. Pray continuously. Pray with your spouse. Jesus knows our spirits are willing to follow Him. He also knows that our bodies are weak. He does not wish for us to fall into temptation. Prayer will strengthen us.

I can do all things though Christ who strengthens me. (Philippians 4:13, NKJV)

APRIL 7

Inside Out

You are like whitewashed tombs, which look beautiful on the outside but on the inside are full of dead men's bones and everything unclean. (Matthew 23:27)

Jesus had some pretty strong words for the Pharisees. This verse has always struck me as one of His strongest reprimands.

The Pharisees were always concerned about what looked right. They took pride in knowing the laws, looking good, and judging others. Jesus, however, was very clear in pointing out the error of their attitudes. Jesus told them it was good that they fulfilled some of the laws, such as tithing, but that they *"neglected the more important matters of the law—justice, mercy and faithfulness"* (Matthew 23:23). The Pharisees looked like they had it all together on the outside, but Jesus told them they were dead on the inside.

Have you ever caught yourself judging others who didn't appear perfect in your eyes? Perhaps you didn't approve of their dress, their choice of church, the amount of work they did, or whether they ate and drank things you didn't approve of. Perhaps you have found yourself admiring and looking up to someone who appears to have it all together. They appear to dress well, work hard, and live a righteous life. Only Jesus knows the entire truth. Try to see others through His eyes, but ours is not to judge others.

What about yourself? Are there areas of your life you try to cover over? Is there anything you do in secret you wouldn't want your Christian friends, leaders, or Jesus to find out about? Are there things you do just to receive approval of man? Are you willing to give Jesus permission to convict you of attitudes, thoughts, and behaviours that aren't clean and pure? Ask Jesus to continue to clean you from the inside out. Don't risk being nothing but dead bones on the inside. Always start your clean-up from the inside out.

APRIL 8

What Did You Say?

Impress them on your children. Talk about them when you sit at home and when you walk along the road, when you lie down and when you get up. (Deuteronomy 6:7)

Here is a command from God to teach our children His commandments. Of course, as Christian parents, that's what we want for our children. It seems quite obvious. However, for those of you who have children, how much do you really talk to them about anything? This doesn't include management time such as "Clean your room" or "Is your homework done?" In North America, we live in a fast-paced society. We hear a lot about the lack of communication in our technological age, but remember that the book of Deuteronomy is dated at 1410 B.C. This issue has seemingly plagued mankind for a long time.

The statistics on how much time, even from infancy, we spend in front of a screen is disturbing. The statistics of how much time we spend with our children outside of corrective time is no more encouraging. We appear to be spending less and less time just sitting, walking, and relaxing together as families. You can change that for your family!

As I reflect again on this verse, I notice the method we are directed to use to teach our children about God and His commands. It doesn't tell us to send them to Sunday School, although that's a perfectly good thing to do. It doesn't say make Christian books or videos available to them, although that's also a good thing. It commands us to spend quality, relationship-building time together, and to use that time to speak into their lives about God.

I also notice that it doesn't say we should only do this between certain ages. It is for *all* your children. Talk to them, regardless of their age. It is God's command. To do that, you must purpose to spend time quality, undivided time together.

Enjoy the blessing God has given you in your children.

APRIL 9

The Lord Knows How to Bless

Now to him who is able to do immeasurably more than all we ask or imagine, according to his power that is at work within us...
(Ephesians 3:20)

God desires to bless us more than we can anticipate. If we ask with the right heart or motive, the Lord will bless us. Our tendency is to tell God exactly what we think we want or need. He is a patient Father, and therefore, in His wisdom, He may only bless us as much as we ask, or He may give us the full blessing in spite of ourselves.

I have two illustrations to explain what I mean. The first is a situation where our Sunday School children offered to raise money for a special project. The person making the request thought they were stretching the children, so they only asked them to raise money for half of what was needed. The timeline for raising it was set. When the time arrived, the children had actually raised twice as much as they were asked to. In fact, they were on God's agenda and raised the total amount that was needed, even though they didn't know what the total need was.

The second illustration is of a person who stepped out in faith. This person believed that the Lord had asked him to do something that included buying a number of books. At the time, he had little financial resources, but he stepped out anyway, trusting the Lord. He contacted the publisher and received a quote for the number of books needed. It would cost five hundred dollars. The books were ordered. Later, he was approached by someone who said that the Lord had told him to give three hundred dollars. As it turned out, when the books arrived, the cost was just under three hundred dollars. God knew that!

This doesn't only apply to finances. When you go to the Lord and ask for His blessing, be careful what you ask for. Allow the Lord to bless you with what He knows you need.

APRIL 10

Yes, I Can

The Lord himself goes before you and will be with you; he will never leave you nor forsake you. Do not be afraid; do not be discouraged. (Deuteronomy 31:8)

This verse comes at a time when Moses was handing off his leadership to Joshua. After all Moses had done in leading the rebellious Israelites out of Egypt, he had displeased the Lord and was told he would only get to see, but not enter, the Promised Land. Can you imagine how Joshua felt? He had some pretty big shoes to fill!

Thankfully, even today, when the Lord asks us to do something, we can trust that He has gone before us. As well, we have the advantage of the Holy Spirit to guide us and comfort us.

So what happens when you hear the Lord directing you through the Holy Spirit? Many of us start out with zeal! "Yes. I can do this with the Lord's help!" Then we allow thoughts of self-doubt to creep in, and we start seeing all the barriers ahead of us. Where do you think those thoughts come from? The evil one doesn't want to see the Lord's kingdom expanded. Put aside those fears and doubts as soon as they crop up. Go back to Jesus and confess your struggles. He knows about them. Don't allow the enemy make you believe for one minute that he can win against the Lord's will. The Lord will *always* go before us. The Holy Spirit will *always* be with us. All we need to do is keep our eyes on Him and not stray from the path.

Here again, we who are married to a Christian spouses are strengthened. Share with your spouse the things you believe the Lord is asking you to do. As you together turn to Jesus, you will find strength in the cord of three.

Therefore encourage one another and build each other up, just as in fact you are doing. (1 Thessalonians 5:11)

APRIL 11

Childlike Faith

I tell you the truth, anyone who will not receive the kingdom of God like a little child will never enter it.
(Mark 10:15)

In my Bible, this verse is in red, meaning that it was words spoken directly by Jesus. That gets my attention! *"I tell you the truth,"* Jesus said. Would He do otherwise? He said this to emphasize what He was about to say.

I know we don't all have the same giftings, nor should we. However, one of my passions is working with young children. As I endeavour to teach children, I learn so much from them. If you have the opportunity to help out with a children's program, even for a short while, I highly recommend you do so.

I remember a time when I was teaching Sunday School to a group of four- to six-year-olds. We were learning how to pray. Each Sunday we would sit in a circle and share what we would like to have prayer for. As we went around the circle, things like sore throats, mean kids at school, and sick family members would come up. As each request was made, I asked who would like to pray for that situation. These little children's prayers were amazing! They were short, direct, and sincere. The children expected their prayers to be answered. Guess what? Their prayers were answered time and time again. The Bible tells us that Jesus hears our prayers, and that when we pray with the right motives, He answers our prayers. These children just believed the word of God.

As we grow older, we tend to start worrying about what others think. Social responsibility is a good thing. What isn't good is when we allow our perceptions of others' opinions to be more important than what we know through the word to be true. When is the last time you looked to Jesus through the eyes of a child?

APRIL 12

The Lord Detests Dishonesty

You must have accurate and honest weights and measures, so that you may live long in the land the Lord your God is giving you. For the Lord your God detests anyone who does these things, anyone who deals dishonestly. (Deuteronomy 25:15–16)

This section of Deuteronomy instructed the Israelites on the Lord's commands regarding human relations. This indicates that some of the Israelites were in the habit of using measures to cheat people. Obviously this was wrong, and the Lord told them He actually detested them for their dishonesty. I'm sure nobody, regardless of what they believe, would want to have God actually detest them! It's not only uncomfortable, but dangerous!

However, when you think about it, we have all fallen into using such measures. What about holding the store door open for a well-dressed, smiling person whose arms are full? Then suppose a dirty, smelly, apparently homeless person approaches, pushing a cart full of items. Do you hold the door open for them? Suppose a distraught, well-dressed elderly woman has lost her car keys. Do you offer to give her a ride or otherwise help her out? Okay, and then say you come across a scruffy-looking person begging for money for bus fare. Do you offer to give them a ride or otherwise help them out? What about a child vs. an adult, a man vs. a woman; a difference in style of dress, or some other determining difference? Yes, we need to be responsible in making decisions regarding the safety of ourselves and our loved ones, and yes, we need to be wise in how we help others for their good. However, do you always approach all people with the same heart attitude or measure?

Is there a situation the Lord is speaking to you about?

APRIL 13

King of Your Life

When you enter the land the Lord your God is giving you and have taken possession of it and settled in it, and you say, "Let us set a king over us like all the nations around us..."
(Deuteronomy 17:14)

This verse refers to the Israelites who the Lord had taken from slavery in Egypt, whom He was leading into the Promised Land. This process had taken years— even generations. They were about to receive all the Lord desired to give them, what's the first thing they do? They want to "fit in" and do things like everybody else.

Think about how this might apply in your life. Where is the Lord leading you? We've already been set free from slavery to sin through Jesus Christ.

But thanks be to God that, though you used to be slaves to sin, you wholeheartedly obeyed the form of teaching to which you were entrusted. You have been set free from sin... (Romans 6:17–18)

Where is the Lord leading you now? When you arrive at the place or area of ministry the Lord is giving you, will you recognize it and receive it? Take hold of the gifts He's offering you!

Why is it that we keep looking around at what everybody else is doing? You may think that what someone else has looks good. You ask yourself, "What harm will it do if I begin to be a little bit like them?" I'm not saying that career success, wealth, or any other attribute is bad; it's where your focus is. In fact, the Lord may grant you those same attributes so you can use them to further His kingdom.

As you and I continue to develop our relationship with the Lord, I pray that we will recognize what He is giving us, not allowing ourselves to be distracted by the worldly things around us.

What is "king" of your life?

APRIL 14

Leading Others to Jesus

So the man went away and began to tell in the Decapolis how much Jesus had done for him. And all the people were amazed.
(Mark 5:20)

I love to read the Gospels! Here is a story of a man who had been possessed by a legion of evil spirits (perhaps three to six thousand). No one had been able to help him. Jesus had just set him free. Of course, the man wanted to stay with Jesus and follow Him. Jesus didn't let him. Instead, Jesus sent him back to his family to tell them about what had happened to him. The man obeyed.

Notice that the man didn't start lecturing everyone else. He didn't try to beat them over the head, manipulate them, criticize them, or threaten them with eternal hell so they would be saved, too. He simply went with the joy of the Lord and told others about what Jesus had done for him. The results were that *"all the people were amazed."* He didn't witness to just one or two people, but *all* the people! His life got their attention and they did the seeking! Luke 8:40 tells us, *"Now when Jesus returned, a crowd welcomed him, for they were all expecting him."* The people went out to look for Jesus!

What parts of your life witness to what Jesus Christ has done for you? Do people see a positive change in you since you received salvation through Jesus Christ? Do people see something different or special in the way you live your life as a Christian versus the rest of the world? Is there something different? Do you still have joy in the Lord? If not, why not? What can you do to refresh that joy and live it out in your daily life as a witness to others?

Dear God, I pray that You would help us realize and remember all that You have done for us. Help us to receive Your joy daily and allow it to shine to those around us. Amen.

APRIL 15

No Other God

I will set my face against the person who turns to mediums and spiritists to prostitute himself by following them, and I will cut him off from his people.
(Leviticus 20:6)

The Lord has called us to turn to Him and no other god!

I have known people who go to psychics or tarot card readers as a fun thing to do. How about horoscopes? You're reading a paper or magazine, and there they are. Just out of curiosity, you check out what they have to say. Then you may start going to that section of the paper or magazine purposefully to check it out once in a while; then daily. What about Ouija boards or others games? No harm, right? Wrong!

Any time we interact with the spiritual world without being under the cover of the Holy Spirit, a lot of harm can and will be done. When we do this, we invite spirits into our lives. If they aren't of God, they are of Satan. Those spirits enter with our permission and begin to do their work. We may not notice anything right away. After all, Satan and his demons are masters at deception. It is not a game to them! They will do whatever they can to turn you away from the one true God and take control of your life. You will find yourself back in the slavery to sin Jesus died to set you free from.

...I, the Lord, am holy, and I have set you apart from the nations to be my own. (Leviticus 20:26)

The Lord loves us and desires what is good for us. He does not demand our undivided attention to feed His ego, but rather desires to show us the way to wholeness and righteousness.

If you have entertained these ungodly spiritual areas before, now is the time to confess your sin, repent, and ask the Lord to free you from any hold these spirits may have on your life. Then invite the Holy Spirit to enter in and fill you now and always.

APRIL 16

Passing the Test

Remember how the Lord your God led you all the way in the desert these forty years, to humble you and to test you in order to know what was in your heart, whether or not you would keep his commands.
(Deuteronomy 8:2)

If I'm a Christian, isn't everything supposed to go perfectly now? I just ask the Lord and He makes everything run smoothly, right? No. The Lord is our strength and He will walk with us at all times, but He doesn't prevent life from happening. In fact, as we can see from today's verse, He allows, and sometimes even leads us through, difficult times to test our faith. He has something more for us!

To some, that may sound mean, but let's take another look at this. If a toddler was never allowed, or encouraged, to try to walk just in case he should fall, he would never learn to walk. If we cut open the cocoon to help the poor butterfly out, it would never be able to fly and would therefore die. If a university graduate was given all intellectual knowledge at birth, they would never learn the process of learning something new, or even to problem-solve.

I know it doesn't feel good when we go through times of testing, but it's ultimately for our good. I'm not saying every bad thing that happens in our life is a test from God, but He's always there with us if we invite Him. We need to *"trust in the Lord with all your heart and lean not on your own understanding"* (Proverbs 3:5).

We should have so much joy when God considers us ready for the next step! Instead of "Why me?" let's try asking, "What would you have me learn, Lord?" In times of difficulty, we need to spend even more time listening and learning. How exciting it will be when we *get it* and pass to the next level of our spiritual walks!

Don't give up or turn away. You are considered ready for a deeper teaching.

APRIL 17

Are You Successful?

You may say to yourself, "My power and the strength of my hands have produced this wealth for me." But remember the Lord your God, for it is he who gives you the ability to produce wealth, and so confirms his covenant, which he swore to your forefathers, as it is today.
(Deuteronomy 8:17–18)

What does success mean to you? Are you successful? As Christians, we must recognize God's hand in our lives. If you consider yourself successful, what were those things that enabled you to reach success? You may have worked hard to reach the place you're at, but be assured that God gave you that ability. It might be your family, your country, your opportunities, the climate, or any other number of contributing factors, but God created and chose each of them for you. If you don't feel successful, what is preventing you? Are you living your life in alignment with all God has for you? Have you asked for His input? Are you listening for His direction? Is He testing you?

Take a moment to meditate on this.

Now let's think about what success means to you. Is it wealth and status? Is it peace, helping others, improving the world around you, and sharing the joy of the Lord to those around you?

Take another moment to really contemplate your answer—not the answer you're supposed to give, but how you really feel. Do you believe your definition is in alignment with God's will for your life?

Thank You, Father, for creating and caring for the whole universe. Thank You for creating and caring for each one of us. Thank You that You *"know the plans [you] have for [us]... plans to prosper [us] and not to harm [us], plans to give [us] hope and a future"* (Jeremiah 29:11).

Father, help each of us to know what it is You would have us do to reach success in Your eyes. Amen.

APRIL 18

God's Laws

Do not add to what I command you and do not subtract from it, but keep the commands of the Lord your God that I give you.
(Deuteronomy 4:2)

Moses instructed the Israelites in the commands and laws of the Lord. He prepared them to enter the Promised Land without him. These laws were instituted for the good of the Israelites, and were meant to set them apart from the corrupt nations around them.

Perhaps you say, "That no longer applies. That was for Old Testament times. I live in the freedom of the New Testament through my salvation in Jesus Christ." If so, I would remind you that the Bible ends in Revelation 22:18–19, with:

I warn everyone who hears the words of the prophecy of this book: If anyone adds anything to them, God will add to him the plagues described in this book. And if anyone takes words away from this book of prophecy, God will take away from him his share in the tree of life and in the holy city, which are described in this book.

In the Gospels, Jesus tells us that He was sent to fulfill the Mosaic Law, but He also instructed us in the way we should live as Christians for our good and for the glory of the kingdom of God. Jesus scolded the Pharisees for adding extra burdens on people, and for ignoring the parts of the law that didn't suit them. The word of God is not fickle, nor is it a menu. We are not to pick out the parts that fit our opinions and wishes, dismissing the parts we consider less tasteful or that don't suit our spoiled attitudes. The word of God is *all* good!

Dear heavenly Father, help each of us to know Your word and keep ourselves in Your will each and every day. Show us where we fall short, and help us to realign ourselves with Your will. Amen.

APRIL 19

What Comes Out of Our Mouths?

The good man brings good things out of the good stored up in his heart, and the evil man brings evil things out of the evil stored up in his heart. For out of the overflow of his heart his mouth speaks.
(Luke 6:45)

These words are taken from Jesus' Sermon on the Mount. He was teaching His followers how to discern the purity of their own heart attitude. Jesus was explaining to them, and us, that we should not judge and condemn others, since we each have work on ourselves to which we need to attend.

If in our pride, we find ourselves being critical of others, what good is that? What right do we have to do so? More importantly, it is our responsibility to keep our own lives and attitudes in check. Jesus taught us to listen to our own words. Do you hear good, loving, and encouraging words coming out of your own mouth, or are you negative and critical? What does that tell you about your own righteousness and attitude?

How do you become a good person? Jesus tells us to seek to store up good things in our hearts. Keep your focus on Jesus! Seek to know God more intimately. Praise Him, read His word, pray, spend time speaking and listening to God, and invite the Holy Spirit into your life. If the Lord reveals sin in our lives, we need to confess, repent, and thank Him for His mercy. Don't dwell on it! That just allows the evil one to continue to put you down, and invites Satan to infect you. Evil, like darkness, cannot coexist with good, or the light of Jesus. Rather than struggling with the evil, seek to be filled with goodness through the Holy Spirit that Jesus has sent to dwell within us.

May our words always express the goodness that overflows from our hearts.

APRIL 20

Easter

The Son of Man must be delivered into the hands of sinful men, be crucified and on the third day be raised again.
(Luke 24:7)

Easter is the day! This is the very key to Christianity. Yes, Good Friday is crucial. It was on Good Friday that Jesus Christ was crucified. He was betrayed, falsely accused, beaten, and finally killed by crucifixion. He took all our sins upon Himself and died that we might be saved and have eternal life with Him in heaven. However, if Jesus didn't break the chains of death and rise again, Good Friday would be meaningless. He would have just been another good and wise man, or a prophet in His time, who was killed.

This is the one aspect all Christians are united in. We may have different ways of receiving communion, different demonstrations of baptism, different times or days for meeting, but being Christian means believing Jesus died on the cross for us and that He rose again.

Jesus tried to foretell to His disciples what must take place. He returned to them for a short time after He rose from the grave. *"Then he opened their minds so they could understand the Scriptures"* (Luke 24:45). He promised two things: to send them the Holy Spirit and to be with them, and every Christian, always. The disciples watched Jesus ascend into heaven on a cloud. Then Jesus did send the Holy Spirit to His disciples. He has made that same offer to each of us.

Easter is definitely a time to solemnly reflect on all that Jesus sacrificed. It is truly amazing! However, it is also a time of great joy. Jesus Christ has broken the chains of death! He has given us eternal life with Him in heaven! You have been set free! Give thanks.

Rejoice!

APRIL 21

The Seeds of Hope (Part One)

As he was scattering the seed, some fell along the path, and the birds came and ate it up. Some fell on rocky places, where it did not have much soil. It sprang up quickly… But when the sun came up, the plants were scorched, and they withered because they had no root.
(Mark 4:4–6)

Jesus presents the parable of the farmer. The farmer represents a Christian who spreads the good news of the word of God to others. The ground represents the people to whom the message is presented. Each seed is the opportunity to receive salvation through Jesus Christ.

In the first verse, Jesus speaks of the seed that falls on a path. The ground is packed down and the seed exposed. The birds can easily find the seed and swoop down to eat it.

Some people are like seed along the path, where the word is sown. As soon as they hear it, Satan comes and takes away the word that was sown in them. (Mark 4:15)

Satan will use whatever strategy he needs to try to rob these people of their newfound faith. He lies, deceives, ridicules, and throws doubts at them.

Then Jesus addresses the seed that fell on *"rocky places."*

Others, like seed sown on rocky places, hear the word and at once receive it with joy. But since they have no root, they last only a short time. When trouble or persecution comes because of the word, they quickly fall away.
(Mark 4:16–17)

These are the people who appear to have life-changing experiences. They are overjoyed and excited about the word. They receive the message with the enthusiasm of the moment, but quickly fall back into their old ways. Maybe they were at a conference, or received help at a low point in their lives. As quickly as they received the word, they forget it.

Can you think of people either of these applies to? Pray that God would renew a steadfast spirit within them.

APRIL 22

The Seeds of Hope (Part Two)

Other seed fell among thorns, which grew up and choked the plants, so that they did not bear grain. Still other seed fell on good soil. It came up, grew and produced a crop, multiplying thirty, sixty, or even a hundred times.
(Mark 4:7–8)

In the first verse today, Jesus speaks of a third category of people.

Still others, like seed sown among thorns, hear the word; but the worries of this life, the deceitfulness of wealth and the desires for other things come in and choke the word, making it unfruitful. (Mark 4:18–19)

These people hear the word and begin to follow it. Then they get distracted by life. They take their eyes off Jesus and return to focusing on themselves and their situations. They start out with good intentions, only to lose the prize in the end.

Finally, Jesus speaks of the fruitful people, those people *get it*! Their hearts have been prepared. They hear the word and receive their salvation through Jesus. They keep their eyes on the Lord and seek to know His ways. They serve Him always, no matter where they are or what's happening in the world around them. As they allow the Holy Spirit to work in their lives, they become fruitful. They spread the "seed."

What type of "ground" do you see yourself being? The truth is that we have all received the "seed" differently at different times in our lives. There may have been times when we allowed Satan to steal some of what has been offered to us, times when we haven't persevered, times when we've taken our eyes off Jesus and focused on ourselves. Hopefully, we've all experienced fruitful times in our lives. Thankfully, we serve a merciful God, and when we turn our eyes back to Him, He is forgiving. Be encouraged. What can you do to spread the seed and be fruitful today?

APRIL 23

The Lord Rejoices

The Lord your God is with you, he is mighty to save. He will take great delight in you, he will quiet you with his love, he will rejoice over you with singing.
(Zephaniah 3:17)

This verse is taken from Zephaniah's prophecy over the Jewish nation, which was under a terrible time of judgement and punishment. Through the prophet Zephaniah, the Lord encouraged them to repent, promising them a better time ahead if they did so. The Lord, through Zephaniah, spoke the above verse in reference to a future time (the millennial age) for those who choose to obey the Lord.

This verse also applies to Christians today. The Bible tells us time and again that the Lord is always with us. We also know that every person can have eternal life through belief in Jesus. Then we are told that *"he will take great delight in you."* That's not just some fictional character, some holier person than you; that is *you*! You and I, as individuals, are important to God. He loves and cares for each of us. He even *delights* in each one of us. *"He will quiet you with his love."*

Do you find it hard to just *"be still, and know that I am God"* (Psalm 46:10)? Allow the Holy Spirit to enter in and bring the love and peace of God. The Lord our God *"rejoice[s] over you with singing."* He is so happy for each one of us who have chosen to receive His love. He treasures each of us as if we were the only one in the world.

It's hard to understand the kind of love that God has for you and me. We don't have the capacity. It's like an unborn child not having the capacity to understand the beauty of colour he will see after birth.

Take heart. You are not insignificant. The Lord loves you, delights in you, and rejoices over you.

APRIL 24

Jesus' Forgiveness

Jesus said, "Father, forgive them, for they do not know what they are doing."
(Luke 23:34)

I am always moved as I read through the account of the events leading up to the crucifixion. Sometimes I see it as a news clip and wonder about the horror of how some humans could treat another human being. Then I think about the mob mentality, which is not so different from allowing our media to slant the way we judge events without knowing the full account. Here was an innocent man, whose death people had been manipulated into demanding! I wonder how I would have responded if I had been part of that crowd.

Then we come to the cross. It was now time for Jesus to be nailed to the cross and crucified with two other apparent criminals. Jesus had been falsely accused, severely beaten, mocked, and deserted. Then He turned to the Father and asked Him to forgive those same people! What?

Well, in fact, I am a member of the crowd. Jesus died for my sins as well. He has asked the Father to forgive me, too. Wow! Then who am I to be unforgiving? It is very humbling.

We have all been hurt, and maybe even afflicted by others. Sometimes those we hurt were even other Christians. What are we called to do? Forgive.

Recently, I was hurt because I felt someone spoke to me sharply. I went away wounded. I was convicted of that. I confessed that hurt to Jesus, asking Him for forgiveness once more. Then I rejected the very thought of the other person hurting me, unintentionally or intentionally. I recognized my fault in allowing that thought to even enter my mind. I emailed the person an encouraging word about what I appreciated about them. I'm sure that person doesn't even know about what transpired in my mind and spirit, but I'm glad Jesus led me to clearing our path of fellowship.

Who are you not to forgive?

APRIL 25

He Is There

When you pass through the waters, I will be with you; and when you pass through the rivers, they will not sweep over you. When you walk through the fire, you will not be burned; the flames will not set you ablaze.
(Isaiah 43:2)

As a scuba diver, I get to enjoy a beautiful aspect of God's world that most people do not. However, I recently had an experience where my regulator broke at eighty feet underwater. That was my life line! If I had darted for the surface from that depth, I would have been seriously injured or drowned. Being aware of the possible dangers, the dive industry includes in their training some safety precautions. One such precaution is to have a second regulator available. I also practise, on a regular basis, switching from one regulator to the other underwater. In this case, rather than panic, I simply removed the malfunctioning regulator and replaced it with my alternate one. Wow! My experienced diving partners expressed how impressed they were that I had been so calm during this emergency. The truth is that I was trained to be prepared. When the time came, I was able to make it through.

How comforting it is to know that no matter what comes our way, our God is with us. He created us, died for us, and wrote our names in His Book of Life. He will not forget about us or the things He knew from the beginning that we would go through. Notice that the Lord didn't say we won't have any troubles. We will still go through the challenges of life, or deep waters.

What are you doing to train, be prepared, and practice knowing where God is? Will you be able to reach His extended hand when you need it? Where is He guiding you to step? What is He directing you to do? Don't panic in the moment.

APRIL 26

Poor Pilate

Finally Pilate handed him over to them to be crucified. So the soldiers took charge of Jesus.
(John 19:16)

I feel sorry for Pilate. He seemed to know that there was something special about Jesus. Pilate, a very powerful man, even seemed afraid of Jesus. He looked for several manipulative ways to avoid having to make a decision and take a stance. He tried to push the decision back onto the Jews who had brought Jesus before him. Then Pilate tried to get Jesus to say something to give him an out. Pilate tried to negotiate with the crowd, to let Jesus go as a favour, even if the crowd did believe that Jesus was guilty of something. In the end, Pilate gave in to the pressure of the crowd and handed Jesus over to be crucified.

So, why do I feel sorry for Pilate? I'm not sorry for him because he faced opposition. I'm not sorry for him because he, a man in authority, caved to the pressures of man. I'm sorry for Pilate because he came so close to knowing Jesus. He appeared to know that he was looking at a great being. He just didn't have a soft enough heart to understand and receive Jesus as his Saviour. Pilate shut himself off from the great love, mercy, and forgiveness of God. Yes, Jesus had to die so we could all be saved, but did it have to be at the hand of Pilate?

I feel sorry for all people who are given the opportunity to know Jesus and yet harden their hearts and not take the step of faith to receive Jesus as their Lord and Saviour. I feel sorry for people who don't realize that they're risking their eternal life for pride or acceptance during their short time here on earth.

Each person is ultimately responsible for making their own decision to receive Jesus or not. I believe that every person in the world will be given the opportunity to know Jesus if it is meant to be. I also believe our prayers can help to soften hearts. For whom are you called to be praying?

APRIL 27

I've Got It Covered

And Micah said, "Now I know that the Lord will be good to me, since this Levite has become my priest."
(Judges 17:13)

Micah was a man who thought he had his bases covered. He had various cast idols in his home, and he even managed to hire a priest to stay in his house. It didn't seem to matter that he stole from his own mother and continued to live a self-serving lifestyle.

When you ask someone if they're a Christian, have you ever been given a rundown about how they cover their bases? "My spouse/parents/children go to such-and-such church." "I go to x-church (at Christmas and Easter)." "I do a lot of volunteer work." "I don't get drunk, steal, etc." They obviously didn't understand the question. At the same time, you may notice that they wear a cross or have a plaque on their wall with a Bible verse on it.

The ticket to heaven doesn't come through controlling God by working the right formula. Godly relatives aren't a "get out of hell free" card. Nor are these relatives or friends a guarantee of future enlightenment and salvation. When they knock on heaven's door, saying "I'm a friend of *(fill-in-the-black)*," it won't get them in.

Are your bases covered? Do you really know Jesus? Do you have an ongoing relationship with our Father in heaven? Do you look to Him for guidance and direction in your life, or do you do it all on your own, or with the help of professionals? It's not wrong to consult a specialist when you have a problem, such as going to a doctor when you are sick. However, is that your first impulse? Is that professional or specialized person you hired a Levite? Let us first seek the Lord in all we do.

Thank the Lord for His work in our lives. Thank Him for our spouses, who can come together with us in prayer.

APRIL 28

Who Do You Say He Is?

"But what about you?" he asked. "Who do you say I am?" (Matthew 16:15)

Jesus asked, *"Who do people say the Son of Man is?"* (Matthew 16:13). The disciples gave various responses to this question. People were trying to place Jesus within their experience or understanding. Then Jesus turned to His disciples and asked, *"Who do you say I am?"* We only know Peter's response: *"You are the Christ, the Son of the living God"* (Matthew 16:16). Now I'm asking you, who do you say that Jesus is?

It sometimes seems easy to say one religion believes this while another religion believes that. What about you? How does your heart tell you to respond to that question? Was He a prophet, a good man, a wise teacher, or *"the Christ, the Son of the living God"*?

Jesus confirmed that Peter had responded correctly through knowledge he had received from the Father, not through other people. Peter was open to hearing from God. We attain knowledge through the work of other people. We read Bibles that have been written by inspiration from God through man. Our Bibles have been translated into our language by man. We study books, listen to speakers, seek out Christian teaching, and learn how to pray. All of that is good. However, we ultimately need to receive Jesus and His gift of salvation directly. We need to develop our own relationship through the Holy Spirit. We need to know Jesus.

Pray that each of you would truly know Jesus, that He would draw you closer day by day. Ask the Lord to continue enlightening you and strengthening your faith. Then go out and share the truth with all those to whom He would send you. Amen.

APRIL 29

What Is Your Faith Worth?

If the bull gores a male or female slave, the owner must pay thirty shekels of silver to the master of the slave, and the bull must be stoned.
(Exodus 21:32)

This is the law of God given to the Israelite people through Moses. Moses was in the process of teaching the people the law and its consequences. Moses had already covered situations such as murder, intentional or not; injury to others, intentional or not; treatment of slaves; and responsibility for the behaviour of their bulls. There were various forms of payment or retribution assigned depending on the circumstances.

If a bull killed anyone, not only was the bull put to death, but also the owner of the bull was put to death, or he had to pay whatever amount was demanded for his life. Then we come to slaves. If a bull gored a slave, the owner only had to *"pay thirty shekels of silver to the master of the slave."* Now, let us fast-forward to the New Testament. What was the price paid to Judas for betraying Jesus? That's right. He was paid thirty shekels, the price of the lowest of people, a slave.

We know as Christians that we cannot put a price on Jesus and what He has done for us. However, like the priests and Judas, our faith can appear worthless to those who do not know Him. What value do you put on your faith in Jesus? What does it cost you when you allow someone or something to damage or weaken your faith?

Take some time of contemplation and discuss with your spouse those people or circumstances who cause you to receive injury to your faith. What can you do to avoid that injury? What are you willing to pay? Are there some people with whom you need to correct your relationship? Are there some activities you need to avoid or stop doing? Are there some activities you need to start doing?

Jesus considered you worth dying for.

APRIL 30

Jesus Is a Friend of Mine

Jesus replied, "Friend, do what you came for."
(Matthew 26:50)

Judas, the one who betrayed Jesus, arrived with a large crowd. The crowd was obviously intent on harm, as they were *"armed with swords and clubs"* (Mark 14:43). Then Judas greeted Jesus with a kiss. Jesus responded to Judas with today's verse, calling Judas a friend.

A friend? From the sin in his heart, this man betrayed Jesus! How could Jesus possibly still consider him a friend? As we read further in the book of Matthew, we find that Judas was horrified to find out that Jesus was actually condemned. We read that Judas was *"seized with remorse"* (Matthew 27:3). Although Judas confessed to the chief priests that he had sinned, that he had *"betrayed innocent blood"* (Matthew 27:4), it was too late to turn back the clock. The deed was done. Jesus had called him "friend."

I'm so grateful that Jesus is so merciful and forgiving. No matter what mistake or sin I commit, when I repent in my heart and ask, He always forgives. What could be harder to forgive than a friend who would betray you to death?

If our desire is to be Christ-like, what does this say to us? Has someone offended or wronged you? Are you willing to forgive? Notice that Jesus had forgiven Judas even before Judas was convicted of his sin and was remorseful. That suggests that we are not to wait for someone else to ask forgiveness before we forgive. It may not be easy, but it's the Christian thing to do. Fortunately, we can ask Jesus to help us with our heart attitude when we are unable to feel forgiveness on our own. This applies especially to your spouse.

Don't hold onto unforgiveness. Be a Christian friend.

MAY 1

The Loving Husband

In this same way, husbands ought to love their wives as their own bodies. He who loves his wife loves himself. After all, no one ever hated his own body, but he feeds and cares for it, just as Christ does the church… (Ephesians 5:28–29)

We all love our own bodies. I can hear the objections already, especially from the wives. "I'm too heavy/light. My eyes are too big/small. My legs are too short/long." No matter what parts you may not appreciate, you still feed, clean, and take care of your whole body. You can't feed your hands and not your arms. When you marry, remember: *"'and the two will become one flesh.' So they are no longer two, but one"* (Mark 10:8). Husbands, your wives are now a part of you.

Paul compares your relationship with that of Christ's relationship to the church (Christians). Try to imagine how much Jesus loves us! Husbands, you are called to be the leaders of the family. Paul isn't just referring to the physical needs of your wife. Jesus demonstrated His concern for the spiritual needs of His people.

What are your wife's needs? Each of us are different and at a different point in our walks with Christ. We are always a work in progress. What greater expression of love could there possibly be than nurturing and encouraging your wife's spiritual growth? In order to serve her needs, it will be necessary to attend to your own spiritual development and awareness. You cannot lead where you have not gone.

Spend time in the word together. Pray together regularly. Ask the Lord to show you how to love your wife more completely. Strengthen the cord of three.

MAY 2

A Loving Wife

A wife of noble character who can find? She is worth far more than rubies. Her husband has full confidence in her and lacks nothing of value. She brings him good, not harm, all the days of her life.
(Proverbs 31:10–12)

What is a wife of *"noble character"*? Being noble is to have or show a high level of character. One's character is the attributes that determine one's moral and ethical actions.

This verse directs a wife to strive to be of noble character and to give her husband reason to trust her and appreciate all that she does to contribute to a loving relationship. Be courteous, respectful, and uplifting. Thank God each and every day for the husband He has provided for you. Does your husband have reason to have *"full confidence"* (i.e. trust and pride) in you? Do you try to always think of your husband's best interest?

Do not be deceived into thinking you can fulfill this command on your own any more than you could fulfill the Biblical law under your own power. Involve the power of the "red strand" in your relationship. Ask for the Holy Spirit to guide you in your responsibilities as a godly woman and wife. Ask the Lord to reveal to you areas in your life where your mind and heart are not in alignment with His will.

Husbands, how can you help your wife attain her noble character? Are there areas in your life where you may be hindering her development? Do you express your appreciation for what she does? Does she know that you consider her *"worth far more than rubies"*? Thank God each and every day for this wife He has provided for you. Ask for wisdom in leading and enabling your wife to be all God would have her to be.

MAY 3

Sacrificing Children

Say to the Israelites: "Any Israelite or any alien living in Israel who gives any of his children to Molech must be put to death. The people of the community are to stone him."
(Leviticus 20:2)

Molech was the Ammonite god who required the people to sacrifice their children by having them pass through fire. Can you imagine a religion that would actually encourage the people to sacrifice their children!

Unfortunately, many people today are sacrificing their children in a more subtle way. They allow others to raise and influence their children on a regular basis. Children are permitted to watch unsupervised television shows and movies, play video games, access the internet, and read all types of magazines and books. Parents in general have stepped back and allowed unknown people in the education system to decide what should be taught to their children and when. We allow the media to teach them how to dress, how to talk, and how to act. Many people spend more and more hours at work or away from home "to get ahead," communicating to their children that work is more important than they are.

What can be done? Take back your children! Be aware of what they're involved in. What are they watching? What are they being taught in school? What are they reading? What are they doing in their free time? Spend quality and quantity time with them. Talk with them. Make an effort to be at their school and sports events. Tell them they are important to you. Take it upon yourself to teach them about Jesus. Teach them how to pray. Show them how to develop a relationship with the one true God.

Let us dedicate our children to God, not sacrifice them to the gods of this world.

MAY 4

Unity in Christ

"Do not stop him," Jesus said, "for whoever is not against you is for you." (Luke 9:50)

Jesus' disciples witnessed a man driving out demons in the name of Jesus. They tried to stop the man, because he wasn't one of Jesus' selected disciples. Jesus told them not to stop the man. Later, Jesus tells them, *"He who is not with me is against me, and he who does not gather with me, scatters"* (Luke 11:23). In other words, you can tell who is a follower of Jesus (i.e. Christian) by his works. You don't earn points towards entry into heaven, but if you believe in Jesus you desire to do His work.

Notice that Jesus wasn't concerned if the man was associated with a particular group of followers (denomination). The important thing was that he was doing the work of the Father in Jesus' name. Jesus encouraged the disciples to have a cooperative spirit with the man. Notice also, in Luke 11, that it didn't matter if a person was associated with the church and didn't do the work of the Father in Jesus' name. The person who didn't do Jesus' work was considered "against" Jesus.

You can be a Christian and not go to any church at all. (This is not advisable, as discussed in other devotions.) You can also be a churchgoer and not be a Christian. If you are going to church to please someone else, look good, or feel righteous, that doesn't make you a Christian.

What would the disciples think of you? Would they recognise you as a Christian by your works? How do you view Christians from other churches or denominations? Are you able to put aside the differences of man and work in a cooperative spirit in unity with Jesus?

MAY 5

Who Is My Neighbour?

He answered: "'Love the Lord your God with all your heart and with all your soul and with all your strength and with all your mind'; and, 'Love your neighbor as yourself.'"
(Luke 10:27)

There was an expert in the law who was out to test Jesus. He asked Jesus what would be required to receive eternal life. These "experts" were charged with knowing the Mosaic Law, teaching the law to others, and were respected as judges of the law. This expert knew it all! Jesus, in His wisdom, turned the tables and asked the expert what the law said. The expert needed to demonstrate that he was knowledgeable in the law, so he replied with Luke 10:27. Jesus then spoke with authority as the expert's teacher, telling him he was correct. Jesus told him, *"Do this and you will live"* (Luke 10:28).

Jesus didn't judge him or lecture him on his behaviour or motives. Jesus simply pointed out that the man already knew the answer. Now the expert began to squirm. He knew he lacked in the area of loving his neighbour and wanted to justify himself. He asked, *"And who is my neighbor?"* (Luke 10:29)

Jesus replied with the parable of the Good Samaritan. A man was beaten and robbed and left on the side of the road to die. Neither a priest nor a Levite stopped to help the man when they passed by. Then a Samaritan man, who would normally have been despised by Jews, came by and had mercy on the beaten man. He took care of the man as best he could without expecting anything in return. Again, Jesus turned back to the expert in the law and asked him who the neighbour was. *"The expert in the law replied, 'The one who had mercy on him.' Jesus told him, 'Go and do likewise'"* (Luke 10:37).

Who are your neighbours? Are you merciful to them?

MAY 6

At His Feet

"Martha, Martha," the Lord answered, "you are worried and upset about many things…"
(Luke 10:41)

Martha and Mary were sisters who had the amazing opportunity to have Jesus over for dinner. Martha was busy trying to get everything ready for the event. Mary *"sat at the Lord's feet listening to what he said"* (Luke 10:39). There's a popular song just now by the group *Mercy Me* called "I Can Only Imagine." It talks about what a person's response will be when they meet Jesus face to face. We can contemplate and anticipate that time, but we can't really know what our response will be until it happens. What would your response be if you were to have Jesus over for dinner? Again, I can only imagine.

Even though I know that nothing I could do to prepare my home, plan a meal, or create that meal would be worthy, I have a feeling I might work myself to exhaustion trying to make things as near-perfect as I could. However, once Jesus arrived, I wouldn't want to miss a second of what He had to say. Hmmm… would I be a Martha or a Mary? Maybe I would do the modern-day woman thing and try to be both at the same time!

We can visit with Jesus through the Holy Spirit. We just need to invite Him into our lives. Submit to Him and wait at His feet in prayer. This is not the wish list prayer many of us fall into. This prayer is that of submission to the Father and stilling ourselves before Him. Allow Him to teach you, direct you, and fill you with His presence through the Holy Spirit.

There was nothing bad about Martha's desire to be a good hostess to Jesus. Of course she would want to honour Him! However, there is a time for action in doing good works, and there is a time to sit at His feet and listen.

How much of your prayer time do you just listen?

MAY 7

Faithful Love

But Ruth replied, "Don't urge me to leave you or to turn back from you. Where you go I will go, and where you stay I will stay. Your people will be my people and your God my God."
(Ruth 1:16)

The book of Ruth is only four chapters long. I suggest you read it through in its entirety. This is truly a love story. It's a story of a family's struggles to survive, the faithfulness of Ruth to her mother-in-law, and the Lord's sovereignty.

Are we as faithful to our spouses as Ruth was to her mother-in-law? In times of trials, are you tempted to leave, or push your spouse away emotionally, or are you willing to go the whole way together? Fortunately for Ruth, and her entire family line, although she entered into a mixed-religion marriage, she came to know the true God. Ruth was willing to stick with her mother-in-law, even though their futures did not look hopeful. God blessed them beyond anything they could imagine.

Many things in this world attempt to assault our marriages. External threats will be applied, such as exposure to sexual temptations, financial burdens, and bigger and better media. There are also the internal stresses of working out our relationships with one another, such as negotiating finances, giving respect, and deciding who is responsible for what. Then there are other internal stresses, such as our own egos and selfishness. "Am I getting all I need? Do I have to give so much? Could I do better or get more somewhere else?"

Reaffirm your dedication to your spouse often. Assure each other with today's verse. Regularly reaffirm your faith in the one true God. Through trials, be assured that your spouse and the Lord will be with you always.

MAY 8

Honest Hannah

In bitterness of soul Hannah wept much and prayed to the Lord. (1 Samuel 1:10)

Hannah was one of two wives in a polygamist relationship. Her husband appeared to love her, but his other wife tormented Hannah because Hannah wasn't able to conceive a child. Even in our culture today, it is painful for a woman who desires to have children to be unable to conceive, but in Hannah's time it was the purpose and ultimate status of a woman to bare children to carry on the family line. In fact, it was so important to have children that a woman's barrenness was reason for a man to marry a second wife.

Hannah was in *"bitterness of soul."* The dictionary defines bitterness as "sharp and unpleasant to the taste; painful; severe; relentless."[7] It's interesting to note that Hannah did not wipe off her tears and paste on a smile before entering into conversation with the Lord, even at church! Hannah *"was pouring out [her] soul to the Lord"* (1 Samuel 1:15). The Lord heard her and answered her prayers. It was prophesized to Hannah that her prayers would be answered. Hannah received that prophecy, and in time she did conceive.

Most of the time when someone says "How are you?" they don't really want to know. You're supposed to answer "Good!" and carry on. When it's a casual acquaintance, you can usually pull off the socially accepted answer without question. However, there are times when someone who knows you a little more intimately will look at you again and question if you really are fine. Jesus knows us more intimately than anyone here on earth. He knows us better than we know ourselves. Be honest in your conversations with Him, and like Hannah, pour out your soul to the Lord. He will not answer what we do not ask for.

---

[7] Ibid., 59.

MAY 9

Our God Is In Control

When the men of Ashdod saw what was happening, they said, "The ark of the god of Israel must not stay here with us, because his hand is heavy upon us and upon Dagon our god."
(1 Samuel 5:7)

It's interesting how many people recognize the omnipotence of our God, but still fail to turn from other gods to follow Him. The Philistines recognized the importance of the Ark of the Covenant to the Israelites as their connection to their God. Therefore, when the Philistines overcame the Israelites in battle, the first thing the Philistines did was capture the Ark of the Covenant and take it back to their temple and place it beside their idol.

The story in 1 Samuel 5 is almost humorous. When the Philistines realised that the God of the Israelites was stronger than their god, they determined to pass the Ark of the Covenant off to their other relatives. The second group also recognized that the Israelite God was more powerful than their god, and they too wanted to get rid of it. They wisely returned it to the Israelites. The Philistines mistake, of course, was thinking that they could control God by possessing the Ark of the Covenant, that they could keep their gods and old ways and still be blessed by the God of the Israelites.

Have you ever had someone come to you and ask for your prayers because they didn't think they could pray directly to God and be heard? Why is that? Have they not accepted the gift of the Holy Spirit? Are they trying to serve other worldly gods and the one true God as well? How about you?

We cannot control or manipulate God any more than the Philistines could. We must surrender all to God, putting aside all the other idols we may be worshipping. God desires to bless us. Read Romans 8:28.

MAY 10

You Have the Power!

The Spirit of the Lord will come upon you in power, and you will prophesy with them; and you will be changed into a different person. Once these signs are fulfilled, do whatever your hand finds to do, for God is with you. (1 Samuel 10:6–7)

These verses were the Lord's promise to Saul, spoken by the prophet Samuel. Saul was to become king. In Saul's words, he came from *"the smallest tribe of Israel… the least of all the clans of the tribe of Benjamin"* (1 Samuel 9:21). The Israelites were pleading for a king, so the Lord chose Saul for the role. We read in chapter 10 that Saul hid when the people wanted to proclaim him king. This isn't exactly the power-seeking type we would picture for leadership. The point is that the Lord chose him and provided for him by promising, and delivering, the power of the Holy Spirit.

We too, as Christians, have the power of the Holy Spirit on our lives. All we need to do is ask and receive what has been promised to us. God has promised that we *"will be changed into a different person"* when that happens. He has told us that you can *"do whatever your hand finds to do, for God is with you."* To the uninitiated, that sounds like foolishness and totally anarchy. However, if we receive the Holy Spirit, it's no longer all about us. The things we find for our hands to do will be the things that the Lord, through the Holy Spirit, inspires us to do. If it's inspired by the Holy Spirit, be assured He will give us the power to carry it out!

When you read on in 1 Samuel, you will discover the mistakes Saul made, and challenges he had along the way, even though the Holy Spirit was on him. As humans, we also will make mistakes and have challenges. However, God is with us. Are you following His lead?

MAY 11

What's Your Assignment?

As for me, far be it from me that I should sin against the Lord by failing to pray for you. And I will teach you the way that is good and right.
(1 Samuel 12:23)

A couple of things come to mind as I read this verse. The first is that Samuel considered it a *"sin against the Lord"* not to pray for the Israelites. If sins could be better or worse, a sin against the Lord would be incredibly big! It's not possible to pray for everyone and everything in the world, nor is that God's plan for you, but Samuel had been called *by the Lord* to pray for the Israelites. His sin would be in the inaction of not obeying the Lord.

Secondly, Samuel recognized that he needed to do more than just talk. Samuel promised to teach the Israelites in the ways of the Lord. They couldn't be expected to be obedient if they didn't know what was *"good and right."* The Israelites were Samuel's calling.

That's all well and good for Samuel and the Israelites, but what is God saying to you through this verse? Who or what is God telling you to pray for? It's very easy to say to someone, "I'll be praying for you," but do you do it? What does that entail? Is God prompting you to pray one time for a given situation, or is there a more involved, continuous assignment? Perhaps there is someone, or a few people, for whom God is prompting you to be more than a role model. He may be telling you to come alongside another Christian in prayer and help them through a difficult time. Perhaps you are to provide more instruction or passing on of the information you've learned and experiences you've had. Maybe God has given you a completely different assignment. Are you acting upon it?

Sin is not always about what we do wrong. Let us not fall into sin by failing to act on God's assignment for us.

MAY 12

Equal in God's Eyes

In the same way, you husbands must give honor to your wives. Treat your wife with understanding as you live together. She may be weaker than you are, but she is your equal partner in God's gift of new life. Treat her as you should so your prayers will not be hindered.
(1 Peter 3:7, NLT)

Can you remember a time when you were talking to someone and realized they weren't even listening? In fact, they may have even left the room! Are there times when you wonder if God can hear your prayers? Well, I assure you that it's not because He left the room. God is never too far away to hear you. He may, however, not be answering your prayers as you wish due to some hindrance.

One such hindrance may be a wrong relationship with someone. A husband's closest, most delicate relationship is that with his wife. Are you treating your wife with love and gentle understanding?

In the beginning, we believe that we will have a "happily ever after" marriage. Then we get familiar with one and other and begin to let our guard down, or drop our best behaviour. We risk taking one another for granted. Perhaps we're less careful about the way we say things, or are less respectful. Feelings get hurt.

How do you handle those misunderstandings? Prayer is good, but is your prayer to ask God to fix the other person? The only side God will take is the righteous one. Are you willing to hear *His* answer to your prayer? Ask the Lord to reveal anything about your marriage He is displeased about. Ask for His help in making it right. Clearing up any misunderstanding in your marriage may be just what's necessary to open the flow of God's grace into your prayer life once more.

Praise God for the *"gift of new life"* you each have in Jesus.

MAY 13

Lift the Veil

When Moses came down from Mount Sinai with the two tablets of the Testimony in his hands, he was not aware that his face was radiant because he had spoken with the Lord.
(Exodus 34:29)

After spending time in the presence of the Lord, Moses' face actually glowed! The Lord's presence lingered on Moses. The people could see the radiance of holiness upon Moses and listened to what the Lord was saying to them through Moses. After relaying the Lord's message, Moses would *"put a veil over his face to keep the Israelites from gazing at it while the radiance was fading away"* (2 Corinthians 3:13). Whenever Moses entered into the Lord's presence, he would remove the veil.

Do people see that radiance on your face? How often do we enter into the presence of the Lord only to pull a veil over our faces immediately afterwards? We allow the evil one to deceive us. We feel unworthy, not good enough to share the light of the Lord. We fear not having all the answers. We look to others who are "more holy" to be our leaders.

Jesus died on the cross for each one of us. He broke the chains of death so everyone could have a relationship with the Father. He removed the veil once and for all! Enter into His presence. Because of Jesus, we have hope and freedom. There is no need to hide, because through the Holy Spirit we have been invited to be in His presence always. As we look upon Jesus, we allow Him to transform us with His ever-increasing glory.

Be bold! Allow others to see the radiance on your face. May it beckon others unto Him. Share the light of His glory. Don't hide behind the veil.

Enter into a time of prayer with your spouse now. Ask the Lord to whom He would have you show His glory.

MAY 14

Obedience Is Best

But Saul and the army spared Agag and the best of the sheep and cattle, the fat calves and lambs—everything that was good. These they were unwilling to destroy completely, but everything that was despised and weak they totally destroyed.
(1 Samuel 15:9)

The Lord had directed Saul to *"totally destroy everything"* (1 Samuel 15:3) that belonged to the Amalekites. So, Saul called together his army and struck out in obedience—sort of. When Saul's army appeared to have won the battle, they looked at what was there and kept the best. What little faith they had! They didn't think the Lord would provide at least as good for them as what they coveted.

Think of the Amalekites as the sin in your life. Perhaps you say, "I'm willing to follow you completely, Lord, and obey all your commands!" But then, a short time later, you say, "Hey, look at that. Nice eh? Surely God won't mind if I keep this little sin in my life. I like it. I've given up most of my bad habits and choices. This little sin can't hurt, right?"

Well, notice what happens to Saul. As we read on, Saul refers to *"the Lord your God"* (1 Samuel 15:15) when speaking to Samuel. When do you suppose the Lord stopped being Saul's God?

Then Saul starts with the excuses: *"The soldiers took sheep and cattle from the plunder, the best of what was devoted to God, in order to sacrifice them to the Lord your God at Gilgal"* (1 Samuel 15:21). Now it's someone else's fault. (Remember Eve?) In addition, Saul tries to claim that his intent was to honour God. Busted! Do you think God really wanted a sacrifice of something that wasn't theirs to give in the first place? As you read on, Samuel tells Saul in very strong words that God prefers obedience to sacrifices.

No more excuses. Are you willing to follow Jesus with all your heart? We all sin; it's our fleshly nature. Has God revealed a sin in your life that you haven't completely dealt with? Thank Jesus that we serve a merciful God!

MAY 15

God's Choice of Family

But in fact God has arranged the parts in the body, every one of them, just as he wanted them to be.
(1 Corinthians 12:18)

Families are our most intimate relationships. We usually have strong emotions in relation to family members. We tend to look at our family members with more intensity than we do the rest of the world. That can be a great blessing, but it can also be very painful.

One day, as I was thinking about a couple of family members who seem to prickle others more easily and more often than other members, I turned to God in prayer. I confessed that I didn't even know how to pray for these people. I asked the Lord to help me. I asked Him to tell me how and what to pray. I gave Him permission to convict me of my attitude or anything I may unknowingly have been doing to contribute to the difficult situations. I also gave Him permission to use me to bring reconciliation if He so chose. His response was, "I have chosen each person to be in the family they are in. No child was born to parents I didn't know about. Nobody became a sibling without my plan."

Today's verse comes from a section of 1 Corinthians that we often refer to when talking about our roles in the church or Christian community. In reflection on God's revelation to me, I can see how this verse also applies to families. Our families are our training ground for how we deal with the rest of the world. Do we treat them with the respect, mercy, and love of Jesus? Some families require more forgiveness than others. Keep in mind that forgiveness doesn't always mean forgetting. We don't need to approve of other family members' choices; we just need to see them through Jesus' eyes.

Thank the Lord for your families. Thank Him for all He is teaching you through them. Thank Him also for your spouse and the family He planned for you.

MAY 16

I Am God-Created!

I praise you because I am fearfully and wonderfully made; your works are wonderful, I know that full well.
(Psalm 139:14)

When you look in the mirror, what do you see? Often, we see what we consider flaws. We might think we would look better with shorter or longer legs, a different colour hair, more or less hair, etc. Do you realize what you're doing? You are critiquing God's work! How are you treating His creation?

Suppose someone gave you a rare and precious vase. What would you say? "Gee, thanks. Too bad the artist didn't make it *this* way instead. Maybe I could paint over it or change it somehow." What would you do with it? Would you use it as a doorstop? No, you would treasure it. You would notice the incredible work and design. You would sit it in a safe place, a place of honour.

Now think again about that image in the mirror. What did God bless you with? Look deeper. What have you been created to be inside? Look at what a wonderful job God has done! Talk with your spouse. Tell each other what great qualities you see in each other. Now, can you tell each other what great qualities you see that God has given yourselves? How are you using God's creation? Are you hiding your skills and abilities because you don't think they're good enough, or are you developing them to be all they were intended to be?

Pray together. Ask God to help you recognize the attributes and skills He has blessed each of you with. Ask God to help you use those gifts to shine His light into the world around you. As spouses, help each other out. Look for opportunities to verbalize to your spouse the qualities and skill you notice God has blessed them with. Encourage each other as you explore ways to honour God's creation.

MAY 17

Doing Your Part

Be joyful always; pray continually; give thanks in all circumstances, for this is God's will for you in Christ Jesus.
(1 Thessalonians 5:16–18)

It is our responsibility to pray. God is able to work without us, but He may not. He will not go ahead and do things according to His will here on earth without our partnership. He has given us a free will and will not treat us like puppets or robots. He wants us to learn and mature in our spiritual development through communicating with Him—in other words, through prayer. He wants us to take responsibility for our prayer lives.

Choosing not to pray is like a child who gathers up all his sports equipment and goes and sits in the car. After a few hours, he goes back into the house and blames his parent for missing the game or practice. He now has to pay the consequence for missing the game or practice and thinks it's his parent's fault. However, the child never told them he needed a ride or what time and place the game was at. Fortunately for us, even if we wait until immediate attention is needed, God doesn't have the time or energy constraints the child's parent may have had. He hears us and is able to respond.

Do you pray continuously? First you must begin. A good starting place is to review the Lord's Prayer. Worship and praise the Father, confess your sins, give thanksgiving, present your requests, and listen for His word. Set aside time each and every day to be alone with God. The more you pray and learn about prayer, the easier it becomes. Pray with your spouse. Jesus told us, *"For where two or three come together in my name, there am I with them"* (Matthew 18:20).

Encourage and remind one another to pray regularly. Take charge of your responsibility to pray!

MAY 18

Spirit of Unity

May the God who gives endurance and encouragement give you a spirit of unity among yourselves as you follow Christ Jesus, so that with one heart and mouth you may glorify the God and Father of our Lord Jesus Christ. (Romans 15:5–6)

The words "unity," "harmony," and "agreement" conjure up feelings of peacefulness. God desires that we live in unity with one another. Unity is something we should all seek.

Today's verses tell you where to find this unity. If we seek to follow Jesus, God will give us the *"endurance and encouragement"* to receive the spirit of unity. He desires that we be of *"one heart and mouth,"* so that we *"may glorify the God and Father of our Lord Jesus Christ."* Out of our heart, our mouth will speak. It is important to be aware of our heart attitudes. Remember that Satan's strategy is division.

Unity involves being willing to give up self for the benefit of all. It involves compromise. It requires a servant's heart. Spending time with the Lord in order to know His will enables you to know when to persevere and when to let go. Unity doesn't mean giving in when it would dishonour God. It also doesn't mean being a doormat for the appearance of peace.

First, we need to be in unity with God's will. Second, we need to be in unity with our spouse. Are there areas of disharmony you need to address? If so, join together in presenting your situation to the Lord and ask Him to direct you in realigning your relationship with *Him.*

Ask God if there is any area where you may not have an attitude of peace and unity. He will help you to correct that attitude if you ask. God desires that you move forward together in unity, bringing glory to *His* name. Finally, are there any other areas in your life in which you need to ask God to help you be more united? Ask for His spirit of unity.

MAY 19

Hole in the Bucket

But in fact God has arranged the parts in the body, every one of them, just as he wanted them to be.
(1 Corinthians 12:18)

Do you remember the children's song that goes, "There's a hole in my bucket, dear Liza, dear Liza"? It goes on and on, with the narrator being unable to solve his problem by himself, and Liza continually giving him more and more hints on what he should do. The bucket is pretty useless until the hole is repaired.

Are you that hole? 1 Corinthians 12 talks about the roles we each play within a church in order for it to function as God planned. First, I would ask, are you attending the church God assigned you to? Second, are you fulfilling your God-arranged part in that church? If not, then you are the hole. That church will not be able to fully fulfill its assignment from God because of the missing piece.

Does that mean God is not omnipotent? No. God is able to do all things. It does mean that your particular church is not able to complete its entire assignment from God. You do make a difference.

So, where do you belong and what are you supposed to be doing? That's between you and Jesus. Ask Him. Spend time listening to what He's saying to you. If you need more hints, like the narrator of the song, ask for them. God is patient and will guide you into discovering your purpose. He will arrange things to come together as they are meant to be. Pray that the things in your life that are of Jesus would flourish and bear fruit. Pray also that the things that are not of Jesus would melt away.

Don't waste another day! Don't miss out on seeing God's name being glorified through you and your church! Your prayers, your ministry, or your smile could make an eternal difference in someone else's life.

MAY 20

The Husband's Substance

A wife of noble character is her husband's crown, but a disgraceful wife is like decay in his bones.
(Proverbs 12:4)

I once saw a series of anti-smoking commercials that showed a computer-generated, timed-elapsed image of the effects of smoking on the body. They would start out with a picture of a beautiful woman or handsome man. Then the person would light up a cigarette and begin to smoke. The following scenes showed their faces begin to wrinkle and their hair dry out and discolour. Then their whole bodies would crumble into ashes. It was meant to shock people into not smoking. It was not a pretty picture.

A wife who behaves disgracefully towards her husband has the same effect. She begins to wear away at him, affecting his attitudes, self-esteem, and character. She can make him feel incapable and useless. It could even affect his physical appearance. He may begin to droop in his stature and pay less attention to how he dresses and takes care of himself. As we look back over the man's married life, we would see how he crumbled over time.

On the other hand, *"a wife of noble character is her husband's crown."* To crown is to bring completion or perfection. She can bring honour to her husband. Her respect can encourage and spur him on to be all he is capable of. He may stand taller, pay more attention to his appearance, and be motivated to work harder. He will speak positively about, and to, his wife. He will aspire to be kind and thoughtful.

Wife, which are you? Are you wearing your husband down, or are you encouraging completion and perfection? What do you see when you look at him compared to when you began your relationship? Pray that God would help you be your husband's crown. Ask God to make you aware of any wrong behaviours or attitudes towards your husband and replace them with a noble character.

MAY 21

Peace of Righteousness

May the Lord be our judge and decide between us. May he consider my cause and uphold it; may he vindicate me by delivering me from your hand.
(1 Samuel 24:15)

We constantly judge and evaluate events based on our viewpoint. Should I continue driving or stop at this intersection? In this circumstance, should I offer to help or not? Should I say something or keep quiet? When we come to a different conclusion than another person involved, we find ourselves in conflict. Sometimes it's no big deal, and other times it is important to us that things are resolved the way we want them to be.

David was being hunted down by King Saul. Saul's intent was clearly to kill David. David believed himself innocent. He had the opportunity to kill Saul, thus ending his cycle of running and hiding. David's men were thrilled that God appeared to deliver King Saul into David's hand, and they encouraged David to end the dispute by taking Saul's life. However, David chose not to take revenge. David was confident enough in his righteousness to allow the Lord to judge between him and Saul. David called on the Lord to vindicate him. When David revealed to Saul the opportunity, Saul was remorseful. Saul commended David, halted his pursuit, and left.

Are you confident enough in your conflict to allow God to be the judge? Remember that He knows all things, including motivations and intentions. If God were to offer to judge between your position and that of another person right now, would you be confident in your position?

In any conflict, particularly any disagreements with your spouse, invite Jesus to be your judge. Ask Him to reveal to you both the right attitudes you need to resolve the issue, no matter who was/is right. May you both be at peace.

MAY 22

Good Stewards

David replied, "No, my brothers, you must not do that with what the Lord has given us. He has protected us and handed over to us the forces that came against us."
(1 Samuel 30:23)

The word "steward" is defined as "a man in charge of another's property."[8] So when we talk of being good stewards, we are referring to managing well that which we have been put in charge. As Christians, we must recognize that we are nothing, and have nothing, other than what God has blessed us with.

"But I've worked hard for what I own," you may say. Well, I suppose David's men, who put their life on the line in 1 Samuel 30, probably thought the same thing: "We were tired, too, but we pushed on and fought in hand-to-hand combat for the plunder we now have." Those men weren't willing to share with the men who were not able to continue to the end. David was a wise leader because he remembered where his success came from. In fact, these men's biggest blessing was in coming back alive! David knew that God had chosen to bless them, and God could just as easily, and quickly, take everything from them.

Notice that neither David nor God told them they weren't to have *any* of the plunder. The men were only being asked to *share* from their abundance with those who were unable to attain what they needed. God desires to bless each of us who choose to follow Him. What these men had not discovered is that the blessing is in the giving, and secondly that they could not out-give God.

Picture the child in the sandbox whose hands are full of his own toys. His hands are so full that he can't actually play with the toys. He misses out on the joy of sharing and playing with the other children! God isn't asking that we give all our time, energy, and money away; He just asks that we be good stewards of all He has provided for us. We are to be willing to give when He prompts us.

[8] Ibid., 703.

MAY 23

Persistent Prayer

Then Jesus told his disciples a parable to show them that they should always pray and not give up.
(Luke 18:1)

Whenever I've had the opportunity to read a book and then see a movie based on it, I have found the book is much better. In the book, you know exactly what each of the characters is thinking as they interact in a scene. In the movie, you only see the action from one viewpoint.

In today's verse, Luke has started out telling us exactly what Jesus' intended lesson was. You can read the actual parable in Luke 18. I thank God again that we have the advantage of the written word to help us understand the lessons He has given us. Jesus wants us to *"always pray and not give up."*

In this lesson, Jesus is talking about praying for justice. This is not to be confused with selfish or unwise prayers. Imagine the child who asks his parent for something that would not be in the child's best interest. "Please, Mommy! Let me have only sweets for supper! I like their taste better than broccoli!"

Jesus' point was that if a corrupt judge would give in to someone's persistent plea for justice, how much more would a loving God *"bring about justice for his chosen ones, who cry out to him day and night"* (Luke 18:7)? When we pray, we must ask God to tell us how to pray. We need to be in alignment with His will. God has read the whole book. He knows what is best and what is just. As we partner with Him in prayer, we come against the evil one's schemes, fighting back the enemy. We release the light of our heavenly Father into this dark world.

God will answer our persistent prayers in His quick and perfect timing, not ours. All that Jesus asked was whether He would find *"faith on the earth"* (Luke 18:8) when He returns.

Pray faithfully and persistently for God's justice.

MAY 24

Who Turned Out the Light?

But whoever hates his brother is in the darkness and walks around in the darkness; he does not know where he is going, because the darkness has blinded him.
(1 John 2:11)

I live in an urban area. We almost always have some form of light around us. In fact, we have so much light noise that it prevents us from having a clear view of the stars in the night sky. Occasionally, we have electricity outages. That sudden and complete darkness is very disorientating. The first response is usually to search for a candle or flashlight to reintroduce some artificial light.

John tells us that hating our brother puts us in spiritual darkness. This darkness can cut us off from God's light. God is still there as always; we just can't see Him or connect with Him. We begin to wander around without direction or orientation. We can end up completely lost because of that darkness. Sometimes we even turn to artificial or incorrect resolutions.

Have you ever noticed that your prayers don't seem to be answered? Does it seem like you aren't able to hear from God? Do you hate anyone? Hate is a strong word. You may think you don't actually hate anyone. Jesus tells us that *"anyone who is angry with his brother will be subject to judgment"* (Matthew 5:22). It's your attitude that Jesus is looking at. Are you angry with someone? Have you allowed a situation to fester and begin to allow sin and darkness into your life?

Are you the one who has turned out the light? Ask God to turn the true light back on. Ask Him to reveal any darkness or unresolved hatred or anger in your life. Forgive and release the flow of the Holy Spirit through you. Receive His freedom and peace. We must desire to live so completely in God's light that we cannot even *see* the darkness.

MAY 25

Jesus' Words in Me

May the words of my mouth and the meditation of my heart be pleasing in your sight, O Lord, my Rock and my Redeemer.
(Psalm 19:14)

What a great prayer to pray at the beginning of every day. Imagine if everyone were to pray this and mean it! Let's look at this in reverse. We recognize that the Lord is our "Rock" and "Redeemer." He is solid, permanent, and our Saviour. If we align ourselves with Him, we stay on the right track. *"We love because he first loved us"* (1 John 4:19). Our love will inspire us to desire to *"be pleasing"* to Him.

How do you know what will please someone? You get to know them. You spend time with them. You listen to them and pay attention to things that are important to them.

This verse speaks of *"meditation of [the] heart."* That means to reflect or consider what things are pleasing to the Lord. Your heart is the organ that pumps blood (life) through your body. The psalmist is indicating a desire to reflect on the Lord with his whole life. If we were able to accomplish that level of devotion, we wouldn't be able to help but speak that which the Lord would have us speak. Our words would be wise and edifying to others, a reflection of Jesus.

In our own willpower, it's not always possible speak and think in ways that are pleasing to the Lord. Thankfully, Jesus understands that. When we make mistakes, we can ask for forgiveness and try again. Like any endeavour, the more we practise the easier it becomes. Jesus has sent us the Holy Spirit to help us. Spend time with Him and your spouse.

MAY 26

Fellowship in Prayer

Do not be anxious about anything, but in everything, by prayer and petition, with thanksgiving, present your requests to God.
(Philippians 4:6)

Often prayer is discussed as something you need to do alone. Certainly I would encourage you to regularly find quiet time to talk with God. However, something very special happens when we share our burdens with someone else, and present them together to God. It brings your relationship with each other to a deeper level.

In the beginning, praying out loud with someone else can be a bit intimidating. However, as you begin, you will understand that there are no right or wrong words. Your focus will move from your own insecurities to focusing on speaking to God in agreement with others. There will be two or more of you to acknowledge and rejoice in answers to your prayers. A special bond will develop. As you share each other's burdens, the load will lighten.

First, I would highly recommend that you spend time in prayer with your spouse. This can be a time to pray about common, as well as intimate, thanksgivings and concerns. Watch and feel your relationship grow even stronger as you join together as a cord of three.

There will also be times when you are given opportunities to pray with other people. Be sensitive to the Holy Spirit's prompting for when you should move from "I will be praying for you" to "Would you like me to pray with you about that?"

Seek out opportunities to pray in group settings. This may be a Bible study, prayer group, or family time or work environment. Notice how friendships deepen and fellowship grows. Notice how much more often answers to prayer are acknowledged and celebrated.

MAY 27

Blessing Our Adversary

Finally, all of you, live in harmony with one another; be sympathetic, love as brothers, be compassionate and humble. Do not repay evil with evil or insult with insult, but with blessing, because to this you were called so that you may inherit a blessing.
(1 Peter 3:8–9)

Peter was addressing the persecuted Christians who had been scattered throughout the world. He was calling for Christians to rise above their situations and bless those around them. Jesus called Christians to do this same thing, even to *"pray for those who mistreat [them]"* (Luke 6:27–28). These directives were given to Christians who were suffering greatly at the hands of others. Even today, Christians risk their earthly lives just for confessing their faith. They, too, are called to bless their enemies.

These verses also apply to those of us who are living in a relatively safe society. Our personal conflicts seem insignificant in light of the bigger picture. However, these little attacks can bring division and separation from God. Song of Songs 2:15 speaks of the *"little foxes that ruin the vineyards."* Our directive is to humble ourselves and bring harmony and have sympathy, love, and compassion. We are also called to bless and pray for those who attack us. We are to surrender our right to repay *"evil with evil or insult with insult."* Somehow, getting even never has the satisfaction we seek, anyway.

So, how do we pray? I would suggest that we confess our true feelings to God. Ask Him to help our attitudes. We need to ask God to tell us how to pray. We need to invite the Holy Spirit to fill us with God's love for our adversaries. We must seek to bless them from the love of God that overflows from our hearts. Do not allow evil to cause you to miss out on your inherited blessing.

MAY 28

Be an Encourager

Therefore encourage one another and build each other up, just as in fact you are doing.
(1 Thessalonians 5:11)

"Great job!" Doesn't that feel good to hear those words? It really makes you want to keep going!

I used to teach a Kindergarten class. We would regularly celebrate little achievements the children attained. Johnny might learn to tie a shoe or zip his own jacket zipper. We would all congratulate him. Then I would encourage him to use his new achievement to help others. What excitement when I opened the door for them to leave and Johnny would burst through the door to tell his parent what he had accomplished!

Everyone loves to receive encouragement from people around them. The more important the encourager is, the more meaningful the recognition. How exciting will be the day when we meet Jesus face to face and we hear His praise, *"Well done, good and faithful servant!"* (Matthew 25:21)

Next to Jesus is my husband. How good it is to hear his praise! He inspires me to push forward and apply myself to whatever it is he has noticed. I'm sure my praise has the same effect on him. Why don't you purpose over the next few days to take notice and encourage your spouse daily in some way? Don't fake it and make things up. Really take notice of all the things they do and express your thankfulness and appreciation of their works.

What about other people in your daily walk? Do you have a boss, employee, or colleague who could use some encouragement? What about that cashier or service provider?

The bonus to encouraging others is how it makes you feel. Blessing others just seems to reflect back and lighten your step as well. *"Well done, good and faithful servant!"*

MAY 29

Contamination or Purification

Therefore, rid yourselves of all malice and all deceit, hypocrisy, envy, and slander of every kind.
(1 Peter 2:1)

A group of people from a congregation approached their pastor with a request. It had come to their attention that members of the congregation had come from a sinful lifestyle. They asked the pastor to identify those people so they would be able to keep their children from interacting with them. The pastor told them he could see their problem and agreed to address the issue at church the next Sunday.

Sunday morning arrived and the pastor was true to his word. He explained the problem to the congregation and then presented his solution. He asked all the people who had committed any sexual sin in their past to sit in a particular section of the church. Then he asked all the people who had ever lied to sit in another section together. Then he instructed all the people who had ever gossiped or spoke badly of their Christian brothers or sisters to sit in another specified section. Well, I'm sure you can see the dilemma. How could each member sit in several sections at once?

This is like the story in John 8 where the Pharisees brought a woman to Jesus and asked Him if they should stone her as the law required. Jesus response was, *"If any one of you is without sin, let him be the first to throw a stone at her"* (John 8:7). Interestingly, all the people began to leave until no one remained.

Two things come to mind here. First, if we have repented of our sins and asked Jesus for forgiveness, He has done so. Who are we to drag someone else's sin back out? Second, none of us are free from sin; how can we judge the sins of another? Our focus should be more on ridding ourselves *"of all malice and all deceit, hypocrisy, envy, and slander of every kind,"* and letting Jesus deal with the sins of others.

MAY 30

Did I Do That?

David thought, "I will show kindness to Hanun son of Nahash, just as his father showed kindness to me." So David sent a delegation to express his sympathy to Hanun concerning his father.
(2 Samuel 10:2)

How kind of David to express his sympathy to Hanun at such a time. Can you believe David's act resulted in over forty thousand deaths? What David meant as kindness was twisted into a series of misunderstandings that caused the death of men not even involved in the original event.

How often in our lives are we misunderstood, or do we misunderstand others, resulting in damage beyond our imagination, or even beyond what we will ever know here on earth? Hanun's nobles twisted David's expression of sympathy. They misled Hanun, attacked David's messengers, and humiliated those messengers. As emotions and misunderstandings continued, a series of battles occurred. We read that at least 40,701 men died. David never could have imagined such devastation!

Has someone reacted poorly to your innocent gesture? It's easy to get defensive or hurt when they strike back. Stop! Take a minute to step back and ask God to help you understand what went wrong. Ask Jesus to go before you and prepare your hearts and minds. Be willing to offer your hand in kindness again, in the peace and timing of Jesus.

I would also hope, when you are offended, that you give the same grace to the other person. Check your reaction and verify whether you could have misunderstood or missed some information. Again, turn to Jesus and ask Him to help you and the other person clarify the interaction. Consider why it offended you.

Let us love one another with the love and grace of Jesus.

MAY 31

I Didn't Mean To

One evening David got up from his bed and walked around on the roof of the palace. From the roof he saw a woman bathing. The woman was very beautiful...
(2 Samuel 11:2)

So far, it could appear that King David hasn't done anything wrong. He had a sleepless night and was just out walking around. It could appear no worse than taking a walk on a beach somewhere. However, sin began to seep into David when he looked at the bathing woman long enough to realize how beautiful she was. Why did David allow his eyes to linger so long? David could have averted his eyes and gone back inside. He could also have sent a messenger to warn the woman that she had been visible to him from his roof. He could have had a barrier constructed to block the view of her roof. He could have avoided going out on his roof again. There were lots of possible solutions.

Next, David allowed that sin to creep in enough to inquire more about this woman. He found out that she, like him, was already married. End of story, right? Wrong! David was giving in more and more to the sin of lust. He had her brought to him and they had an affair. His lust resulted in sin. David and Bathsheba went too far.

There were further consequences to their sin. Bathsheba became pregnant. Instead of stopping at any of these points, confessing the sin, repenting and receiving forgiveness, David continued to spiral down. David drew other people into his mess and arranged to have Bathsheba's husband killed. Things continued to go awry. What a mess! Horrible consequences resulted from that original unplanned look.

What harm is a little sin, especially an unintended one? David's story is a reminder to stop sin as soon as possible. Don't allow Satan a foothold in your life.

JUNE 1

A Loved Wife

Under three things the earth trembles, under four it cannot bear up: a servant who becomes king, a fool who is full of food, an unloved woman who is married...
(Proverbs 30:21–23)

Blessed is the woman who knows she is loved by her husband. We all like to be made to feel special. Husbands, the above verse gives some indication of how incredibly important it is in God's view to love your wife.

Men and women typically process emotions differently. For example, women generally are more relationship-oriented than their male counterparts. It doesn't instill reassurance for a husband to say to his wife, "Well, I married yah, didn't I?" or "I told you I love you. If I ever change my mind, I'll let you know." That's not the kind of love his wife is looking for.

In any interaction, the facts of what has happened aren't the most important thing; rather, it's how a person perceived it. People develop actual illnesses based their negative emotional experiences. In contrast, when a word or action is received positively, it builds them up.

Husbands, do you purpose to express your love to your wife daily? Have you checked with her to see if she receives your words and actions as an expression of your love for her? Take time to discuss with your wife what you say and do that says "I love you." What words or actions speak loudest to her? Keep track on how often you express your love for her.

In addition, although the earth may tremble under an *"unloved woman who is married,"* the world will seem to rejoice with a married woman who is loved.

JUNE 2

Love Is an Action Word

Dear children, let us not love with words or tongue but with actions and in truth.
(1 John 3:18)

In this verse, John teaches how we should love one another as Jesus loves us. He is spurring his followers on to demonstrate the love of Jesus to those in their circle of influence. What better place is there to start than with your spouse? As you demonstrate the love of Jesus to your spouse, not only will your own relationship be blessed, but many people around you will witness that you walk the talk, and they will emulate your behaviour.

When our children were young, I was a fulltime, stay-at-home mother and homemaker. My husband was a shift worker. Unfortunately, there were many times that my husband would come home from a dayshift to find that dinner wasn't ready; in fact, sometimes I hadn't even begun to make it. His loving response was, "What would you like me to make for dinner?" Never did I receive criticism or an impatient "Call me when it's ready!" The love and respect I received in his actions spoke volumes.

We have many opportunities to love others in our church or in the community with our actions. My husband and I enjoy walking, running, biking, and other outdoor activities. As we make use of the trails in our neighbourhood, we always greet the people we meet along the way with a "Good day!" or "Hello." It's always interesting to see how long it takes for it to catch on. At first, we're usually met with shock, and then a greeting in response. Before long, we notice that people are greeting us before we get a chance to initiate it, and that they're greeting others along their way!

Wives and husbands both can put their love into action for one another in big or small ways. What love action can you do for your spouse today?

JUNE 3

The Wise Parents

Then Manoah prayed to the Lord: "O Lord, I beg you, let the man of God you sent to us come again to teach us how to bring up the boy who is to be born."
(Judges 13:8)

Do you remember the story of Samson? He was the Biblical hero whose strength was attributed to his hair never being cut. Samson had the hand of God on his life from conception. His mother was sterile but Jesus (*"the angel of the Lord,"* Judges 13:3) appeared to Samson's mother and told her she would conceive and have a son. Since she had been childless long enough to be considered sterile, this was exciting news indeed! When she shared the news with her husband, Manoah, he believed her. Then they begged Jesus to return and teach them how to raise their son. What wise parents!

We can gather that Samson's parents believed in the one true God. They desired to be the best parents they could be, so they wisely asked Jesus to teach them. In Old Testament times, their direct encounter with Jesus would have been very unique. There is no further mention in the Bible of Samson's parents having direct conversation with Jesus again. However, we read that Samson was blessed by the Lord and the Holy Spirit stirred within him (Judges 13:24–25). It seems his parents did receive wisdom to raise him.

We are fortunate to live in the New Testament times. Jesus has already come to earth in the flesh, conquered death, risen back into heaven, and sent the Holy Spirit to guide us. We have the privilege of speaking with God any time we choose. If you've been blessed with children, I would strongly advise you to also ask Jesus to teach you how to raise them. You have the blessing of being able to ask Jesus for help at any time. Your child may be an adult who doesn't live in your home anymore, but Jesus is still able to give you wisdom in your relationships.

JUNE 4

It's Too Much!

For I am poor and needy, and my heart is wounded within me.
(Psalm 109:22)

When David wrote this psalm, he was feeling pretty low. He was unable to provide for his own needs, and had been emotionally hurt. Can you relate? Have you experienced a time when everything seemed to be going wrong? Perhaps it was work, family, finances, or a combination. When we have one crisis, we're usually able to problem-solve our way through it, but when our troubles multiply, the weight can seem to be too much. We sometimes add to our woes by being self-centred and cranky to others, or perhaps spend more than we should trying to make ourselves feel better.

David, however, knew where his strength would come from. He turned to God. David recognized his human weakness, calling out, *"Help me, O Lord my God; save me in accordance with your love"* (Psalm 109:26). He continued to praise God and surrender everything to God, trusting that God would bring justice.

Where do you turn? I suggest you do the same as David, and always praise God. I'm not saying you should praise God for your troubles, but during your troubles. Continue to praise and worship our God, who is omnipotent, all-knowing, all-wise. Trust that He will be your protector, comforter, provider, defender, healer, peacemaker, and guide.

Reach out to your spouse or other prayer partner, surrendering everything to the Lord. Your prayer might be as simple as David's: *"Help me, O Lord my God."* Listen for His answer and direction. You may not find Him in the wind, earthquake, or fire, but in *"a gentle whisper"* (1 Kings 19:12).

Peace be yours.

JUNE 5

Under Attack

For I will give you words and wisdom that none of your adversaries will be able to resist or contradict.
(Luke 21:15)

Think of a time when you were called to justify yourself. Perhaps it was time for a job evaluation, or you were in a personal conflict, or even facing a court situation. You may be facing such a situation now. Who better to stand in your defence than Jesus Himself? That is what we are promised!

In Luke 21, we are encouraged not to worry, preparing in our mind what we will say. How much time do we waste thinking, *And if he says that, I will say this.* Often, our previews only serve to work us up and make us feel worse about the situation. We don't know what's going to take place in our future; Jesus does. He already knows the outcome, so He knows what is best to be said or not said. Just think of the wise responses Jesus gave in the Gospels. I would dearly desire to have such wisdom! Instead of fretting, God would have us spend our energy and thoughts aligning ourselves with Him. When we prepare ourselves in prayer, we have the peace that passes all understanding, and we will be less reactive.

If you know you have a troubling situation ahead, I would encourage you to gather prayer support. Start with those who are the most intimately connected to you and know your heart, like your spouse. The greater the intercession, the lesser the effect Satan will be able to bear on the situation.

When the time arrives, take a moment to make sure you've set aside your worries and thoughts, having come into His presence. Watch Him work in your defence.

JUNE 6

Kings and Governors

> *...you will be brought before kings and governors, and all on account of my name. This will result in your being witnesses to them.*
> (Luke 21:12–13)

Jesus foretold of persecution and troubled times for His followers because of their belief in Jesus. Those Christians did, in fact, face persecution, and that persecution continues today. That's because Satan, the ruler of this world, is not happy. Jesus encouraged Christians to seize every opportunity to witness to those in leadership.

Who are your kings and governors? Who in your life takes you to account for your faith? Do you have colleagues, friends, or family members who challenge your belief in Jesus? Don't be distressed or afraid. Jesus would say, *"This will result in your being witnesses to them."* Please continue reading Luke 21. He promises to give you *"words and wisdom"* (Luke 21:15).

I once attended a workshop that I thought was going to give me the recipe to make a loved one receive Jesus. I was so disappointed! The speaker didn't have all the answers! In fact, she told me that leaving the right book lying around and battering the person wasn't going to be effective. How was I ever going to make him understand? Well, Jesus tells us: when challenged on our faith by the *"kings and governors"* of our lives, we are to witness the way Jesus tells us. That's the only recipe we need.

Jesus will go before us and prepare their hearts. If we rely on Jesus, He won't only protect us from being defeated, He'll guide us in how to witness to them. Our part is to pray for them. Surrender them to Jesus and listen carefully to what He directs you to do or say. We will rejoice when our *"kings and governors"* receive Jesus, too!

JUNE 7

Sincere Love

Love must be sincere. Hate what is evil; cling to what is good. (Romans 12:9)

Through the Apostle Paul, we have been directed to love one another sincerely. Well, that's easy to say, but what about those people who come into our lives who just aren't very loveable? Yes, we are to love them, too. Not just pretend to love them and then grumble under our breath, but sincerely love them. I would encourage you to ask Jesus to give you that love when you're unable to attain it on your own.

We are to *"hate what is evil."* Do not allow Satan to infiltrate and plant negative thoughts in your mind. Be aware of your attitude towards the behaviour and words of others. Why is it we can accept comments or teasing from some people, and take offence at the same comment or teasing from others? Sometimes it might even be the same person, but our present emotional state affects how we perceive things. Do not allow Satan to inflict that jab!

Instead, *"cling to what is good."* Look for the good. Focus on the other person's good qualities. Your first response might be that you don't think they have any good qualities, but really look for the good. Ask Jesus to reveal the positive to you. Bless and pray for that person. Do they need healing, acceptance, reassurance? Ask Jesus to show you how to encourage and love them.

We will at times be in conflict with those we sincerely love. Satan loves to create disunity and build up walls to prevent communication. Let us remember that we can do all things through our one true and loving Father in heaven. Ask Jesus to help you recognize poor attitudes or walls to loving communication that may exist in your life. Ask Him to help you remove those walls and see others through His eyes. Embrace the good, and seek to love.

JUNE 8

Unity for Christ

May the God who gives endurance and encouragement give you a spirit of unity among yourselves as you follow Christ Jesus, so that with one heart and mouth you may glorify the God and Father of our Lord Jesus Christ. (Romans 15:5–6)

I remember the first time God called me to join a missions team overseas. That was definitely way out of my comfort zone! I had all kinds of objections, but knew in the end that I had to trust in Him and follow where He led me. How exciting and reassuring to know that God provides the *"endurance and encouragement"* for the things He asks us to do! Therefore, we don't need to worry about feeling capable or adequate for what we've been called to do. We just need to step out in faith. What has God called you to do?

Who have you been called to work with? What is your role? How is His work to be accomplished? Notice He has called us to have *"a spirit of unity."* There aren't any lone rangers or glory in having your own way. If you find disunity in an area which you believe God has called you to, then you know something isn't in alignment with His will. Pray that each member of the team would hear clearly from God, and that all other things would fall away. If each member follows Christ, you should all be headed in the same direction!

Ultimately, we are to join together *"with one heart and mouth [to] glorify the God and Father of our Lord Jesus Christ."* It's not about what building is built, what song is sung, or what program is provided. It's about obediently following Jesus in unity with other Christians, to bring light into the dark places of this world and bring glory to God. In the process, you will be blessed. Each time you follow the will of God, you will draw nearer to Him.

God rewards obedience and faithfulness.

JUNE 9

Valley Times

In my distress I called to the Lord; I called out to my God. From his temple he heard my voice; my cry came to his ears.
(2 Samuel 22:7)

David was at a very low point when he wrote this psalm.

As blessed and powerful as David was, there were still things that were out of his control, beyond his ability to fix on his own. Even when David didn't understand why things were going wrong (e.g. people he loved trying to kill him), he trusted in the Lord. He knew God could hear him, and that the Lord would bring justice.

What about your times of trial? Despite your best efforts, with all the resource you gather, have you found yourself in a distressing situation that is out of your control? Where have you turned? I'm referring to the times when you're knocked off your feet—hopefully, onto your knees or face-first on the floor in prayer. Know that the Lord can always hear you. Cry out to Him. You don't need to know how to overcome everything on your own. These valleys are the times when we are teachable by God. He is able to do amazing things! We just need to ask Him and trust that He can, and will, bring good.

Our hope and answers are in our Lord Jesus Christ.

JUNE 10

Delighted

He brought me out into a spacious place; he rescued me because he delighted in me.
(2 Samuel 22:20)

Do you realize God delights in you? He does! Each and every person who has received Jesus Christ as their Saviour is like His precious child.

Many times, we think of the Lord as being way up there somewhere, busily running the whole world. I'm grateful that He knows everything that's happening here on our little plant called earth, and that He is ultimately in control. Amazingly, as big as a task as that is, He's not too busy to know exactly what is going to happen here in Canada, and even in my community. Wow! That's great!

God also knows what's happening in the lives of my family and friends. He cares enough to watch over them, and hear their prayers and my prayers for them. He knows me, and my needs and concerns. He doesn't put us on the pending pile because of time constraints.

The most amazing thing to me, though, is that He delights in me. He delights in you, too! Delight means that He sits back and takes great pleasure. Our Father in heaven sits back and just enjoys you and me. He smiles at us! He picks us up and holds us, not just when we need comforting, but just to enjoy being with us.

Can you find time in your schedule for Him? Do you have time not just to take care of business (prayer requests), but to just enjoy His presence? This isn't the time to remind Him of all the things you believe you have messed up. Nor is it the time to beg Him to tell you where He would have you be, or what He would have you do. You may find playing worship music, retreating to a quiet spot, or just being intentionally quiet helps.

Take the time to enjoy His attention on just delighting in you.

JUNE 11

The Power of Prayer

Simon, Simon, Satan has asked to sift you as wheat. But I have prayed for you, Simon, that your faith may not fail. And when you have turned back, strengthen your brothers.
(Luke 22:31–32)

Why do bad things happen to Christians? Jesus told us that sometimes it's because Satan has asked to challenge our faith. It is apparent here that God was going to allow that challenge in Simon's life. What was Jesus' response to that testing? Prayer!

Simon (Peter) didn't see it coming. Jesus prophesied this straight out to Simon. His response was to assure Jesus that he was ready to follow Him, even *"to prison and to death"* (Luke 22:33). It appears that Peter meant what he said with all his heart, but as we read on, we see that he did indeed stumble. However, we also know that the Christian church was built on Peter's work. Jesus' prayers were answered. Peter not only retained his faith, he provided strength and leadership to his fellow Christians.

Is there anyone in your circle of influence who is going through a time of testing? Is there anyone struggling with their faith? Perhaps you observe someone giving in to the distractions and temptations of Satan. What should you do? What would Jesus do? Pray!

At times in your Christian responsibilities, you will be called to come alongside another Christian, perhaps by bringing a meal to someone who is laid up or helping someone find a job. Then there are times when all you can do, and all you are called to do, is pray for them. At those times, you may find that praying this verse, replacing Simon's name with theirs, is a good place to start.

Will your prayers matter? What happened to Simon, who didn't even know he needed that prayer?

JUNE 12

Tradition vs. Grace

No one sews a patch of unshrunk cloth on an old garment. If he does, the new piece will pull away from the old, making the tear worse.
(Mark 2:21)

New fabric shrinks once it's been washed and dried, some fabrics more so than others. Different fabrics shrink at various rates and for various reasons. Some, like wool, shrinks progressively as the fibre itself shrinks. Other fabrics, like cotton, have tension applied to the fibres during the weaving. These fibres then relax over time and shrink back to their natural size. If you take a new piece of that same fabric and sew it on older garment made from that fabric, over time the new piece will shrink and pull, possibly tearing the original item.

Jesus used this illustration to explain how the new grace He was teaching was not applicable to the old religious system. The Pharisees were concerned with the religious traditions that had been created to fulfill their interpretations of the old Mosaic Law. Jesus taught that religious tradition should not be placed above a relationship with God Himself. Jesus didn't say that traditions such as fasting were wrong. What He did say was that relationships with God are of utmost importance.

For example, Jesus gave us the Lord's Prayer as a model of how to pray. If we recite this prayer by rote, it's of no value. However, if we pray from our heart or use it to understand how to pray with our own words, the Lord will hear our prayers.

Is there an aspect of your spiritual life you do strictly because it's traditional or habitual? How might you break loose from that tradition to draw closer to Jesus? Meditate on this. Discuss it with your spouse.

JUNE 13

What Would You Ask For?

At Gibeon the Lord appeared to Solomon during the night in a dream, and God said, "Ask for whatever you want me to give you."
(1 Kings 3:5)

This sounds a bit like a magic genie, doesn't it? God told Solomon to ask for what he wanted from God. Take a minute to think about some of the things you might have considered if you were in Solomon's position.

Well, most of us are familiar with Solomon, so we know that he asked for *"a discerning heart to govern [God's] people"* (1 Kings 3:9). God was pleased with Solomon's heart attitude. The Lord blessed Solomon with wisdom (a discerning heart), and in addition, wealth and a long life.

Our Father in heaven has also made us this offer: *"For everyone who asks receives; he who seeks finds; and to him who knocks, the door will be opened"* (Matthew 7:8). Does that mean we should just quote Solomon and God will give us wisdom, wealth, and a long life? That would be good, wouldn't it?

What it really means is that we are to ask and seek things of God from a pure heart. Our heart attitude should be that of bringing glory to His kingdom, not just selfish pursuits. What is it you intend to do with that for which you ask God? He knows your heart. He's just waiting for you to ask.

Notice also that this offer pertains to you. God didn't say, "Ask me to manipulate others." He won't impose His will on others just because you ask. God will not answer the prayer, "Please give Johnny the gift of speaking in tongues," if Johnny doesn't seek it himself from his own pure heart.

No, our Father in heaven is not a genie. He is so much more.

Each of us walks our own path. Ask for everything you need to walk in His ways, and you will receive.

JUNE 14

Who Is Worthy?

But the other criminal rebuked him. "Don't you fear God," he said, "since you are under the same sentence? We are punished justly, for we are getting what our deeds deserve. But this man has done nothing wrong."
(Luke 23:40–41)

Who is worthy to receive the message of Jesus Christ? No one. Only by the grace of God, through the sacrifice of Jesus Christ, are we able to have the faith to receive the gift of eternal life. Who needs to know about Jesus? Everyone. To whom can Jesus Christ be revealed? Anyone.

I know of a man who says he received Jesus Christ when he was in solitary confinement in prison. I know of another woman who used to work the streets. She heard someone call her by her birth name. Since nobody in her current environment knew her by that name, she looked around. She knew it was Jesus. She believed and began the difficult climb back from that lifestyle. I also know people who considered themselves too intellectual to believe in the nonphysical presence of Jesus, and then something happened. They too believed.

Today's verses are the words of one of the criminals, crucified with Jesus Christ, to the other criminal. Even he believed, and Jesus promised him that he would go to paradise. Notice the other criminal missed the opportunity. It's not about how good or bad a person has been in the past. It's about the condition of their heart, which only Jesus knows.

To whom should you be willing to share the message of Jesus Christ? To anyone you can, to everyone the Lord sends you to. It's not for you to judge by what you can see. Your role is to be ready and willing when the opportunities present themselves. Salvation is between that person and Jesus. Remember, the second criminal wouldn't hear the message even from Jesus Himself.

JUNE 15

It Is Good

Shimei answered the king, "What you say is good. Your servant will do as my lord the king has said." And Shimei stayed in Jerusalem for a long time.
(1 Kings 2:38)

When we ask Jesus into our lives, we know that He intends good for us. As we invite the Holy Spirit into our lives, we anticipate that He will guide and direct us in ways that will benefit us. We would be in agreement that what God says is good. Our intention is to follow Jesus now and always.

Shimei aligned himself against King David. Although King David did not punish Shimei, King David instructed Solomon that he was not to consider Shimei innocent. Shimei deserved death, but Solomon spared his life under specific conditions. We too deserve death for our sins, but God has spared us because of Jesus. He considers us innocent.

Shimei meant to abide by the conditions set out for him. However, as time went by, something happened. In his self-righteousness, he forgot his promise and broke those conditions. His reaction resulted in death.

At times, we too forget our promise to God. Things happen in our lives and we react. We fall back into sin. Jesus knew we would be weak. He tells us that every time we sin, we can return to Him in confession and repentance. He will again forgive us and wash us clean.

If we confess our sins, he is faithful and just and will forgive us our sins and purify us from all unrighteousness. (1 John 1:9)

Thank You, Lord God, our heavenly Father, for Your unconditional love. Thank You for Your mercifulness. Thank You for Your patience in teaching us Your ways. It is our desire to follow You and be obedient. Thank You for Your infinite forgiveness. Thank You for being willing to hear our cry and set us back on the right path. Amen.

JUNE 16

A Prayer for Churches

For this reason, since the day we heard about you, we have not stopped praying for you and asking God to fill you with the knowledge of his will through all spiritual wisdom and understanding.
(Colossians 1:9)

When I read Paul's prayer for the Colossian church, I want to yell, "Pick me! Pick me!" I would love to be filled *"with the knowledge of [God's] will."* No more doubts, insecurities, or confusion about what His will is for me! No more internal conflict. I would love to have *"all spiritual wisdom and understanding."* Yes, what a blessing!

What an awesome prayer this is for me to pray for my church, and you for yours. I don't mean pray for the building, but for each and every person who gathers there to celebrate our faith in Jesus! The purpose of Paul's prayer was for the church in Colossus to be pleasing to God, be fruitful, gain knowledge of God, and be powerful in Him. Paul's desire was for the church to be strong, joyful, and thankful to God. Imagine the amazing work that would be done in the name of Jesus if my church, your church, and other churches for which we are impressed to pray, received these blessings. Imagine the unity, the light in dark places, and the peace!

Each church group, just like each individual Christian, has a purpose. Prayer brings each of us into alignment with our heavenly Father. If each member is in alignment, the church as a whole will be in alignment. Prayer is the source of the church's power. Prayer will make weak churches strong and strong churches stronger. Prayer will bring clarity of purpose. We are all called to pray. Prayer does change things.

I want for my church what Paul wanted for the Colossian church. Don't you?

JUNE 17

The Loving Truth

Instead, speaking the truth in love, we will in all things grow up into him who is the Head, that is, Christ.
(Ephesians 4:15)

Like Jesus, we are to speak the truth in love. I am one of those people that would rather avoid confrontation, so this sounds so right and peaceful. I imagine Jesus speaking softly, patiently, and with great wisdom. I imagine that the person He is speaking to received His words calmly, with new understanding. It appears simple and effective.

Why then do I fear that I won't have the right words when witnessing to others? Why do I fear not having the right words when someone asks me to pray with them? Why do I fear disagreement with a fellow Christian? I believe the answer lies in the fact that although we may be seeking to be like Jesus, we are influenced by the ruler of this world. Satan loves conflict. He uses confusion, manipulation, and any other form of deception to draw us away from the truth.

In today's verse, the Apostle Paul encourages the Christians in Ephesus not to be deceived by the teachings of evil men. We too must watch that, as we seek enlightenment, we don't become entrapped by self-seeking, deceitful people. We must weigh all things against the word of the Lord. We know His word to always be true.

I pray that the Lord will continue to give me a better understanding of His truths. I pray that He will protect me from being confused and deceived by other teachings. I pray that He will so mould my heart that I won't be tempted to add my own words and thoughts, confusing His message. I pray that He will give me the wisdom, discernment, and the right words at the right time to help others know the truth as well. I pray that He will reveal His truths to others around me. Then *"we will in all things grow up into him who is the Head, that is, Christ."*

JUNE 18

Living for a Purpose

Before I was born the Lord called me; from my birth he has made mention of my name.
(Isaiah 49:1)

On days when you're floundering around, you wonder what it is you're supposed to be doing. You wonder if you're in the right relationships, career, ministry, etc. You doubt whether you're having any effect on the world. What's your purpose, anyway?

Well, be assured that you are important to God. He knew when and where you would be born. He *"created [your] inmost being; [He] knit [you] together in [your] mother's womb"* (Psalm 139:13). He has called you from birth! You weren't a mistake that God has forgotten. You are important to God! He has a purpose for your life!

Start from right where you are. God can use you anywhere at any time, if you allow Him. You are to be His light in this dark world. Ask for His direction and trust that He will answer. Then just listen. Listen for what He says rather than telling Him what you want Him to do. Allow God to work in His timing, not yours.

Do you need encouragement? Ask the Lord to show you some fruits of your labour for Him. Watch with His eyes, listen with His ears. Ask Him what you should be praying about and how He would have you pray.

The Lord really does have exciting plans for your life! I'm not suggesting that everything is pre-planned and that you have no choice or effect. As long as your choice of career, relationship, etc. is not ungodly, He can use you there. For example, both a teacher and a doctor may be called to witness to a friend or colleague, or be called to short-term missions. Both a letter carrier and an engineer can be called to pray for their country or a sick friend.

He knows you by name. He loves you and knows the plans He has for you. Trust in Him.

JUNE 19

Understanding the Word

Then he opened their minds so they could understand the Scriptures. (Luke 24:45)

I have been a Christian for a number of years. I have gone to innumerable church services, Christian courses, Bible studies, and read through the Bible many times. Why is it that I still get an "Aha!" moment when I read or hear a verse?

Jesus spent three years teaching His disciples daily. He taught, modelled, and corrected them. In Luke 24, He was approaching the day of His earthly death. It was at this time that Jesus *"opened [his disciples'] minds so they could understand the Scriptures."* Why now? Why didn't Jesus just open their minds from the very beginning? One reason, I believe, is that we learn better by experience. The learning goes deeper.

Suppose you were going in for surgery. Would you want your surgeon to have only listened or read about how to perform surgery? I would prefer that he had some real, supervised experience before he took a knife to me! Suppose we show a child how to perform addition. We just tell him that 2+2=4. Then we walk away. Do you really think that child would have a grasp on how to do addition correctly?

I believe those "Aha!" moments are when Jesus is opening my mind. Based on my past experience, current state, or spiritual development, Jesus knows when I'm ready to understand the Scripture the way He intends for me to. This is one way Jesus is able to speak into my life and continue to teach me.

That being said, if I don't continue to expose myself to His word in various modalities, how do I expect to understand all that He has for me? I would encourage you to seek out ways to continually sit at the feet of Jesus and learn from Him. Ask Him to open your mind, so that you may understand.

JUNE 20

By Whose Advice?

The king answered the people harshly. Rejecting the advice given him by the elders, he followed the advice of the young men…
(1 Kings 12:13–14)

Decisions! Decisions! We can't avoid them. We need to make decisions every minute of our lives. We begin every day with them by deciding when to get out of bed. Most of our days are so filled with decisions that we don't even give them conscious thought. However, there are other decisions into which we must put much thought and consideration.

When faced with these major decisions, we turn to others for help. "What do you think? What do you see as the consequence of deciding this way or that?" Whose advice do you seek?

In 1 Kings, we read of one of King Rehoboam's major decisions. He first asked the elders for advice. These would have been experienced men with a proven track record for wisdom. Then he asked his young companions. Just as we may, he received conflicting advice from the different people he spoke to. He unfortunately went with the ill advice of his young companions, which resulted in tragedy.

Sometimes what appears to be the right decision isn't. For example, I have known people who chose not to pursue an awesome looking job when they had a chance. Shortly afterwards, that company laid off employees or closed down. Obviously, they made a good decision.

So, I ask you, who do you go to for advice? How do you sort out what the best advice is in each situation? Who knows more than our Father in heaven? Ask Him. Pray that He would direct you to the best answer, and that He would give you peace about the decision when you make the right one.

JUNE 21

Be Joyful and Amazed

And while they still did not believe it because of joy and amazement, he asked them, "Do you have anything here to eat?"
(Luke 24:41)

What an emotional roller-coaster ride Jesus' followers must have experienced when He was crucified. They had thought He was going to bring them deliverance from their current political situation. He was their leader who was going to bring them victory! Then He was gone. Then He reappeared in flesh and blood! They could see the scars, touch Him, and He even wanted something to eat! How could this be? I'm sure there was great *"joy and amazement"*! As you read the story, you may wonder why they were so surprised. Jesus had already told them what was going to happen. Didn't they believe?

What about you? Is Jesus your leader, the king of your life, your Saviour? When you pray and talk to Jesus, do you believe He will listen? Do you believe He will answer? Do you believe you will understand His answer? Do you believe what He tells you?

What happens when He answers your prayers? Do you remember what you asked Him for? Do you recognize His answer and how He perhaps provided more than you even asked? Do you remember to praise God and thank Him like the man healed from leprosy in Luke 17? Or do you receive the blessing and then carry on with life, taking His blessing for granted like the other nine men who were healed?

I continue to be joyfully amazed at all that God does in and through my life. He is so faithful to answer prayers. May we all continue to seek to understand Him and what He desires to bless our lives with. As the old hymn goes "Praise God from whom all blessings flow."

JUNE 22

Understanding the Light

The light shines in the darkness, but the darkness has not understood it. (John 1:5)

Some people are more observant than others. They can just walk into a room and take in the whole picture in one glance. They are great at memory games, such as when you show a tray of items, then take the tray away and ask them to tell you what all was on the tray. Some people will even be able to tell you the colour or orientation of each article. Other people struggle to remember what was there.

This is how the good news of Jesus works. Some people have the blessing of being born and raised in an area where they have every opportunity to hear and learn about Jesus, but they don't understand. They have never asked Jesus into their lives. The light has been there all along, but they just don't understand it

Other people are born into less fortunate situations. Their country and families may be living in complete darkness. There are places where people believe in witchcraft and worship local witchdoctors. Sexual abuse, incest, and other dark practices are just the way it is. However, even there, God can provide a means for someone to hear the good news of our Saviour Jesus Christ. They can be given the flicker of light and receive Jesus. They understand immediately and become the light of Jesus in their own dark world.

People may receive the same opportunities to be exposed to the light, but each one will understand it in their own timing. Our job is to continue to walk in the light and allow Jesus to shine through us, whether that be through prayer, modelling, or direct evangelism. Sometimes you may shine the light of Jesus and not know its effect until you reach heaven.

JUNE 23

Walking Together

But God has combined the members of the body and has given greater honor to the parts that lacked it, so that there should be no division in the body, but that its parts should have equal concern for each other.
(1 Corinthians 12:24–25)

Paul is writing here of God's plan for each of us in the Christian body. God has a role for each of us to play. Some people will be called to perform those upfront roles that everyone sees. Others will perform supporting roles. Still others will have roles that are not as well-known. Your role might be welcoming newcomers or recognizing a fellow member in pain and quietly walking alongside them. You are not honoured more or less or have more or less "pull" with God due to the visibility of your role. We are to work together and *"have equal concern for each other."*

The same can be said for our families. God has known which family we would be part of. Each of us is of equal value to God. It doesn't matter who brings in the most money, who is the oldest or youngest, or who appears to take on the role of coordinating roles and responsibilities. Each one is precious to God. We are meant to work together and have concern for each other in our family units, as well as in our church families.

What are your roles? Do you value your roles as God does? What do you see as each of your family member's roles? Do you value them as God does? If you puff yourself up or cut yourself down, you are not seeing yourself as God does. Likewise, if you hold one family member in higher or lesser importance, you are not seeing them as God would have you see them.

Thank You, Lord, that You love me just the way I am. Thank You for helping me work through my walk with You. Thank You for the family, church, and friends You have placed in my life, that we may work together for Your glory. Amen.

JUNE 24

Jesus Loves You

For God did not send his Son into the world to condemn the world, but to save the world through him.
(John 3:17)

On occasions, I've heard a backsliding Christian say something like, "You don't want me on your prayer team" or "If you mention my name at church, you might burst into flames." It breaks my heart. These people pretend to be making a joke, but in their hearts they feel condemned and unworthy of the love of God. They know they have wandered away from righteousness and truth.

However, I'm not the one who matters. I'm sure Jesus Himself cries out for these lost souls. The condemnation is not of God! Satan has deceived these precious children of God into believing they are unlovable. Satan would have them believe they are hopeless failures. Satan doesn't want them to know they are forgiven, loved, and missed.

Well, I have a message for these people: Jesus loves you! He misses you and is waiting to hear from you. As long as we have breath, it is not too late to turn back to Jesus. He will welcome you back with open arms! Time and again, the word tells us that if we repent and turn back, He will hear us. For a few examples of this promise, see 2 Chronicles 7:14, Proverbs 28:13, and 1 John 1:9.

Jesus did not come to condemn. He came to earth to save us! He loves each of us, cherishing each and every one of us. No matter what horrible thing someone thinks they have done, it's not too big for Jesus to forgive. He will lead them back to the right path if they are willing.

I would call you to pray for the wayward children of God. Join together with your spouse so that two or more may be gathered together. Pray against the lies of the enemy, and for the light of Jesus to reveal the truth. Pray that they would receive the love Jesus so dearly wants to give.

JUNE 25

God Can Provide

For the jar of flour was not used up and the jug of oil did not run dry, in keeping with the word of the Lord spoken by Elijah.
(1 Kings 17:16)

This is the story of the poor widow who was about to use the very last of her provisions to make a final meal for her and her son. She expected for them to both die of starvation afterward. Along came Elijah, a prophet, who asked her to give him something to eat. She had lost all hope for herself and her son, and now this man was asking for her help?

Through Elijah, God assured the woman that He would provide. In faith, she went away and made some bread for Elijah. God provided not only enough to go around for the three of them, but He miraculously continued to provide for them throughout the entire drought! The woman received food and hope.

God created the world. Why would we ever doubt that He can provide the little bit we need? We are to trust in Him and obey whatever He directs us to do. It may not be lack of food that we face. We have many needs—physical, emotional, and spiritual. God can provide for *every* need. He knows our real needs and He is ready, willing, and able to provide. We must trust in Him.

Discuss with your spouse what needs you each are facing right now. What needs are you facing together? Ask God for His direction and provision.

Notice that the widow in this story didn't just sit and wait. She was willing to take action as the Lord directed. Nor did she go off and do her own thing, like search the fields for what food she might find to provide for the three of them. She did what would seem ridiculous in man's eyes, and was willing to use her last bit of food to feed a stranger.

God cannot be used up, nor will He run dry. Praise God!

JUNE 26

Are God's Commands Good?

Teach me knowledge and good judgment, for I believe in your commands. (Psalm 119:66)

This is an interesting verse to meditate on. At first glance, one might be quick to agree with it. Of course the knowledge of God is good! Of course having good judgement inspired by God is desirable! And naturally, a Christian believes in God's commands. But are you truly ready for God's lessons?

This means being willing for God to reveal any areas of wrong thinking in your life. It means giving up all sinfulness—greed, lust, jealousy, entitlement, and other self-centred thoughts. It means being willing to experience the life lessons God needs to impose on you for your development. It means giving undivided time and attention to God. It means giving up your will. Wow! That's a big commitment!

I'm so grateful that I serve such a good God. I trust He will not give me more than I can bear.

> *No temptation has seized you except what is common to man. And God is faithful; he will not let you be tempted beyond what you can bear. But when you are tempted, he will also provide a way out so that you can stand up under it.* (1 Corinthians 10:13)

He will not crush me.

After giving this verse careful consideration, I hope you would still agree with it and be willing to pray this prayer for yourself. He is a good God and His commands are good and true. Yes, it is a big commitment, but one that is well worth it. Why stumble about on your own and deal with damage control when you could do it the right way, God's way, the first time?

I'm not always successful, but I desire to always align my thoughts and will with God. I desire to shine His light in this dark world to bring health and wholeness to others and glory to God!

JUNE 27

There Is Hope

O Israel, put your hope in the Lord, for with the Lord is unfailing love and with him is full redemption.
(Psalm 130:7)

The book of Ruth is a story of a woman who experienced many loses. She lived in difficult times and experienced the sorrow of having her husband and both of her sons die before her. On top of her grief, in Ruth's time (1000 B.C.), there wasn't much hope for a childless widow. Broken and hopeless, Naomi sent her daughters-in-law back to their families, and headed back to her homeland.

Thankfully, we serve a God of hope and restitution. Ruth, one of the daughters-in-law, determined to stand by Naomi and walk with her through her valley. Ruth set out to find a way for Naomi and herself to survive. She looked for a way to provide food for Naomi and herself. God provided so much more!

It turns out that Ruth went to a field to glean the leftovers (much like dumpster diving, in our time) and ended up winning the heart of a rich land owner. They married, had children, and became part of the ancestry of Mary, and thereby Jesus. God not only restored hope to Naomi and Ruth, but provided hope for all generations by sending His son Jesus to earth through their linage.

Whether it's your own situation, or that of a loved one, that seems hopeless, do not give up hope. Seek God's help, and He will provide hope in ways you may never have imagined. Surrender your cares to Him and expect restoration! Our God is a mighty God. He can *"bestow… a crown of beauty instead of ashes, the oil of gladness instead of mourning, and a garment of praise instead of a spirit of despair"* (Isaiah 61:3). He reaches beyond our vision and brings not only restoration, but redemption.

JUNE 28

Praise and Worship

I will be glad and rejoice in you; I will sing praise to your name, O Most High.
(Psalm 9:2)

Praise and worship means different things to different people. It can mean everything from the music churches play so latecomers have time to get settled before the sermon, to entering into His presence. It can simply mean Christian music, or it can mean honouring and revering God with music and prayers.

I love listening to Christian music for the shear enjoyment of it. I find it very uplifting to have Christian music play in the background as I go about my housework or other chores. I may not be consciously focusing on God during that time, but I'm unconsciously setting my mind towards right thinking. Often during those times, I hear God speak to me.

I end up learning the songs so well that when I do enter into a time of worship, I can focus on God and not have to busy myself with reading the words or trying to remember them. Learning the songs by heart allows me to close my eyes, focus on God, and truly worship and honour Him. Furthermore, whether in times of trouble, anxiety, or great joy, knowing worship songs is as encouraging as memorized Bible verses.

The mornings when I wake up with a worship song already going through my head are the most joyful and peaceful. It does make me *"glad."* I am encouraged and lifted up. I am more likely to spend time praising God in song or in prayer. When my mind wanders, it's more likely to wander back to God, not away.

How do you praise and worship? What music are you immersed in?

JUNE 29

Put It in Writing

You are beautiful, my darling, as Tirzah, lovely as Jerusalem, majestic as troops with banners.
(Song of Solomon 6:4)

The Song of Solomon (written in 965 B.C) is full of beautiful expressions of love in courtship and marriage. It can also be seen as an illustration of the love of God for His people. King Solomon and the woman who became his wife pour out their love and admiration for one another. This is a wonderful love story to read together with your spouse.

Husbands, one of the best ways to get your wife's attention is to write her a love letter. The letter doesn't have to be long. Perhaps just write your own words in a blank card instead of signing your name to a store-bought one. Or maybe surprise her with a love letter when it's not even her birthday or your anniversary.

She may not want to hear that her *"hair is like a flock of goats descending from Mount Gilead"* (Song of Solomon 4:1) or that her *"teeth are like a flock of sheep just shorn, coming up from the washing"* (Song of Solomon 4:2), but she does want to hear that you love her. What is it that drew you to her? What is it you admire about the way she has developed? What do you enjoy about the way she looks or the things she does?

God has provided His written words of love to each of us through the Bible. How do you know He loves you? What do you think He loves specifically about you? What do you think He loves specifically about your spouse? Tell them.

If you were to write a love letter to God, what would you write? What is it you would like Him to know about your admiration and love for Him? Tell Him.

JUNE 30

How Much Faith Do You Have?

Elisha replied to her, "How can I help you? Tell me, what do you have in your house?"
(2 Kings 4:2)

This is the story of a woman who came to God's prophet, Elisha, asking him to solve her problem. Elisha's response was to ask her what she had to contribute to the solution. Then he gave her specific instructions. This is not unlike when we turn to God for help.

The woman was right to seek God's help. Her problem seemed beyond what she could handle. It's interesting to notice, though, how God responded through His prophet. Nothing is too difficult for God. He could have raised her husband back to life, provided the money she thought she needed, or softened the creditors' hearts to forgive the debt. However, God had something more to teach in this situation. The question was, how much faith did she have?

First, Elisha asked her to recognize what God had already given her. Was she aware of God's blessings and gifts? Then he specifically told her, *"Go around and ask all your neighbors for empty jars. Don't ask for just a few"* (2 Kings 4:3). Ask and trust God for a lot. The woman's oil lasted just until the last jar was filled. God provided as much as she took action for and she had faith for.

Oftentimes, we are the same way. God only answers our prayers as much as we recognize the blessings we already have, and that we have faith for. "God, please let me get this specific job I applied for." Okay. You have determined that you've been blessed with the talent and skills for the position. You trust that God can help. However, is that the best job God foresees for you? Is there something you don't know about the company down the road? Is there a better job you will miss out on because you stopped looking where God was directing you? When you pray, be willing to take action, and try not to limit God's blessings.

JULY 1

Who's in Charge? (Part One)

Wives, submit to your husbands as to the Lord.
(Ephesians 5:22)

Why do we hear this verse so often quoted as a standalone verse? It's usually used when insinuating that the wife should yield control and be nothing more than a slave to her husband. Often I see men smirk and women appear shocked or horrified by this verse. In truth, this interpretation is completely off the mark.

This verse doesn't say wives should be *slaves* to their husbands, right or wrong. I would pray that you're never put in the situation of your husband requesting that you tolerate abuse or compromise your moral or legal conscience. The loving response in those situations would be not only to refuse, but to seek help.

I refer people to the book of Ephesians and ask them to read the verse in its context. The word "submit" is not a negative thing. It's more appropriately interpreted as referring to another person for a decision or judgment. When you read what the husband is called to be, who wouldn't want to consult him? If my husband is striving to love me as much as the Lord loves the church, His decisions and judgment can only be for my good.

Take your focus off the negative connotations of the word "submit" and instead look at the words "as to the Lord." Do you resent the Lord's direction in your life? Why? How should that apply to your husband's direction?

I respect and treasure the advice of my husband. I trust that he would never intend to harm me in any way. If I disagree with him, we've likely had a misunderstanding. Rather than becoming resentful, this signals an opportunity to lovingly clarify our communication.

JULY 2

Who's in Charge? (Part Two)

For the husband is the head of the wife as Christ is the head of the church, his body, of which he is the Savior. Now as the church submits to Christ, so also wives should submit to their husbands in everything.
(Ephesians 5:23–24)

Typically, when someone is told he is the "head," this infers that he's in control or in some way powerful. Sounds good, doesn't it? "I'm the boss! Do things my way!"

Oh, wait a minute. This compares the husband's role to that of Christ's relationship with the church. What kind of a leader is Christ? Well, one example is found in John 10:11, where Jesus said, *"I am the good shepherd. The good shepherd lays down his life for the sheep."* Jesus is telling us that He's responsible for the wellbeing of the church, to the point of dying for it. What does that say about husbands?

Ephesians goes on to talk about Christ's love for the church, His sacrifices, and how He nurtures the church. Husband, you are called to love your wife, be willing to sacrifice for her, and lead her in developing her spiritual walk. Your position of authority is one of leadership. Do you really want your wife and family to follow in your ways, or do you need to make some course corrections? You have a position of responsibility, and it is your responsibility to love, guide, and direct your wife in her walk and spiritual development. When Jesus was here on earth, His mode of leadership was instructional, but gentle and loving.

Thankfully, if your marriage has that third strand and is Christ-centred, you aren't left on your own to figure out how to be the leader. Stay in the word, united in Christ, and He will guide your way.

JULY 3

Investing in Children

Jesus said, "Let the little children come to me, and do not hinder them, for the kingdom of heaven belongs to such as these."
(Matthew 19:14)

Studies have shown that children need quantity *and* quality time with the adults in their lives. If you have children, discuss with your spouse what each of you is doing to invest in your children. If you don't have children, have you considered investing your time in other children? This involvement might be direct or indirect, perhaps by pitching in to allow another parent more time to invest in his or her children.

The above command seems pretty straightforward. Jesus Himself has commanded us to not stop children from coming to Him. You may not be directly inhibiting a child from knowing Jesus, but are you enabling any?

As Christian parents, that would entail teaching them the word of God. Spend time talking with your children about Bible stories, pray with them, and role-model a godly life. Perhaps you need to make sure they get an opportunity to go to Sunday school and/or a Christian children's club. Is there a child in your family or neighbourhood who doesn't have those opportunities? How about befriending that family and asking permission to take their kids with yours to Christian events?

Parent or not, could you give of your time and energy to teach Sunday school or be a youth leader? Have you considered a mentorship program such as Big Brothers or Big Sisters? How about financially and prayerfully sponsoring a child from a less privileged family or country to enable them to learn about, and receive, the love of Jesus through you?

These children are precious to Jesus right now, and they are our tomorrows. We can invest in them or allow them to be tossed about in worldly values. When someone says "What's wrong with this world?" ask if they have invested in a child.

JULY 4

Prideful Independence

But Naaman went away angry and said, "I thought that he would surely come out to me and stand and call on the name of the Lord his God, wave his hand over the spot and cure me of my leprosy."
(2 Kings 5:11)

Naaman was the commander of an army. He was used to telling people what to do and expected them to obey him. He was also well-off. He thought he could take care of everything he needed on his own. Then he became leprous. This problem was one Naaman was unable to fix. No amount of money, knowledge, or strings to pull could help him.

Then along came a little hostage slave girl. She suggested that Naaman go to Elisha, a prophet of God. Naaman thought he was ready to try anything. He gathered up much of his wealth and headed off to pay for a cure.

Elisha didn't even receive Naaman face to face. Elisha just sent Naaman simple directions to go wash in the Jordan. Now the truth begins to be revealed! Naaman was offended because he had already determined the regal method that he expected God to use to heal him. How humiliating!

Naaman was eventually convinced by his servants again to obey God's instructions. He was cured. Naaman immediately wanted to pay for the services. He would earn the right to be healed. Imagine his surprise, and the blow to his pride, when Elisha refused the payment. Naaman finally began to understand. He desired to worship the one true God, and God only. Naaman recognized how little he was and how big God was.

How many times do we try to take care of things ourselves? We forget to ask God what His will is. What areas of your life might you be prideful in? What is God saying to you about that? Do you expect God to do things your way, or are you humbly willing to do things His way?

JULY 5

Fear Not

And Elisha prayed, "O Lord, open his eyes so he may see." Then the Lord opened the servant's eyes, and he looked and saw the hills full of horses and chariots of fire all around Elisha.
(2 Kings 6:17)

An army was sent out to capture Elisha. When he and his servant came out in the morning, they saw that they were completely surrounded. Not surprisingly, the servant was very distressed! Elisha, a prophet of God, comforted his servant, saying, *"Don't be afraid... Those that are with us are more than those who are with them"* (2 Kings 6:16).

Our God is not a God of fear. When we are fearful, we know that the enemy is trying to intimidate us. We must trust the Lord our God, who is all-powerful! Ephesians 6:12 reminds us,

For our struggle is not against flesh and blood, but against the rulers, against the authorities, against the powers of this dark world and against the spiritual forces of evil in the heavenly realms.

You don't have to battle alone! God provides heavenly support which is so much greater than the enemy.

This servant was able to temporarily see into the heavenly realm. We may not receive the opportunity to see with our physical eyes all the support God is providing us, but we can trust that He's there when we call out to Him. I truly believe God has changed many events because of prayer. We will never know all the tragedies that have been averted, but we can witness amazing circumstances that provide help at just the right time.

God reaches beyond our physical needs and meets our spiritual needs. Think about the circumstances that led you to Christ in the first place. Try to imagine the prayers that went before you and continue to be lifted up in your name.

What an awesome and powerful God we serve.

JULY 6

God's Plan

However, as it is written: "No eye has seen, no ear has heard, no mind has conceived what God has prepared for those who love him."
(1 Corinthians 2:9)

I remember a time when I thought I had finally figured out the role God had for me. I was to teach Sunday School forever! I was trained as a teacher, loved children, and had taught for many successful years. Suddenly, something happened to bring all that to a halt. My first response was to fight for the right to continue. Surely there was a mistake. I knew Sunday School was my calling.

Although it was painful at the time, I can look back and see God's hand in it. I had become reliant on my skills and my success. Even though I was involved in a good thing, God needed to get my eyes fully on Him. After surrendering to Him, I finally received peace. He even restored relationships that had been strained because of my attitude.

God has since allowed me many opportunities to work with children again, but to this date, never again in the same way. He has also called me into many other areas of ministry. He has taken me places I would never have imagined! He has blessed me in so many ways!

We must listen to where God is calling us, not hanging on to things beyond what He has asked. By studying His word and spending time with Him, we must strive to be in tune with His will and His timing. We must trust that God's plans are better than anything we can come up with or even imagine. Know that He loves us and desires to use us for good.

In what ways has God used you in the past? What are your current ministries? Are you willing to surrender all to Him and trust that He has good things planned for you? Are you looking forward to all that He is calling you to in your future?

God loves you!

JULY 7

Ambassadors

All this is from God, who reconciled us to himself through Christ and gave us the ministry of reconciliation: that God was reconciling the world to himself in Christ, not counting men's sins against them.
(2 Corinthians 5:18–19)

God—the pure, holy, perfect God—chose to be reconciled to sinful man. He chose to completely forgive us and make peace with us. He has done so in love, not "Oh fine, but don't let it happen again" condemnation. Why? He did so to give *"us the ministry of reconciliation."* Now it's our turn!

I hope and pray I have never done, and never will do, anything to turn others away from God. I pray I have never hurt or angered someone to the point that they would say, "If that's what a Christian is, I don't want anything to do with it." If I have, I pray that God would provide a way to overcome my inequities and provide that person with an opportunity to be reconciled to Him.

We are God's ambassadors! An ambassador is a person who represents his country in foreign places. An ambassador is equipped with a high level of authority from his government. We, as Christians, are just that! We are God's representatives on earth. We are here to tell others of our heavenly home with Christ. We have been given authority through the Holy Spirit to do God's work here. We are to tell the people they are welcome to our homeland, and also how to get there. We are to help reconcile others with God. In God's love, we are to help reveal the truth, heal the broken-hearted, and set captives of the enemy free.

An ambassador also has diplomatic immunity—that is, he is under the protection of his home government (in our case, God). We have been given special privileges and aren't subject to the laws of this government (Satan).

May each of us continuously carry the message of God's love, grace, and forgiveness.

JULY 8

What Does God Say?

Jesus, knowing that they intended to come and make him king by force, withdrew again to a mountain by himself.
(John 6:15)

The people Jesus was teaching and ministering to recognized the good in Him. They received Him and wanted more of His leadership. They wanted Him to be their King! That's good, right? Jesus knew what they intended to do and He hid from them. He withdrew from the very people who wanted to honour Him. Instead He chose to spend time alone with the Father. Jesus knew that the Father had much more planned for Him. He was to be the Saviour of the whole world, not just these people's King.

How many times are we caught up in these types of situations? We purpose to do God's will and find ourselves doing well in a particular area. As God blesses the work of our hands, other people begin to recognize us. We are encouraged to move on to a seemingly better or higher level. Stop! Have you taken the time to check in with God to see if that's where He wants you to be? It may appear to be a good move. God wants us to do well. Perhaps you can see potential for so much more you can accomplish in that new position, but does God have something better planned—Not just for you, but for others as well?

I know a woman who stepped down from a very godly ministry. She has done amazing work in the name of Jesus. However, she believed God was telling her that some people were beginning to believe in her. She would be the first to say it was not her work, but that of God! Others have taken their eyes off Jesus and put their hope in her. She believed God was telling her that this was the time to remove herself from the ministry so that those people could be redirected back to their Father in heaven. She is now waiting on the Lord to see what new, exciting plans He has for her life. What is He saying to you?

JULY 9

How Much Longer?

I will add fifteen years to your life. And I will deliver you and this city from the hand of the king of Assyria. I will defend this city for my sake and for the sake of my servant David.
(2 Kings 20:6)

Hezekiah was a good king. 2 Kings 18:3 tells us, *"He did what was right in the eyes of the Lord…"* Then he became very ill. The prophet Isaiah came to Hezekiah and told him that the Lord said he should get his house in order, because he was about to die. Hezekiah wept and prayed. The Lord sent Isaiah back to tell Hezekiah that He would heal him and give him fifteen more years to live.

None of us knows how much time we have here on earth. As Christians, we know God has prepared a better place for us to go when we leave. However, most of us tend to want to hang on to our lives as long as possible. What would you do if you knew exactly how much longer you had? Would you do anything differently than you are doing now? Why or why not?

What if you knew how much longer someone else had to live? Would it change anything about your relationship? Like most people, I have experienced someone very dear to me going on to their heavenly home. It has given me the opportunity to think about when I will be separated from the people I love for a time. I'm so joyful for those who get to go and meet Jesus face to face and begin their time of reward in heaven!

This has also made me very aware that each time we say goodbye to someone, it may well be the last time. I want my family and friends to know I love them. I want the people I've been blessed to know to be aware that I love Jesus. I want them to know that Jesus loves them even more than I do! I want as many people as possible to receive their gift of salvation, that we may all be reunited with Him when it is our time.

What if Jesus returns today? Are you ready?

JULY 10

God's Requirement

Then they asked him, "What must we do to do the works God requires?" Jesus answered, "The work of God is this: to believe in the one he has sent." (John 6:28–29)

Life can seem so complicated! "What should I be doing? What is the right decision? Where should I be spending my time, money and energy?" Jesus kept it simple and gave us the straight answer: *"Believe in the one he [God] has sent [Jesus]."*

To believe in Jesus is to trust in Him. We are to trust that what He tells us is true and right. How do we know what that is? Read the Bible. By reading the four Gospels, we can learn from what Jesus taught while He was here on earth. We can also learn from those He enlightened by reading the rest of the New Testament. I love spending time in the New Testament! At one point, I considered the Old Testament difficult and boring. I'm not much of a history buff, and I squirmed at all the death and bloodshed. As I drew closer to Jesus, however, I understood that I needed to know the Old Testament to better grasp the teaching of the New Testament.

If we believe in Jesus, we will also want to spend time with Him in prayer. This is our time to worship God, thank Him for all our blessings, and spend time in conversation. I can be quite a talker once I get to know someone well. For me, I need to remember to take a breath and just listen to what Jesus would say to me. I have found that the more time I spend with Jesus, the more easily I remember that He is with me always. I can turn to Him at any time. It's better than the instant messaging so many people use today. Jesus is never too busy to receive an incoming message and respond.

If you're a Christian, then you believe in Jesus. How well do you know Him?

JULY 11

Our Secrets

The Israelites secretly did things against the Lord their God that were not right.
(2 Kings 17:9)

If you spend time in the mud, you're going to get dirty. The Israelites actually thought they could hide their disobedience from God. The fact that they tried to hide it indicates that they knew what they were doing was wrong and shameful. The Lord even sent them warnings through prophets, but they didn't listen. The Israelites rejected the ways of the Lord in favour of worthless idols. As a result, they too *"became worthless"* (2 Kings 17:15). The Israelites wanted to "fit in." They chose acceptance from the nations around them over the privileged relationship with God and His blessings.

As an adult, we may find ourselves criticising young people. We shake our head at how they are influenced by the media and peer pressure. We disapprove of their music, their dress, and their expressions of individualization. We remember our youth and wanting to be accepted by the group. How different are you now?

If Jesus was to show up at any point in your day, would there be anything you would try to keep secret? Is there a little corner in your heart you have denied Him access to? Are there areas in your life you have compromised, knowing they're not in alignment with the Lord's will? You are not alone. You have been accepted by Jesus, the only one who really matters. He loves you and treasures you for who you are. He has sent the Holy Spirit to be your friend and counsellor.

We are in this world, but we are not of this world. Our work is here. Our desire should not be so much to be taken out of the world, but to be protected from the evil one (John 17:15). May our Father in heaven guide us, strengthen us, and protect us as we shine His light in this world.

JULY 12

A Parent's Influence

Josiah was eight years old when he became king, and he reigned in Jerusalem thirty-one years. His mother's name was Jedidah... He did what was right in the eyes of the Lord and walked in all the ways of his father David, not turning aside to the right or to the left.
(2 Kings 22:1–2)

Many bad kings reigned over Jerusalem. Some reigned for a very short period of time. Then along came Josiah. He was eight years old! How much wisdom do you think an eight-year-old could possess when it came to being in charge of an entire kingdom?

I find it interesting that we are also told who Josiah's mother and father were. At eight years of age, who do you think has the greatest influence in a child's development? His parents! David had died by this time and couldn't have been part of Josiah's daily life, but his influence was still felt. We learn that when Josiah was about sixteen years old, he *"began to seek the God of his father David"* (2 Chronicles 34:3). We are not provided any more information on his mother, but his life gives us an indication of her character. Josiah not only sought God, but cleansed his kingdom of all the foreign idols and restored the Lord's temple. Josiah concerned himself with bringing his own life into alignment with God's will, as well as the people he had influence over.

If you are a parent, aunt, uncle, or other person with influence over a child, I urge you not to take your role lightly. Those children will have an influence on many others in their lifetimes. Take each opportunity afforded you to direct them to the one who will keep their feet on the right path—Jesus. Pray for God's wisdom and protection over their lives.

They are never so old that they won't need your prayers.

JULY 13

Be Encouraged

A bruised reed he will not break, and a smoldering wick he will not snuff out. In faithfulness he will bring forth justice.
(Isaiah 42:3)

There may be times in your life when you feel bruised, crushed, and ineffectual. You might be going along just fine, and then bam, everything seems to fall apart. I would encourage you to turn to God and hold on! The Lord has promised that He will not allow us to be broken or extinguished. He has promised justice to those who are faithful to Him.

I once went through a difficult time when I felt deserted, persecuted, and abandoned by those I thought were friends. I cried out to God, but I couldn't hear what He was saying to me. I *chose* to continue studying His word, praising Him, and seeking His will. He provided for me. Like a drowning victim, I was so busy thrashing around that it took a while for me to recognize the help He was offering. He never left me. He brought me through and restored me.

I have known people who believed they had gone too far astray for the Lord to know them or want them. Not so! God created the universe! There is no place you can go where He won't know. He knows everything each one of us has been through. He has promised that even when we wander away, if we turn back to Him, He will hear us.

If you are the *"bruised reed"* or *"smouldering wick,"* be encouraged. God is faithful and will bring justice. If your friend or loved one is in this situation, continue to pray for them. When the opportunity arises, let them know you were talking to Jesus and that He wants them to know He still loves them. There is hope.

JULY 14

Everlasting Way

See if there is any offensive way in me, and lead me in the way everlasting. (Psalm 139:24)

Being human, we experience conflict. We each approach a situation with different experiences and thought processes. We stand the chance of seeing the same thing differently. There is a saying that goes, "His view, her view, and the real event." Have you ever witnessed a car accident? The fact is that the cars came in contact with each other, but each person will have seen the approach differently. Some may have seen others not leaving enough room, differ on who had the right of way, or even what the road conditions were. Who is right?

If there is a disagreement, the first response is to believe you are in the right. The other person misunderstands, doesn't know as much as you about the situation, or has an impure motive. You say to yourself, "If they just did it my way, everything would be fine!" But is your view or opinion perfect? Do you always see the whole picture? Does it really matter in God's view?

Some conflicts are resolved quickly upon communication or submission. Then they are quickly forgotten about. Other situations are not so easily resolved. We hold grudges and build upon past events. Satan is quick to build on the division!

I would suggest you take those unresolved issues right to the top. Ask God for His help. Ask Him to help reveal the truth. That means you will have to give Him permission to convict you of anything you need to address in yourself. Ask Him to help you forgive. Ask God to bring restitution and harmony. Is it really important in eternity? Allow Him to *"lead [you] in the way everlasting."* Experience His peace.

JULY 15

Today, I Choose

Through Jesus, therefore, let us continually offer to God a sacrifice of praise—the fruit of lips that confess his name.
(Hebrews 13:15)

Each and every day, we make choices. God created man with his own will. We are not robots or puppets for Him to manipulate and control for His entertainment. Free will comes with responsibility. It's up to you whether you will follow the one true God or not.

Have you ever heard someone say, "You make me mad!"? Perhaps you even heard those words come out of your own mouth. If fact, no one else can make you feel anything. You manifest your own emotions. Your emotions flow out of your own mind and heart attitude.

You can *choose* to spend your day praising God. Praise God for who He is and give thanks to Him. Give thanks to Him that He would have a relationship with you though Jesus. Lift His name on high and worship Him.

Choosing to praise God and be in constant communication with Him affects your outlook, bringing your attitude and mind in alignment with His. In fact, praising God will help your attitude be more like His. It's hard to be in praise and in a foul mood at the same time. Even when events cause you to allow negative thoughts or feelings to emerge, it's so much easier to recover when you practice choosing to continually offer praise to God.

Discuss with your spouse things you could do to help you get into, and stay in, an attitude of praise. Is there anything you could do to help each other remember to make that choice each day?

The Lord lives! Praise be to my Rock! Exalted be God, the Rock, my Savior!
(2 Samuel 22:47)

JULY 16

Set Free

"Then neither do I condemn you," Jesus declared. "Go now and leave your life of sin."
(John 8:11)

Here is the story of a woman caught in the act of adultery. I have always found it interesting that only a woman was brought before Christ. With whom did she commit this sin? I feel certain Jesus didn't miss that little oddity, either. How often do we, in our self-righteousness, judge one person's sins and not another's for the same thing, or what we consider a slightly lesser sin?

I notice the wisdom in which Jesus responded. He didn't get defensive for her by bringing up all the sins of the people in the crowd. He knew her remorse and shame. Jesus also knew that there was not one person in the crowd who was free of sin. When nobody was left who was worthy to judge her, Jesus pointed out to the woman that she wasn't alone in her sin. He forgave her.

However, He also commanded her to *"leave [her] life of sin."* It's not good enough to ask for forgiveness without repentance. Why would we expect the Lord to forgive us if we intend to return to those same sins over and over again? If we cry, "Lord, Lord forgive me," while having no intention of correcting our ways, He will answer, *"I don't know you or where you come from"* (Luke 13:25). How devastating! However, if you truly repent, Jesus has promised us forgiveness. In our flesh, however, we are weak. We will find ourselves needing to return to the feet of Jesus again and again to seek His forgiveness. It is our heart attitude that Jesus is concerned about.

Thank the Lord for His great mercy and forgiveness. Pray that He will help you to stay close to Him and walk in His ways. Pray for His wisdom and discernment. Ask Him to help you see others through His eyes.

JULY 17

Arise from the Mire

And the God of all grace, who called you to his eternal glory in Christ, after you have suffered a little while, will himself restore you and make you strong, firm and steadfast.
(1 Peter 5:10)

When we find ourselves in the murk, it is important to keep our hope in the Lord. I think of the story of Job. Here was a righteous man who found himself in an unimaginable pit of devastation. He lost all his wealth, his family, his health, and the support of his closest friends. He did not, however, lose his faith in the Lord. Although he didn't understand why all this had happened, his attitude was: *"I know that my Redeemer lives, and that in the end he will stand upon the earth"* (Job 19:25).

We will each face our own times of struggles. Hopefully you'll never find yourself pushed down as far as Job. For some, you may feel you can relate to Job's horror. You must remember that which you know to be true: your faith.

In 2 Corinthians 12, the Apostle Paul speaks of his plea for Christ to remove the thorn in his flesh. This is thought to mean some physical aliment. Paul was not healed. God answered him, saying, *"My grace is sufficient for you, for my power is made perfect in weakness"* (2 Corinthians 12:9). Paul chose to be delighted, because he said, *"For when I am weak, then I am strong"* (2 Corinthians 12:10). I'm not saying you will not receive healing or restoration from your situation. I'm saying that you should put your trust in God and choose to continue believing in Him. The Lord is concerned for our wellbeing, and our ultimate freedom is in Him.

You don't have to wait for the circumstances to be fixed to move on into freedom.

JULY 18

Celebrate!

David and all the Israelites were celebrating with all their might before God, with songs and with harps, lyres, tambourines, cymbals and trumpets. (1 Chronicles 13:8)

I love to celebrate! I so enjoy the opportunity to join together with others to acknowledge and celebrate special events like weddings, graduations, anniversaries, and birthdays! I love to bless people with cards, gifts, music, decorations, and food to set apart their event with special acknowledgement and rejoicing!

What could be more exciting than celebrating our God? King David and the Israelites were celebrating the return of the ark, the return of the presence of God into their midst! It was not a solemn event. David, the king himself, danced with joy. He put on his special linen robe and ephod. The people made sacrifices. King David called forward the musicians. We read that they were *"celebrating with all their might before God."* Jesus has sent the Holy Spirit to be with us, and in us, always! Do you celebrate His presence? Do you celebrate the presence of God with all your might?

We don't need to wait for a significant religious day such as Christmas or Easter. We can celebrate any and every day! It's fun to have a crowd, but it's not necessary. Go ahead! Turn up the worship music and dance in your living room! Dance like only God can see. Sing like only God can hear. You don't need to know the lyrics. Sing to the Lord *your* words of praise. Sing in tongues. Praise God!

This is the day the Lord has made; let us rejoice and be glad in it. (Psalm 118:24)

JULY 19

Spiritual Passion

And you also are among those who are called to belong to Jesus Christ. (Romans 1:6)

Thankfully, we're not all exactly the same. God has created us in unique, but purposeful ways. He has created the Christian body to work together in harmony. We are all called to Jesus, but each church, ministry, and individual's giftings and talents are unique. When each Christian is fulfilling their calling, all things work together in God's plan.

What is your spiritual passion? What ministries have you chosen to dedicate yourselves to? Why? Are you merely filling a need in your church because you have the training, because someone has to do the job, or because you were specifically asked? Are you feeling discouraged, unappreciated, overwhelmed, or ineffective? Perhaps you need to reassess where you believe God has called you. Keep in mind that as we mature and develop, God may draw you on to new areas. You will know your spiritual passion by your enthusiasm. Your work will seem natural and ordinary, but will get others excited to support your ministry.

I would encourage you to spend time with God discovering your spiritual passion. Perhaps you could discuss with your spouse what excites you. Why? For example, you may love children, but not be fulfilled teaching Sunday School. Why or why not? When does your spouse notice the light in your eyes and the bubble in your voice? How might things be changing in your calling from what you have been passionate about and called to do in the past? Are you willing to allow God to direct your steps down a new path? I can only imagine the exciting things God has planned for my future. What about you?

JULY 20

Do Not Be Outwitted

If you forgive anyone, I also forgive him. And what I have forgiven—if there was anything to forgive—I have forgiven in the sight of Christ for your sake, in order that Satan might not outwit us. For we are not unaware of his schemes.
(2 Corinthians 2:10–11)

Ouch! You've been hurt again! It may have been a misunderstanding, or you may have every earthly right to be upset. What you choose to do about it is up to you.

In the Apostle Paul's letter to the Corinthians, he urges them to be forgiving towards one another. Paul even promises to be in agreement in their forgiveness. His reasoning isn't what one might think, though. He agrees to be forgiving for the sake of the person offended! The Apostle Paul understood the schemes of the enemy in bringing division and hurt amongst the Christians.

Think about it for a minute. When you believe you have been wronged, what does that do to your mood? If you allow your mind to go over the offence again and again, where do you find yourself? How does that affect your approach to the rest of your experiences? How does it affect your communication with God?

There is a prayer called "The Serenity Prayer," by Reinhold Niebuhr. It goes, in part, "God grant me the serenity to accept the things I cannot change, courage to change the things I can, and the wisdom to know the difference." Surrender the situation to God. Ask Him to help you forgive. Be forgiving and move on. Don't allow Satan to win at creating division amongst you, nor separation from God. Do not be *"unaware of his schemes."*

Not only is it important for each of us to be forgiving, but we must encourage the same in others. Like the Apostle Paul, you should offer to come into agreement with them in their forgiveness. Is it time for you to defend someone you know from the schemes of Satan?

JULY 21

Safety

The name of the Lord is a strong tower; the righteous run to it and are safe. (Proverbs 18:10)

I remember the house I lived in as a young child. We had a playroom at one end of the house off the kitchen. You had to go through the kitchen, and then the dining room, to get to the living room. The stairs went off the living room to the upstairs bedrooms.

We would occasionally have thunder and lightning storms. Often that meant our power would go out. I quickly learned that the loud bang of thunder and the flash of lightning meant that I might soon be in total darkness. To this day, my heartbeat skips when I remember the mad dash from the playroom to find a parent somewhere in the house the instant I heard thunder. I remember the fear that the lights would go out before I was safe in the arms of a parent. I believed that if I made it to a parent, everything would be okay and they would take care of all my needs.

Today's verse reminds me of those events. I'm no longer terrified of thunder and lightning storms or the likely results of physical darkness. There are other fears, however, that I've had to deal with as an adult, and I suspect I will face more in the future. I still make that mad dash for safety, but now it's into the arms of the Lord. As a child, I believed that my parents would protect me from all harm. I now know that only in the arms of our Father in heaven am I truly safe.

What are some instances in your past when you were afraid? How did you handle that fear? In what instances might you not be able to find safety or peace on your own? Where do you run when you're afraid? How will you be able to find the Lord when you need His protection?

JULY 22

Encouraging Lives

But as for me, I will always have hope; I will praise you more and more. (Psalm 71:14)

Have you ever known someone who seems to find peace and hope no matter what their circumstances? Someone who hasn't been spared the pains of this world, but confidently holds on to the promises of the Lord and looks forward to the future with great hope and anticipation? What pleasure it is to be in their mist! Their passion and overflowing joy is such an encouragement!

On more than one occasion, I have felt that I should reach out to comfort someone in their sorrowful situation, only to leave having them encourage me! How do they do that? What is their secret to happiness? The consistent qualities I've witnessed in those people are their faith, trust, and hope in the Lord. They have a close and very personal relationship with our Father. When life throws dirt at them, they don't wallow in the mud; they turn to God. Under God's direction, they build sandcastles!

That's what we have all been called to do. We are to continuously praise the Lord. Spend time with Him and learn to see the world through His eyes. As we align our hearts with His will, we will know His peace and joy more readily. In Romans 15:2, the Apostle Paul reminds us, *"Each of us should please his neighbor for his good, to build him up."*

To whom is the Lord calling you to lift up today? I'm not suggesting that you manipulate or create an encounter to practise being an encourager. Just be aware of whom the Lord is bringing into your life so that you may fulfill your assignment to spread the peace and joy the Lord has poured upon you.

Anticipate with great excitement all that He has for you!

JULY 23

Refining

Test me, O Lord, and try me, examine my heart and my mind. (Psalm 26:2)

Anybody who knows Jesus soon realizes that Jesus knows all there is to know about you. He knew you before you were created in your mother's womb (Psalm 139:13). He knows the number of hairs on your head (Matthew 10:30). He even knows the number of days you have here on earth.

When we pray today's psalm, the intent is not for God to learn anything new. This prayer is for the person who desires to grow in the ways of the Lord. It is admirable to strive for a pure heart and mind. However, when you ask to be tested, don't be surprised at what comes your way. I'm not saying this to make you fearful; the Lord will always be with you. However, you can't pass the grade without taking the test. The exciting part is, like refining precious metal, when you pass through to the other side, you become purer and stronger. You draw closer to all you were meant to be.

Can you recall past experiences when you went through times of testing? What happened? What instigated the test? How did you handle it? What helped you through that experience? What did you learn from it? Keeping those experiences in mind, what might you do to prepare for future times of testing?

I have heard that we remember ten percent of what we hear, twenty percent of what we see or read, and about seventy percent of what we do. It's also interesting that we apparently remember about ninety percent of what we teach to others. So, we can listen to sermons, read the word (repetition improves retention), and go through the experiences, but it appears the best strategy for remembering the lessons God teaches us is to help others along their spiritual walks. Never stop learning!

JULY 24

The Conflict Within

What causes fights and quarrels among you? Don't they come from your desires that battle within you?
(James 4:1)

We are in a constant state of tension between our fleshly desires (lust and pride) and the new creation we are in Jesus Christ. In James' letter, he addressed this struggle. He told the Christians that the root of their quarrels was the *"battle within."* He told them that the reason they weren't receiving what they wanted was because they weren't asking God (James 4:2), and that they were asking *"with wrong motives"* (James 4:3).

Think of a recent conflict in your own life. What is it that upsets you about that issue or event? What do you suppose the root of that issue is? These don't necessarily have to be big conflicts.

I recently observed someone doing a job. It wasn't even anything particularly important, but it needed to be done. I so wanted to express my opinion of how I thought it should be completed. As I wasn't doing the job, I decided it was best to keep my mouth shut. I initially felt very good about that decision. However, in the back of my mind, I continued to think my way would be better. As I carried on about the work at hand, God spoke to me: "Not saying anything is not the same as letting go." Ouch! That was so true. Why had I even entertained such controlling thoughts? It was, as James said, a *"battle within"* me. Thankfully, this time my new creation won.

I know that just acknowledging the sinful root of a conflict won't make it go away, big or small. That's when we need to turn to our new creation and ask God for what we really need. We must consider whether our motives are right, and what God would want for the situation. May you always seek victory in Christ, and have His peace.

JULY 25

Why Do I Need To Read the Bible?

It is to be with him, and he is to read it all the days of his life so that he may learn to revere the Lord his God and follow carefully all the words of this law and these decrees…
(Deuteronomy 17:19)

There are numerous excuses for not reading the Bible. "We never did that when I was growing up, and I've turned out okay. I don't understand it. The Bible is boring. I don't have time…" However, we are called to read God's word all the days of our lives. I can suggest several reasons why it is critical that you read the Bible regularly.

…the message is heard through the word of Christ. (Romans 10:17)

Man does not live on bread alone, but on every word that comes from the mouth of God. (Matthew 4:4)

…cleansing her by the washing with water through the word, and to present her to himself as a radiant church… (Ephesians 5:26–27)

Sanctify them by the truth; your word is truth. (John 17:17)

Take the helmet of salvation and the sword of the Spirit, which is the word of God. (Ephesians 6:17)

Your word is a lamp to my feet and a light for my path. (Psalm 119:105)

And we have the word of the prophets made more certain, and you will do well to pay attention to it, as to a light shining in a dark place… (2 Peter 1:19)

The best time to start your regular Bible reading is today. Don't listen to the condemnation of the enemy if you miss a day. Pick up and start again the next day.

Start by asking the Lord to reveal whatever it is He has for you in today's reading. You may not get something earth-shattering or life-changing every day, but sometimes you will find a verse that takes on a new meaning, even though you know you've read it before. Always thank God for what He's teaching you through His word.

JULY 26

Our Defender

...Satan [stood] at his right side to accuse him. The Lord said to Satan, "The Lord rebuke you, Satan!... Is not this man a burning stick snatched from the fire?"
(Zechariah 3:1–2)

You know when you get negative thoughts? When you think poorly of yourself or something you have or haven't done? When you start out enthusiastically in an area you feel God has directed you to, and then begin to have doubts or fears? Where do you think that comes from? That's Satan trying to derail you from the good path God has set out for you.

Fortunately, the Lord is our defender! He would not wish to lose even one of us who have received our salvation and have had our names written in the Book of Life. Jesus said, *"My Father, who has given them to me, is greater than all; no one can snatch them out of my Father's hand"* (John 10:29). Our Lord can always win!

Know the Lord's promise for you. When you're experiencing accusations from the enemy, turn him over to the Father. Yup! It's okay to be a tattletale. Take those negative thoughts captive and refuse to receive them. Let the Father take care of the enemy. Now is the time to remember how much Jesus loves you, and all He did and is doing for you. Go ahead and sing the children's song "Jesus Loves Me," and take it personally.

Then, in confidence, present yourself before the Father. Ask Him to set you free from those false accusations. Ask Him to help you to recognize any areas you need to change to get back on the solid foundation of the path He has set before you.

Live your day as if you really believe Jesus loves you, and that the Lord has good plans for you. Rejoice!

JULY 27

Women in Leadership

There is neither Jew nor Greek, slave nor free, male nor female, for you are all one in Christ Jesus.
(Galatians 3:28)

That's right. No matter who you are, if you have accepted Jesus Christ as your Lord and Saviour, you are the same as any other Christian in God's eyes.

But isn't "man" supposed to be the head? Aren't women supposed to submit to men? No. Actually, women are told to submit to their husbands, not all men. Women and men alike are instructed to submit[9] to those in authority over them, whoever that might be.

There are many great examples of women to whom God assigned leadership roles in the Bible. Women played important teaching, preaching, prophesying, and other roles. God chose Mary to give birth to and raise Jesus, the Son of God. Then, of course, there is Eve. Eve was chosen to be the mother of all living beings. God gave Eve and Adam equal partnership in ruling over all creation. There is Sarah, Abraham's wife; Deborah, the judge and leader over Israel; Queen Esther, who saved the whole Jewish race from obliteration; Anna, the prophetess; and many more.

Please note that this doesn't mean women are superior to men, either. Both men and women are meant to consider the ways of the Lord. They are to imitate Jesus Christ whether in leadership or not. They are to lead by example, humble themselves before God, be accountable for their ministries, and not neglect their own families.

Similar arguments can be made for Jew or Gentile, or any other defining human attribute. All Christians are *"one in Christ Jesus,"* but we are not all given the same assignments.

---

[9] Submit means to respect or turn to for advice, not necessarily meaning being lesser or slave to.

JULY 28

Showers of Blessings

I will bless them and the places surrounding my hill. I will send down showers in season; there will be showers of blessing.
(Ezekiel 34:26)

The Lord has brought a very special woman into my life. I am blessed to know her and spend time listening to all the Lord has done and is doing in her life. Every time I start the conversation with the typical "Hello, how are you doing?" she seizes the opportunity. Her response is, "I'm so blessed I can hardly stand it!" And she means it!

This is not to say everything goes perfectly in her life. She has had trials, hurts, and illnesses like everybody else. However, she has a very close relationship with the Lord. She trusts in the Lord with all her heart. She is willing to make sacrifices to learn whatever it is the Lord would teach her.

I just love being around her. Her joy in the Lord is very contagious. I can't help but feel encouraged and challenged in my spiritual walk and excited about our precious Jesus! Her *"showers of blessing"* seem to splash all over those who get near her. She is such an awesome witness for Christ, just by being who she is.

I don't ask that God make me just like her. We are each uniquely designed by God for our own purpose. Instead I ask God to help me be in alignment with what He would have me be. If I stay in His will, then that joy and excitement should shine through my life as well. I would love to have people drawn to Jesus because of that light.

Who are your spiritual mentors? Why? What is it about how they face life that you admire? What is it in your life that might attract others to want what you have?

May you, and all those who surround you, be blessed. Amen.

JULY 29

Successful Ministry

For God did not give us a spirit of timidity, but a spirit of power, of love and of self-discipline.
(2 Timothy 1:7)

The Apostle Paul wrote these words in his letter to Timothy, who was like a son to him. Paul was encouraging Timothy to move out in the ministry to which he had already been ordained. When God calls us into a ministry, no matter what it might be, we are to put aside any timidity and doubts. Those are not of God, but are the schemes of the enemy to prevent us from accomplishing all that God would have us do. God would not call us into a ministry and not equip us to fulfill it.

Notice the attributes Paul grouped together. The spirit of power is accompanied by the spirits of love and self-discipline. We are not to be offensive, manipulative, or bullies in doing God's work. We are to have the heart attitude of the love of Jesus, and not let our "self" interfere. Instead, we are to ask for God's wisdom, discernment, and that His will be done. Even the Apostle Paul recognized his need to be God-led. In Ephesians 6:19, Paul asked for the prayer support of the church of Ephesus. He asked them to pray that the words he spoke be of God. Paul asked them to pray that he, too, would not be fearful in his ministry.

In our ministries, if we keep ourselves in the spirit *"of love and of self-discipline,"* God will give us the power and authority to be successful. He has given us talents, skills, and knowledge which He will direct us in the use of. Like the Apostle Paul, ask for the prayer support of other Christians. Use the army of God available to you for your protection and direction. Involve others for accountability and encouragement along your way.

Talk (pray) to God continuously. Make sure you know His voice. Thank God that He has specifically chosen you for the privilege of your ministry. He has the authority to give that assignment to anyone He chooses. He chose you!

JULY 30

Time of Beauty

He has made everything beautiful in its time.
(Ecclesiastes 3:11)

What an encouraging verse! It is wonderful to know that God has everything under His control! If we were able to see life from His eternal prospective, we would understand this. However, God has chosen not to reveal all of life's mysteries to man. I trust that is because He knows the right timing for each of us.

This may be a hard reality to accept at some points in our lives. When you're feeling mired down, struggling through some difficulty, or simply feel like you're being blown about by the storms of life, you may think it would be nice to know that the outcome will eventually be positive. Take heart! In His time, God will reveal the beauty!

If you think about it, I'm sure you can all think of times in your past when you weren't seeing the beauty. However, even with limited human hindsight, we can see the blessing of the sequence of events.

I can think of situations when new jobs didn't work out, only to find out later that the position didn't turn out well for the successful candidate—or perhaps an even better job came up. There are times when a housing purchase didn't work out, only for the prospective purchasers find that the housing market dropped, or a better house location became available. I know a woman who was involved in a car accident that took the life of her husband and unborn child. It nearly took her life as well. Her toddler survived, and eventually, with God's strength, she healed beyond anything her doctors expected. After a time of growth and healing, her son prayed that God would give him a daddy here on earth. Shortly afterwards, she met a widower with children of his own. They fell in love and eventually married. There is much joy in that blended family! How beautiful!

No matter where you find yourself today, take joy in knowing the beauty in God's timing.

JULY 31

Celebrating the Lord

On the eighth day they held an assembly, for they had celebrated the dedication of the altar for seven days and the festival for seven days more. (2 Chronicles 7:9)

In Old Testament times, the people would gather to celebrate the Lord. This verse comes from the celebration of the completion and dedication of the temple Solomon had built for the Lord. These people *"saw the fire coming down and the glory of the Lord above the temple"* (2 Chronicles 7:3). Wow! How amazing it must have been to actually be present to experience seeing the glory of the Lord! Their response was to kneel to the ground and worship, giving thanks to the Lord. They continued to give sacrifices and sing praises to the Lord for days! Can you even imagine such a celebration?

Today, although we might gather together for times of worship, praise, and celebration, we don't even contemplate setting aside days at a time for such activities. Although it would be quite the experience, we are now fortunate to be able to be in God's presence no matter where we are. Through the sacrifice of Jesus Christ, we have been given access to God through the Holy Spirit. No longer is it necessary to travel to one specific location at set times to ask a priest to intercede for us.

That's not to say we shouldn't continue to join together with other Christians in times of worship and praise. We are called to continue to meet together (Hebrews 10:25). The freedom, though, is that we can praise, worship, and pray to (talk with) God anytime! That is something the Old Testament believers never could have imagined!

We, too, can experience the glory of the Lord. As we enter into praise, thanksgiving, and worship, we need to linger awhile in His presence. Psalm 37:7 tells us, *"Be still before the Lord and wait patiently for him."* God tells us, *"Be still, and know that I am God"* (Psalm 46:10). You may not remain still for days at a time, but don't rush away.

AUGUST 1

Don't Look Back

Jesus replied, "No one who puts his hand to the plow and looks back is fit for service in the kingdom of God."
(Luke 9:62)

Jesus spoke this verse at a time when He was calling people to follow Him. The people He had just called had seemingly good worldly excuses for not dropping everything and following Him immediately. Jesus was requesting their complete faith and trust in Him, and a complete commitment.

As we recall, Jesus also told us that our marriages are like His relationship with the church. We need to be fully committed to our relationship with our spouse before all else, except Christ. Are there areas in your life where you look back? "Before I was married, I could go hunting with my buddies every weekend. If it wasn't for my responsibilities to my spouse, I could spend as much money as my banker would allow debt. I would rather travel, but my spouse wants to save towards owning a home. Maybe this isn't the spouse God intended for me. Maybe my spouse would have been better off with someone else."

Don't look back. Right now, God knows exactly where you are in your marriage. He knows what has come before, and He sees where your marriage is headed. He is there to rejoice in the good times and help you through the bad. Embrace your marriage and look forward together. Communicate with each other about your hopes and dreams. How can you reach the important goals happily together? If your marriage is drifting, ask God what He would have you do to get it back on track. If you are blessed with a good marriage, ask what you can do to make it even better.

AUGUST 2

Trusting Our Children to God

By the word of the Lord were the heavens made, their starry host by the breath of his mouth.
(Psalm 33:6)

I recently heard from a mother whose heart was broken for a family member. She had an adult son who was going through a very difficult time. Her maternal instinct to want to make things better was in conflict with her son's desire to work through the situation without his parent's involvement. There are various reasons why he may not have wanted his parents involved. One important one is that the parent and child may have been too closely involved to allow him to think clearly.

What's a mother to do? The mother only wanted to help make everything work out for the good of their child. It can hurt to be excluded. Satan began his work to convince this mother that she was somehow not wanted or loved—and indeed, maybe she was even responsible for the situation. I say, "Don't receive those accusations!"

There are some things a parent just cannot fix. That doesn't mean we can't do anything. If you find yourself in this situation, lift your child to Jesus and surrender the situation to Him. Ask the Lord to protect and guide your loved one through the situation. Ask the Lord for wisdom and strength in keeping out of the situation unless He says differently. We all know our Father in heaven loves us deeply. He also loves our children more than we ever can.

Our God is a big God! He created the heavens just by speaking them into existence. I know I can't do that. Neither can you. Trust in Him always. Read Psalm 13 for encouragement. You don't need to wrestle with your thoughts or allow the enemy to triumph. *"Trust in [His] unfailing love"* (Psalm 13:5) and *"sing to the Lord"* (Psalm 13:6). Our God is mighty!

AUGUST 3

Words of Life and Death

The tongue has the power of life and death, and those who love it will eat its fruit.
(Proverbs 18:21)

How refreshing and encouraging it is to be around a positive person. I don't mean someone who says flattering things to gain their own rewards. I mean those people whose hearts seem to genuinely overflow with joy. Their minds and words are full of gratitude and appreciation. They don't try to see their cups half full; they're just happy people.

Then there are the people who have cups half empty. These people are angry and disgruntled. They feel the world hasn't been fair to them. Out of their negative state come their thoughts and words. They tear people down and leave others feeling like they have just had garbage dumped all over them. These people don't tend to draw a lot of people to themselves.

So, we just decide to be the positive life-giving type of person, right? It's not that easy. Trying to continually manage our mouths to speak words that are completely different than our thoughts only creates conflict within us. We could try to think only positive thoughts. When we find ourselves thinking negatively, it is good for us to desire to put those thoughts aside. If we aren't feeling positive from our hearts, though, we may find ourselves in a state of denial, feeling like failures.

Only through our God can we truly succeed in eating the fruit of life. As we develop our spiritual walks and align ourselves with God, becoming more Christ-like, will our heart attitudes create life-giving thoughts and words?

Dear God, please help me have an attitude of a life-giving heart. Forgive me for things I have allowed to dwell within me that produce death. Reveal to me any of Satan's arrows that I have held on to. Help me to release them all into Your care. Amen.

AUGUST 4

What Do People Say?

He was a good man, full of the Holy Spirit and faith, and a great number of people were brought to the Lord.
(Acts 11:24)

What do you think people say about you? Have you ever given thought to what will be said in your eulogy? What will you be noted for? As the song goes, do they "know you are Christian by your love"?

I'm sure you and your spouse can come up with a list of positive attributes. Take a few minutes to share each of your lists. Go ahead and add to each other's! Then take a few minutes to think about which attributes are most important to you. Are those attributes easily recognized by others? Are they godly values?

Today's verse was written about Barnabas. Luke, the author of Acts, liked Barnabas and thought of him as *"a good man, full of the Holy Spirit and faith."* Now, those are honourable attributes for which to be known! As a result, Barnabas influenced many people to come to the Lord and receive their salvation. There is no greater accomplishment than that!

I know we cannot please all people all the time. I also know that people receive what we say and do from their own viewpoint. Sometimes our intentions are misconstrued. However, one would hope that the majority of the people we come in contact with would see the love and light of Jesus in our lives. We will never know all the influence we have, both good and bad. If even a few people are drawn to Jesus, or stay on His path because of you, then you will hear the Lord say, *"Well done, my good servant"* (Luke 19:17). Who knows how many lives those people will touch in turn?

What do you hope to be recognized for? More importantly, what does Jesus say about you?

AUGUST 5

Accountability

As iron sharpens iron, so one man sharpens another.
(Proverbs 27:17)

The word "accountability" tends to bring to mind legalities. It might sound like you're asking someone to boss you around or constrain you. In fact, this proverb is meant to encourage like-minded people (Christians) to help keep each other on the path of righteousness. It is for your benefit. I would much rather be warned that the water is deep and the current swift than find out too late.

Obviously, the person closest to you who should be able to speak into your life is your spouse. When you're struggling with sin in an area of your life, you should usually be able to confide in your spouse and ask for their prayer support. They are also the one who will most likely spot any signs of impending slippage, and lovingly warn you.

However, at times you may be struggling with sin that's best shared with another. Don't make assumptions of your current friends. Choose your "sharpeners" wisely. Really think about a Christian, or a couple of Christians, who you consider wise in the Lord, people you would be comfortable confiding in, who you trust to be honest with you, who won't just tell you what you want to hear. Ask God to bring to mind people with whom He would have you work. In some situations, you might specifically ask those people if they would be willing to work with you to keep each other accountable.

Being accountable should not always be about correction. These relationships should be encouraging in areas that are going well. They should provoke you to think about the things the Lord is saying to each of you. They should spur you on to fulfill your calling and help deflect the arrows of the enemy.

Who is your iron, and whose iron are you?

AUGUST 6

Is God Punishing Me?

I no longer call you servants, because a servant does not know his master's business. Instead, I have called you friends, for everything that I learned from my Father I have made known to you.
(John 15:15)

I recently received a call from a distraught friend. She was facing a huge challenge in her life and couldn't understand why it was all happening. In her despair, she blurted out, "Maybe God is punishing me for not doing my devotions for a couple of days!"

No! Our God doesn't need our devotion and praise for His ego. In fact, He doesn't *need* us at all. Our time with Him is for our benefit, that we may draw closer to Him and better understand His "business." Some of us have better earthly fathers than others, but none is perfect. Therefore, it is sometimes hard for us to understand our heavenly Father's perfection. He is not going to punish us like bad servants for not doing as we are ordered.

Instead, Jesus has told us that He considers us friends, not servants. He has come alongside us by coming to earth in the flesh and experiencing what we experience. Jesus has tried to help us by teaching us all He can about the ways of our heavenly Father. Furthermore, He has sent the Holy Spirit to be with us.

Who of you would not be there for a friend when they are in need, if you could? Suppose you are a well-trained and highly experienced scuba diver. A friend decides to take up the sport, too. Would you just stand back and watch as they grab some equipment, put it together as best they can figure out, and jump in the water?

Jesus considers you a friend. He desires to help you along your walk no matter where you are. He's not looking to punish you like some abusive master. He loves you. Reach out and take His hand. Ask for His direction.

AUGUST 7

What is Your Calamity?

If calamity comes upon us, whether the sword of judgment, or plague or famine, we will stand in your presence before this temple that bears your Name and will cry out to you in our distress, and you will hear us and save us.
(2 Chronicles 20:9)

What great faith, the people of Judah, under the leadership of Jehoshaphat, declared that their only real hope was in God. Thankfully, we don't need to stand at the temple (church, or any other building) in order for God to hear us. Because of the sacrifice of Jesus Christ, the Holy Spirit allows us to talk to God directly any time, any place. As Christians, we already bear His name.

So, what is the calamity that you or a loved one is facing today? Fill in the blanks. "If (crisis) comes upon (name), we will stand in your presence, through the Holy Spirit, and will cry out to You in our distress, and You will hear us and save us."

Each of us will have our own calamities, big and small. It's not up to us to judge whether or not someone else's situation qualifies as a calamity. Nor should we receive Satan's ridicule concerning what we feel is a calamity. It may be an individual need or a group need. God is our judge. As our Father in heaven, God can, and will, answer our needs by opening doors, lifting us from the muck, saving us from drowning, or whatever else is required. We need only call out to God, whether for ourselves, or in unity with someone else in need. God *"will hear us and save us."*

God not only answers our cries, He will exceed all our expectations if we allow Him. Sometimes we only get by, because that's all we asked for. Allow the Holy Spirit to guide your prayers in communicating to God what you want His help for, and allow Him to fully bless you with an answer in His way.

AUGUST 8

Sing onto the Lord!

As they began to sing and praise, the Lord set ambushes against the men of Ammon and Moab and Mount Seir who were invading Judah, and they were defeated.
(2 Chronicles 20:22)

King Jehoshaphat was facing a battle he knew he and the men of Judah had little chance of winning. He called upon the Lord. God told them, *"Do not be afraid or discouraged because of this vast army. For the battle is not yours, but God's"* (2 Chronicles 20:15). Being the wise king that he was, Jehoshaphat encouraged his people to have faith in God. The king appointed men to sing praises to the Lord as they led Judah into battle. God took care of the rest. King Jehoshaphat's army never had to lift a weapon of war, yet the opposing armies were completely defeated.

Our God will be there for you as well. As you face battles in life that you cannot win by your own strength, turn to the Lord. Hold on to your faith and be encouraged. Sing praises and be thankful to the Lord! Allow Him to go before you and slay the enemy.

When the army of Judah arrived at the battle, they found their enemies already dead. Not only was the battle over, *"There was so much plunder that it took three days to collect it"* (2 Chronicles 20:25). God will go before you as well. God will ambush Satan's workers and defeat them. He can, and will, deliver blessings to you during a difficult time in your life.

I would encourage you to keep your eyes on God. Sing to Him and praise Him as much as you can! Immerse yourself in worship. If you aren't very musical on your own, or can't remember the words to the worship songs, put on worship music. Find a Christian radio station, play worship CDs, and seek out church events where you can join others in singing to the Lord! Great is our God!

AUGUST 9

Ending Well

The anger of the Lord burned against Amaziah, and he sent a prophet to him, who said, "Why do you consult this people's gods, which could not save their own people from your hand?"
(2 Chronicles 25:15)

King Amaziah started out well. *"He did what was right in the eyes of the Lord"* (2 Chronicles 25:2). The Lord was with Amaziah and brought his people victory over their enemies. Then something happened and Amaziah got distracted. He looked on the things of his enemy with lust. He coveted what he saw and took their gods. He set those gods up and began to worship them. This eventually led to Amaziah's death. What a sad ending. Isn't it amazing that someone could turn away from God even when he was being so blessed?

Well, the truth is that this often happens even today. Consider, for example, the lives of many of our movie stars and pop artists. We watch them and see all the glamour and glory. We look at their clothes, cars, homes, money, and time in the limelight. Often we see how their fame brings destruction upon their lives. However, we continue to watch them and try to dress like them, talk or sing like them, and gather material things like theirs. We get distracted from the things of God.

Uzziah, Amaziah's son, also started out well. *"But after Uzziah became powerful, his pride led to his downfall"* (2 Chronicles 26:16). Amaziah set a bad example. Not only did Amaziah's life end poorly, so did his son's.

Who is watching you? If you should get distracted and end your life poorly, who else might it affect? Who are you looking at? Ask God to help you keep your eyes on Him. Give God permission to convict you when you get distracted. Ask Him to keep you focused on Him alone, that you may glorify His name. You will save more than just your own life.

AUGUST 10

Help Me Be Just

Now let the fear of the Lord be upon you. Judge carefully, for with the Lord our God there is no injustice or partiality or bribery.
(2 Chronicles 19:7)

King Jehoshaphat appointed judges in his land. He warned them, *"Consider carefully what you do, because you are not judging for man but for the Lord, who is with you whenever you give a verdict"* (2 Chronicles 19:6). The Lord was with them to direct their judgement, but He was also aware if they judged corruptly.

Jesus has left us with the same edict. He has sent the Holy Spirit to be our friend and counsellor. When we judge others, we can bring either eternal life through Jesus Christ or separation from God. Therefore, we are to judge very carefully! 2 Timothy 4:2 calls us to *"be prepared in season and out of season; correct, rebuke and encourage—with great patience and careful instruction."* We must take great care that we don't judge others to please man, but to glorify God. We must not condemn or criticize someone just to improve our own standing in our own eyes, or in the eyes of another person.

As we draw closer to God through the Holy Spirit, we will more readily be able to judge as He would have us judge. We will not only better know what is right or wrong for ourselves, but with the Holy Spirit's guidance we will begin to judge what we witness in others.

It is always important to lift our concerns to God. It is a privilege and blessing to be able to intercede in prayer for others as well. However, be very careful that prayer concerns and requests don't merely become gossip sessions. Let us not join with others in carelessly condemning others or being wrongly influenced. Even Jesus declared, *"For I did not come to judge the world, but to save it"* (John 12:47). He went on to say that those who reject Jesus convict themselves. Holy Spirit, help me be just!

AUGUST 11

Put Aside False Gods

But didn't you drive out the priests of the Lord, the sons of Aaron, and the Levites, and make priests of your own as the peoples of other lands do? Whoever comes to consecrate himself with a young bull and seven rams may become a priest of what are not gods.
(2 Chronicles 13:9)

Sometimes when you look around, it might appear that those who have turned their backs on God are the ones who are prospering. They may rely on their "lucky" idols, or regularly check their horoscope or other such sources of supposed wisdom. Then they just go for it and hope to be "lucky"! It may even appear that their system is working—usually. They take their chances. What about when their idols don't work so well? What about that inner peace and joy they can't seem to grasp?

Someone may say, "I had a great time at Saturday night's event!" What they don't share is the bitterness and anger they're holding inside. "I won a huge amount of money last week!" Never mind the money they lost the week before or after. Oh, and let's not talk about the amount it cost to gain that sum. Let's not think about the lack of satisfaction they feel or their desire to constantly need more.

Those of us who keep our eyes on Jesus and seek His wisdom are the real winners. We have the promise and hope of eternal life. We also have a direct, personal relationship with the only truly wise God. It is through Jesus that we find inner peace, joy, and true success. In John 17:19, Jesus says, *"For them I sanctify myself, that they too may be truly sanctified."* The word "sanctify" means to be set apart. We who choose to follow the one true God, are set apart for God and His purposes. We aren't taking chances; we have a sure thing!

Ask God to help you keep your focus fully on Him. Ask Him to reveal to you if you are in any way turning to false gods.

AUGUST 12

Be Prepared to Encourage!

"With him is only the arm of flesh, but with us is the Lord our God to help us and to fight our battles." And the people gained confidence from what Hezekiah the king of Judah said.
(2 Chronicles 32:8)

Hezekiah was a man of God. He understood the importance of staying close to God to be prepared for all things. He understood God's timing and His blessings when we endeavour to do His work. Hezekiah also understood that when the enemy challenges and tries to intimidate or otherwise prevent us from doing the work of God, God will help fight those battles. Because Hezekiah knew God, he was confident God would help them succeed in the work they were doing. Hezekiah encouraged his people by sharing his belief and trust in God. As a result, the people *"gained confidence"* and were not defeated by the threats and discouraging words of the enemy.

As we read our Bible, worship God, do regular devotions, and just spend time getting closer to God, we will find ourselves better prepared when faced with hard times or challenges from the enemy. We will build our confidence in God's provision. Not only will we be better prepared for ourselves, God will be able to use us to encourage others! In Ephesians 6, we read about how to put on the full armour of God. We are told to *"pray in the Spirit on all occasions with all kinds of prayers and requests. With this in mind, be alert and always keep on praying for all the saints"* (Ephesians 6:18).

May you be fully equipped with the armour of God. Be prepared to share your faith. Be alert to the struggles of the people the Lord brings into your life. Be prepared to speak the encouraging words of the Lord to them. I pray that the Holy Spirit would grant you wisdom and discernment in your ministry. Seek to equip others with the knowledge of, and confidence in, our great Lord! The battles are His, and He is always victorious!

AUGUST 13

To Whom Do You Turn?

Then Asa called to the Lord his God and said, "Lord, there is no one like you to help the powerless against the mighty. Help us, O Lord our God, for we rely on you, and in your name we have come against this vast army. O Lord, you are our God; do not let man prevail against you."
(2 Chronicles 14:11)

Way to go, Asa! He knew exactly where to turn for help when facing a huge battle while performing the work of the Lord! What a great role model, right? Unfortunately, King Asa, like the rest of us, did not keep his focus. King Asa falters and even takes the treasures that belong to the Lord, using them to bribe other men to come to his aid. 2 Chronicles 16:7 tells us,

At that time Hanani the seer came to Asa king of Judah and said to him: "Because you relied on the king of Aram and not on the Lord your God, the army of the king of Aram has escaped from your hand."

Oops! That should have brought King Asa back into repentance and onto the path God laid out for him. Instead he got angry at Hanani! How many of us have made that mistake? Suppose someone does try to warn you of your sin, or perhaps you feel convicted by the Holy Spirit directly. How do you respond? Do you repent and turn back to God, or do you ignore them or get angry with the messenger?

As we continue the story, we find that King Asa becomes severely ill. Now his heart is so hardened he doesn't go to the Lord for help. He still turns to man (so-called physicians who likely used magic), which meets with failure, and King Asa dies.

Even when you get off-course, if you humble yourself, confess your sins, and repent, God will hear you. When you walk in His ways, He watches over you and fights the enemy for you. God is willing and able to help you in the big battles for His name's sake, and in the little battles in your personal lives. To whom do you turn?

AUGUST 14

A Time of Rest

He brought me out into a spacious place; he rescued me because he delighted in me.
(Psalm 18:19)

Everything seems so fast nowadays! Hurry and do this! Hurry and do that! This person needs you to do this right now! That person needs you to do that immediately! Oh yeah, you need to squeeze this in some time, too! Sometimes we can be tired before we even get out of bed, just thinking about everything that needs to be done. If you throw in something unexpected or an emergency, you're really in trouble! Don't you just feel like stepping off the world for a little while sometimes? Well, you can.

Take that little bit of time at the beginning of the day, or when you feel overwhelmed, and sit down with Jesus. Go ahead and take a break. Turn everything off, sit down, and enter His presence. Allow the Holy Spirit to bring you *"into a spacious place."* He would delight to do so. Spend time just receiving the peace, comfort, and wisdom of the Father.

When it's finally time to leave, take the Holy Spirit with you. You will approach each aspect of your day in a calmer, wiser way than if you continue to rush through on your own. Be prepared to be amazed at how well you handle the things before you. At the end of the day, you will find those things that really do need to get done, did. You will go to bed and rest. If you find yourself drawn back into a frazzled state of the hustle and bustle, step off again and sit down with the Holy Spirit. His timetable is not too full.

Try a prayer like this: Thank You, Lord, for all the amazing blessings You pour into my life each and every day. May I never be too busy to invite You in and sit with You for a while. Thank You for being with me through my day and always being available to me. May Your will be done. Amen.

AUGUST 15

The Peace of God

He makes me lie down in green pastures, he leads me beside quiet waters... (Psalm 23:2)

Close your eyes for a moment and imagine your place of rest and peace. Where is it and what does it look like? I tend to imagine something like warm sunshine on a beautiful field of tall grass and wild flowers, or a beautiful rushing waterfall. I can definitely relate to the peaceful vision of today's verse.

King David was known to have a soft heart towards the things of God; however, he was no stranger to life's struggles. David spent a good part of his life in hiding because King Saul was trying to have him killed. Yet David knew God well, and he was able to write this well-known psalm. David recognized that his peace was in the Lord. David depicted the Lord as the shepherd, who provides *"green pastures"* and *"quiet waters"* as peaceful provision for His sheep.

The Lord beckons us to His refuge. Do you seek peace? Do you trust in the Lord to protect you? If you listen to the Holy Spirit and follow His counsel, that peace and protection are yours. If you find yourself stressed out and vulnerable, it's time to take an inventory of where you are. Are you where God has called you to be? Do you really expect to have God's peace if you have chosen to play on the freeway instead of going where He leads you?

I realize that real life is not a surrealistic experience with soft music playing in the background. I also realize that we humans have a hard time always staying on the path God has prepared for us. However, our amazing Lord can *always* provide us with His peace when we are willing to receive Him, no matter what storm or circumstance we find ourselves in. May you know His peace always.

AUGUST 16

Praise God!

Through Jesus, therefore, let us continually offer to God a sacrifice of praise—the fruit of lips that confess his name.
(Hebrews 13:15)

As a young couple, when we bought our first home it was about an hour and a quarter drive from our places of work. My husband bought a motorcycle as an economical way to get from our home in the suburbs to his job in the city. Early one holiday Monday, he was headed to work on an almost deserted freeway. At some point, a large bus approached from behind. The driver had either fallen asleep or had highway hypnosis and he hit my husband on his motorcycle. My husband slid some distance down the roadway but survived. In fact, he was checked at the hospital and released with minor injuries! When the shock of the initial story sunk in, I realized the protection of God was the only possible way he could have escaped with his life. A motorcycle versus a large bus! Thank You, God!

Sometime later I spoke to a Christian friend of ours. This friend commented on how lucky my husband had been. I looked at this friend and said, "You know that 'luck' had nothing to do with it." He smiled and acknowledged that I was right. God is good!

How often in life do we attribute the blessings of God to good luck or coincidence? How often do we accept that conclusion from others? Instead, let us give acknowledgement and praise to God! When we say "Thank God" for something, let us mean just that, and not simply throw it out as an absent-minded expression. Praise God for His provision and protection. Isn't God, good!?

There are many ways of praising God. Confess His name verbally with praise and thankfulness. Be a reminder to yourselves and to those around you of from where all blessings flow.

AUGUST 17

Act of God

In all this, Job did not sin by charging God with wrongdoing.
(Job 1:22)

I really dislike the insurance term "act of God." It's used to refer to tragic environmental events of which man had no forewarning, nor can he explain. It makes it sound like God just gets distracted or bored so He decides to create some great calamity for His amusement or something. I don't have an answer for why various weather conditions occur and create disasters. Nor do I have an explanation for any other sudden disaster. I do know, however, that God isn't a god of confusion and evil. He is a loving, orderly, and all-powerful God!

Job *"was blameless and upright; he feared God and shunned evil"* (Job 1:1). God was pleased with Job. Satan challenged God on Job's motives for being such a righteous man and asked permission to test Job's true motivations. Satan then attacked Job's possessions and family. In this case, God permitted the attacks to test Job's faith. Job passed the test. Satan then challenged the purity of Job's motives based on the fact that God had protected Job's health. God again permitted Satan to test Job, whom He knew would remain faithful; however, God limited Satan from taking Job's life. Job suffered greatly at the hands of Satan, but he proved his faith unshakeable. In the end, Job became a stronger person, and God rewarded him beyond anything Job had previously experienced.

Please understand me! I'm not saying that all disasters are the work of Satan to test people's faith. My point is that although Job went through more suffering than most of us can imagine, he never blamed God of any wrongdoing. We may suffer for many reasons—Satan's challenges, our own misguided choices, the poor choices of other people, or even just the nature of a sinful world. God is always just and righteous.

AUGUST 18

Gehazi Didn't Get It

Gehazi, the servant of Elisha the man of God, said to himself, "My master was too easy on Naaman, this Aramean, by not accepting from him what he brought. As surely as the Lord lives, I will run after him and get something from him."
(2 Kings 5:20)

Naaman was not the only one who learned an important lesson from his encounter with Elisha, the man of God. Gehazi was also to learn something very important.

Naaman was naturally very grateful for being healed from leprosy. He was used to relying on his own power and wealth, and so had offered to pay Elisha for the healing he received. Elisha was very clear about not accepting any reward from Naaman. Firstly, Elisha wanted Naaman to understand that he could not buy God's blessings. Secondly, Naaman was to understand that the healing was from God, not Elisha. Naaman vowed to *"never again make burnt offerings and sacrifices to any other god but the Lord"* (2 Kings 5:17).

Then Gehazi had something to learn. He resented that Elisha hadn't accepted Naaman's gifts. Gehazi secretly went to Naaman to get whatever he could from him. Naaman gladly presented Gehazi with the gifts he asked for. Gehazi then went home and hid what he had received. He obviously knew what he did was wrong or he would not have felt the need to hide it. As a result of Gehazi's greed, he was cursed with Naaman's leprosy.

God does not *owe* us anything. We do not *deserve* special treatment or blessings because we do the work of God. We are accepted because of what Jesus did for us, not because of anything we have done. We are blessed because of God's grace and mercy. We are privileged to be able to partner with God in His work to bring glory to Him, not ourselves. It's not about me or you.

AUGUST 19

Humility of Jesus

Your attitude should be the same as that of Christ Jesus.
(Philippians 2:5)

As Christians, we are called to have Christ-like attitudes. Jesus humbled Himself and took on the form of man for our sake. He put aside His rights and status as God to take on the nature of man so we could relate to Him. He graciously demonstrated the ultimate self-sacrifice to teach us how to live servant-hearted lives here on earth.

Many times, Jesus confessed that He had no special powers or knowledge of Himself while here on earth (John 7:16, 26, 28). He said that He only knew what the Father told Him (John 14:10, 15:15) and did what the Father said to do (John 5:19, 36, 38, 10:15–18, 12:27). Jesus said that *"the world must learn that I love the Father and that I do exactly what my Father has commanded me"* (John 14:31). Jesus denied Himself in obedience to the Father, even to death. Did Jesus have supernatural peace about His impending death? No. In Luke 22:42, Jesus prayed, *"Father, if you are willing, take this cup from me; yet not my will, but yours be done."* But He chose obedience.

Are you willing to put aside your rights and privileges for the sake of the work of God? If God calls you, are you willing to give up your vacation time and funds to go into the mission field? What if God asks you to be forgiving in a situation where you don't believe you have done anything wrong? If God asks you to speak into someone's life, are you willing to put aside your pride, fear, or any other hindrances and obey? Trust in God. He will not ask you to say or do anything for which He does not already know the final outcome.

Have you learned to love the Father as Jesus does? How much do you value your salvation? Are you obedient to God's calling and servant-hearted for the glory of God?

AUGUST 20

A Recipe for Joy

I have told you this so that my joy may be in you and that your joy may be complete.
(John 15:11)

Can you imagine the money you could make if you could develop a recipe for joy? You wouldn't be able to print it fast enough to keep up with the demand. You would have speaking engagements all over the world!

Jesus gave us such a recipe. The world just hasn't received it. When speaking to His followers, Jesus told them that He loved them like the Father loved Him. His words apply to all of us who have chosen to believe in Jesus. Now that's reason to be joyful!

Jesus went on to tell His followers that they would remain in that love if they obeyed His commands. That doesn't mean that Jesus' love is fickle. If we sin, as we all do, and fall short of what Jesus would want for us, He will not desert us. We are the ones who choose to step outside His love when we sin. It's like a child choosing to throw sand in the sandbox after being told not to. The parent will not stop loving the child; the child just chose not to stay in that place of love. When the child (us) repents and turns back to the parent (God), the parent and his love is still there.

Jesus told His followers that they didn't choose Him, but that He chose them (John 15:16)—just like a child doesn't first choose to love his parents, but his parents choose to love him. Jesus commands His followers to love each other as He has loved us (John 15:12). Jesus said, *"You are my friends if you do what I command"* (John 15:14). He has *"appointed [us] to go and bear fruit—fruit that will last"* (John 15:16).

So, what's the recipe for joy? Stay in the love of Jesus through obedience to Him. That's it! Receive His love and be joyful!

AUGUST 21

Friendship

He who covers over an offense promotes love, but whoever repeats the matter separates close friends.
(Proverbs 17:9)

The definition of "friendship" is "the relationship between persons who like and respect each other."[10] Certainly our spouse should be our most treasured friend here on earth. We should "like" (love) and "respect" each other. Today's verse from Proverbs advises that we *"cover over an offense"* rather than *"repeat the matter."* What sound advice!

Have you ever had the misfortune of being trapped listening to someone tear down or repeat what they believe to be another person's errors? It is never pleasant, especially when that person is their spouse, the one they are supposed to be closest to. It's one thing when it happens on one or two occasions, but when their topic of conversation each time you meet is to relate more failures, then red flags should go up. My first caution is not to share what your spouse might have done wrong. The session can soon become a rally against all people of the opposite sex.

Ask yourself why this person is sharing these things with you? Are they looking for help, or justification for their negative attitude? Are they looking for objective and respected words of advice, or sympathy? If their motive in sharing is not for help, then my advice is to close down the topic immediately. Let them know that you do not wish to take part in such negative activities. If they are seeking help to restore their relationship, however, then seek God in what He would have you do. You can pray with them, point them to God, encourage them to work out their difficulties in honest and loving ways, or help them find confidential outside help if needed.

Overlooking small offenses may save a relationship, but perpetuating an offense can cost the relationship.

---

[10] *The Winston Dictionary of Canadian English* (Toronto, ON: Holt, Rinehart and Winston of Canada, 1969), 264.

AUGUST 22

Courage

When they saw the courage of Peter and John and realized that they were unschooled, ordinary men, they were astonished and they took note that these men had been with Jesus.
(Acts 4:13)

I, like Peter and John, have no paperwork to prove my understanding of God's word. I have never received credit for Bible school courses. Many of you will be able to relate. I'm just an "ordinary" person.

How did Peter and John do it? What gave them the authority to speak out about their faith and perform miracles in the name of Jesus? Let's remember that Peter and John were being questioned by the rulers, elders, and high priests. These judges held a lot of power! Let's back up to verse 8: *"Then Peter, filled with the Holy Spirit, said to them…"* It was the Holy Spirit that enabled them to speak with authority, wisdom, and knowledge. These judges commanded Peter and John to stop teaching and speaking of Jesus. Peter and John denied these judges right to their faces! Then the disciples were released. Does that make sense?

Notice also that people *"took note that these men had been with Jesus."* They knew Peter and John were followers of Jesus and were impressed with the courage the disciples had. People were drawn to the disciples and wanted to know more because of what they witnessed.

We, too, can speak and act with courage in what we are told by the Holy Spirit. You may find your faith questioned by people in authority over you, or people close to you (family and friends). When you do, call on the Holy Spirit. He will fill you with wisdom in how and when to respond. The Holy Spirit will guide and protect you.

It is my hope and desire that people will take note that I am a Christian. I don't need any paperwork. Jesus is with me.

AUGUST 23

What Is Holding You Back?

For if their purpose or activity is of human origin, it will fail. But if it is from God, you will not be able to stop these men; you will only find yourselves fighting against God.
(Acts 5:38–39)

The Bible warns us many times about false teachers and prophets. None of us want to be tricked or fooled into believing lies. It is good to be discerning. That's what we are called to do. However, are we so hesitant that we also miss out on all God has called us to?

Remember the Israelites as they stood at the entrance to the Promised Land. After all the Lord had done for them to bring them out of oppression and into His blessings, they were still uncertain. They sent in twelve scouts to check out the Promised Land, even though God had told them it was theirs. Caleb and Joshua recognized God's promise and His power to provide it. They came back all excited and ready to go! However, the other ten were held back by their own insecurities. They were uncertain and discouraged the rest of the Israelites. The fear of a few caused all the Israelites to miss out on God's blessings.

When God calls, are you ready to be unstoppable? God's wish is for each one of us to overcome our self-imposed restrictions of fear, doubt, anger, bitterness, ingratitude, jealousy, pride, and ignorance. He has sent us the Holy Spirit to move us into a realm beyond our human weakness. We are not to be discouraged because of our own, or other people's, imposed restrictions.

When faced with a decision of what is of the Lord, ask Him. He knows our struggles. Pray that He would give you wisdom and confirmation. You don't need to send someone else in to check it out. Based on today's verse, you might pray something like this: "Lord, if this is not of You, may it dissolve away, but if this is of You, Lord, may it blossom!"

AUGUST 24

Speaking Boldly

After they prayed, the place where they were meeting was shaken. And they were all filled with the Holy Spirit and spoke the word of God boldly. (Acts 4:31)

After being released from prison, Peter and John went back to their people. They reported all that had happened to them, which included the authorities' threat that they were to stop speaking and teaching about Jesus. Now what? The entire group gathered together in prayer. They felt a shaking, and all were filled with the Holy Spirit. As a result, they *"spoke the word of God boldly."*

What does this mean for us? Well, firstly, when we are challenged regarding our faith and work for God, we are called to come *together* in prayer. Gather Christian support and pray! What do you expect to happen? You may or may not feel a physical shaking, but trust that God is shaking up the spiritual realm! Expect things to start happening! Secondly, be prepared to be filled with the Holy Spirit. Jesus promised to send Him as our friend and counsellor. Receive that gift with confidence and joy! The Lord will go before us as we follow in the ways the Holy Spirit leads.

Well, that all sounds great, but why? It is so that we can speak *"the word of God boldly."* We will know what and when we are to speak for God. Our whole purpose is to bring glory to God. We are to encourage one another. We are to reveal the truth to all those to whom God calls us. We are to point all eyes to Him, for His glory!

You may not even know all the lives you touch in Jesus' name. You will be empowered to bring glory to Him when you answer God's calling, invoke His intervention through prayer, and receive the help He sends through the Holy Spirit!

AUGUST 25

Offering from the Heart

With his wife's full knowledge he kept back part of the money for himself, but brought the rest and put it at the apostles' feet.
(Acts 5:2)

Before I get into discussing offerings, I wish to make very clear that this doesn't refer to tithing. Tithing has been discussed on other days' devotions. Offerings are above and beyond tithes, and in fact I believe you cannot truly give an offering until you have fulfilled your tithe.

That being said, we come to today's verse. In the early church, the Christians chose to contribute to the good of all Christians. Those who could provide did so out of their financial wealth (an offering) to meet the needs of others. It was a choice they made. They were never required to give up all they had been blessed with. They maintained the right to their personal property.

Then why was Ananias and his wife killed when they didn't give all they had? Their sin was not in keeping some of their money or personal wealth for themselves. In fact, it was very charitable of them to give even part of their wealth to benefit others. We don't know from this passage if they had fulfilled their tithe, but the insinuation is that this was an extra gift or offering. Their sin was in lying to God. Their hearts were not pure.

Ananias planned to lie about the price they made on the land they sold. He wanted it to look like he was keeping up with the Joneses and was righteously giving everything, too. However, his wife had full knowledge of what he was doing. She missed her opportunity to warn Ananias of his sin. She had the opportunity as his closest confidant to lovingly point out to him the deception he was being entrapped in. Then they could have decided to give the full price, or honestly donate the portion that their heart prompted. She could have saved the lives of both her husband and herself.

God doesn't need your offerings; He needs your heart.

AUGUST 26

The Possible

But during the night an angel of the Lord opened the doors of the jail and brought them out.
(Acts 5:19)

I had the fortune of being raised in a family that took me to Sunday School right from the beginning. I heard Bible stories and became familiar with all the main characters of the Bible. I learned about what we should and shouldn't do to be good people. Then, one day, it occurred to me that these weren't just stories. All the Biblical events I had learned about were true. They actually happened!

As I continued to learn, I came to the realization that the morals of the Bible weren't just intended for Biblical times. The God-inspired words of the Bible (2 Timothy 3:16) were provided for us, for the here and now! God didn't just work through holy Biblical heroes; He continues to work through ordinary Christians.

Today's verse tells us that even the apostles weren't miraculously self-sufficient. *"An angel of the Lord"* was sent to intervene on the apostles' behalf. Yes, the apostles endeavoured to do the work of God. Yes, the apostles spent time in prayer. Yes, the apostles requested and were granted the interceding prayers of fellow Christians. How is that any different from you or me?

We should all endeavour to be in alignment with God's will for our lives. We should all spend time in prayer and pray for one another. *"With God all things are possible"* (Matthew 19:26). They were possible when He created the world, in Old Testament times, when Jesus came to earth, ever since then, now, and forevermore.

Our God is not just a god of the past. He is omnipresent and prepared to send us any help we may need to carry out His work here on earth. He may even send *"an angel of the Lord."* The words of the Bible are real now!

The Bible isn't just stories.

AUGUST 27

Ordinary Christians

And who knows but that you have come to royal position for such a time as this?
(Esther 4:14)

Imagine a story about a little orphan girl who rises up to become an honoured queen. What are the chances of that happening? We all love a story about a good person who overcomes obstacles to attain their reward in the end. This story, however, isn't about some fictional character developed in someone's imagination. This is a true story.

Esther was orphaned, taken from her relatives, and brought into a strange place to be groomed by a stranger. She had to spend twelve months being prepared to be presented to a king to see if she pleased him or not. She did please him, and he made her queen. She made it past all those hurdles and then she was asked to go to the king *"to beg for mercy and plead with him for her people"* (Esther 4:8). If anyone entered into the king's presence uninvited, the consequence was death. Esther was her people's only hope. She gathered the support of her people in fasting, and presumably prayer. Then she took action as she felt led by the Lord. She was successful in saving the lives of her people (the Jews), defeating their enemy at the same time.

God loves and provides for all of us whether we are a little orphan, royalty, or something in-between. He can use any one of us who are willing to do His work to bring great victory for His kingdom. It is hard to imagine that something an ordinary Christian does can bring defeat or victory in the heavenlies, but it's true! However, we must remember that it is not by our strength or wisdom, but His. He has empowered us in the name of Jesus through the Holy Spirit. It is His wisdom and power in us at work.

Why are you where you are right now? Is it *"for such a time as this"*?

AUGUST 28

The Lord's People

I will give them a heart to know me, that I am the Lord. They will be my people, and I will be their God, for they will return to me with all their heart.
(Jeremiah 24:7)

If you have a child or loved one who seems to have wandered or turned away from God, take heart! God's hand is upon them.

The Lord gave the prophet Jeremiah a vision of good and bad figs. He compared the good figs to His people, those who knew Him. Although the people appeared to be separated from God for a time, He promised,

My eyes will watch over them for their good, and I will bring them back… I will build them up and not tear them down; I will plant them and not uproot them. (Jeremiah 24:6)

Then God gave today's verse. God has promised that He *"will give them a heart to know [Him]"* and that they will *"return to [Him] with all their heart."*

God will allow His people to make decisions that take them off His path for a time. They may suffer some consequences for those decisions, but God will use those things for their good.

You can claim this verse for anyone who has known God but now appears to have gone off His path. Thank God that *He* watches over them in ways you cannot. Thank God that *He* will bring them back and build them up. You don't have to manipulate or plot their return. Thank God that *He* will firmly plant them in His word. Thank God that *He* will give them a heart to know Him, and when He does, they will return to Him with all their heart.

Do not be anxious about anything, but in everything, by prayer and petition, with thanksgiving, present your requests to God. And the peace of God, which transcends all understanding, will guard your hearts and your minds in Christ Jesus. (Philippians 4:6–7)

AUGUST 29

Knowledge or Wisdom

If any of you lacks wisdom, he should ask God, who gives generously to all without finding fault, and it will be given to him.
(James 1:5)

Knowledge isn't the same as wisdom. Both are good, but wisdom is far more beneficial than knowledge. Knowledge is becoming informed. It is the learning process. Wisdom, however, is knowing how to use knowledge for the good judgement of what is right and true. True wisdom is God-inspired insight of the truth.

We can study and learn many things. Life is an ongoing learning process. Whether formally attained for academic credit, or gained informally, knowledge is good. We want to avoid continuously learning but never being able to come to the knowledge of the truth, as spoken in 2 Timothy 3:7. Without a soft heart for the things of God, which permits the indwelling of the Spirit of wisdom, it is all for nothing!

The Apostle Paul blessed the church in Ephesus by interceding for them:

I keep asking that the God of our Lord Jesus Christ, the glorious Father, may give you the Spirit of wisdom and revelation, so that you may know him better. (Ephesians 1:17)

The Apostle James, in today's verse, encourages us to ask God directly for His wisdom.

For the Lord gives wisdom, and from his mouth come knowledge and understanding. (Proverbs 2:6)

Continue to seek knowledge of all kinds. Read God's word and seek knowledge of our Christian faith. I would encourage you to then join together with your spouse in petitioning God for the outpouring of the Spirit of wisdom into your lives. Receive the gift that God will *"generously"* give to you. May that God-inspired wisdom guide you in how to think, act, and live every day.

AUGUST 30

The Face of an Angel

All who were sitting in the Sanhedrin looked intently at Stephen, and they saw that his face was like the face of an angel.
(Acts 6:15)

We are told in Acts 6:8 that Stephen was *"a man full of God's grace and power."* However, he came up against some evil men. These men were unable to *"stand up against his wisdom or the Spirit by whom he spoke"* (Acts 6:10). Therefore, they plotted to discredit Stephen and distort the truth in front of the Sanhedrin (the elders and teachers in authority). The Sanhedrin wouldn't have been Christians, but evidently even they were able to see the purity of Stephen just by looking at his face. At this point, Stephen was given an opportunity to witness to the leaders publicly. Stephen recounted events from Abraham to the crucifixion of Jesus Christ. We know of at least one person who was changed by Stephen's witness. His name was Saul, who was eventually known as the Apostle Paul.

It makes you wonder what people see when they look at you, doesn't it? Do they see *"the face of an angel"*? Is the purity, honesty, and integrity God has filled you with evident on your face? Can people witness God's grace and power in your life? Is the evil one able to stand up against the wisdom or the Spirit by whom you speak? What effect do you have on the people in your life?

I hope that you will be blessed with knowledge of some of the fruits of your labour. If you need encouragement, ask God to reveal some of those fruits to you. However, like Stephen, you will never know all the people whose lives are affected by you and your choices. Thank God for those whose attention is drawn to the light they see in you. As you keep your eyes on God, may you continue to demonstrate His grace and wisdom. May those who look upon you see *"the face of an angel,"* and be drawn to that which you have in Jesus Christ. Amen.

AUGUST 31

Never Gives Up

My Father, who has given them to me, is greater than all; no one can snatch them out of my Father's hand.
(John 10:29)

The other day, my husband and I went for a run. My health had been suffering a bit lately, so I found the run more of a challenge than I usually did. It was hot, but I was determined to push through and complete the run. Unfortunately, I had to stop two or three times and walk for a bit. My husband refused to go on without me, even when I told him to. Instead, he stopped to walk when I walked, encouraged me to try again when I could, and said lots of encouraging words along the way. When we finished, he cheered for me! I'm so thankful that God has granted me a husband who never gives up on me.

We service a God who never gives up on any of us. Jesus said,

> *Suppose one of you has a hundred sheep and loses one of them. Does he not leave the ninety-nine in the open country and go after the lost sheep until he finds it?… I tell you that in the same way there will be more rejoicing in heaven over one sinner who repents than over ninety-nine righteous persons who do not need to repent.* (Luke 15:4, 7)

Jesus also said, *"And this is the will of him who sent me, that I shall lose none of all that he has given me, but raise them up at the last day"* (John 6:39).

We may not always get it right. We may not always be in alignment with God's will for our lives. But our Father in heaven never gives up on any of us. He seeks us when we go astray. He searches for us and calls us back. He encourages us to persevere.

> *…let us throw off everything that hinders and the sin that so easily entangles, and let us run with perseverance the race marked out for us. Let us fix our eyes on Jesus…* (Hebrews 12:1–2)

Thank God that He never gives up on us! I would encourage you to fix your eyes on Jesus and preserve! You can do it!

SEPTEMBER 1

I'm Not a Nag!

...a quarrelsome wife is like a constant dripping.
(Proverbs 19:13)

Ouch! Can't you feel the grating on the nerves when you read this verse? "I'm not his mother!" screams the frustrated wife. No, you're not. God created woman to be man's companion, not his overseer. However, if you see your husband partaking in behaviour that's detrimental to his wellbeing, that doesn't mean you close your eyes or turn your back on him. Fear of being a nag shouldn't keep you from acknowledging areas of concern, whether they be physical, emotional, or spiritual.

What does your attitude say? Are you approaching your husband with an attitude of control? "You're blowing it! Just do it my way and everything will be fine!" Or rather, are you approaching your husband with an attitude of love? Are your intentions corrective, or of concern and encouragement?

For example, if your husband is overweight, an attitude of control may be quarrelsome or nagging if you constantly criticise what or how much he chooses to eat. An attitude of concern would be to lovingly tell him that you love him and want him to be around for a long time to come. Tell him you are concerned about his weight in relation to his health and wellbeing. Encouragement might take the form of noticing and positively commenting when he makes attempts to bring his weight under control. You could perhaps offer to join him in physical activity. Ask him if there's a way he would like you to support him in his efforts to bring himself into a healthier lifestyle.

Ask God to help you be a companion and encourager to your husband.

SEPTEMBER 2

So You Want Wisdom

But where can wisdom be found? Where does understanding dwell? (Job 28:12)

Seeking wisdom and understanding is an admirable goal. It is an exciting endeavour to be a lifelong learner. No matter your IQ or place in this world, there is always something new to learn. From the moment we are born, we are learning new things.

So, wisdom and understanding are good things, but as Job asks in today's verse, where can we find it? In the next verse, Job tells it like it is: *"Man does not comprehend its worth"* (Job 28:13). Job goes on to explain that man looks for wisdom and understanding in all the wrong places. *"God understands the way to it and he alone knows where it dwells"* (Job 28:23). The obvious answer is to turn to God. In fact, according to God, *"The fear of the Lord—that is wisdom, and to shun evil is understanding"* (Job 28:28).

Don't misunderstand me! God set humans apart from other creatures by giving us a mind and intellect. All the knowledge we seek is admirable, but true wisdom and understanding can only come from God. Spending time in His presence, reading His word, and learning His truths will lead you to wisdom.

As we gain His wisdom, we recognize what is true and what are the lies of the enemy. God has told us to shun evil—that is, to avoid and stay away from it deliberately. Don't knowingly submit yourself to situations that will tempt you towards evil. God has told us that if we avoid evil, we will gain understanding.

Ask the Lord to give you His wisdom and understanding. In so doing, ask that you have discernment. Ask for revelations of His truths.

Wisdom and knowledge come from God alone.

SEPTEMBER 3

Signs and Wonders

So Paul and Barnabas spent considerable time there, speaking boldly for the Lord, who confirmed the message of his grace by enabling them to do miraculous signs and wonders.
(Acts 14:3)

This is truly an exciting topic! It is so encouraging to see and hear of the Lord's miraculous works! Unfortunately, many people think the Lord will only work through "special" people, like His communication with the priests of the Old Testament. The truth is that He can and will work through any Christian.

Let's look at a few aspects of today's verse to help us better understand how this all works. Notice that Paul and Barnabas didn't just show up and start behaving like magicians. They invested *"considerable time there."* They took action by teaching the people about the Lord. That was their whole point! They were trying to help people come to know the Lord personally! Notice also that they spoke *"boldly."* They weren't wishy-washy or uncertain about what they had to say. They weren't secretive (in case things didn't work out). There are many cases in the Bible of people being bold in their requests for miraculous healing. They had the faith that it could happen—for example, the miraculous healing of the woman's daughter in Matthew 15:25–28 and the miraculous healing of the blind man in Matthew 20:29–34.

Why did the Lord enable them to perform miraculous signs and wonders? It was as a confirmation. It proved Paul and Barnabas's authority and the truth of what they had been preaching. It was to draw the people to Jesus and eternal life with Him.

Don't you think it would be wonderful if the Lord would do *"miraculous signs and wonders"* through all Christians more often? Why? Will you allow Him to use you? Do you take the time to know what and where the Lord has called you? Do you speak boldly what the Holy Spirit inspires you to say?

SEPTEMBER 4

Be Encouraging and Alert

But encourage one another daily, as long as it is called Today, so that none of you may be hardened by sin's deceitfulness.
(Hebrews 3:13)

I can talk to the Lord directly. Why do I need anyone else? It's true that we no longer have to go to an appointed temple priest to hear from God, but the Bible does teach us about the value of sharing each other's burdens. We need to encourage one another and help others to avoid being *"hardened by sin's deceitfulness."*

I recently received a call from someone who had to make a decision about her ministry. She had been called to her ministry and had a heavy heart about letting go, although she had begun to feel burdened by it. She was uncertain of what lay ahead. As she shared with me what was happening, I felt a quickening in my spirit. I was inspired to suggest that it may be time for her to release her ministry into the hands of someone the Lord had already put in place. I sensed that the Lord was calling her on to a bigger ministry! I was excited for her!

I was by no means telling this person what to do. That was between her and God. However, by calling on a Christian friend for prayer, I was able to give her a word of encouragement. I was able to caution her not to hang on to her ministry just because that was what she knew and was comfortable with.

Satan will use anything to hold us back from doing the Lord's work! I will continue to intercede in prayer for those whom the Lord would help make the right decisions and give them peace. Trust that God knows what He is doing, and that He will not ask you to do more than He enables you to do. Reach out to others and ask them to join you in prayer. Be prepared to pray for others. Be encouraged and be an encourager!

SEPTEMBER 5

Different by Chosen

God, who knows the heart, showed that he accepted them by giving the Holy Spirit to them, just as he did to us.
(Acts 15:8)

I find it interesting how quickly people look for the differences in each other. What about starting from what is the same? As a teacher of children with special needs, I am constantly reiterating this message. Each child is the same as other children in many ways. They may have one or more exceptions, but they have more things in common than are different or special. People tend to look for differences in others, be it cultures, race, or some other aspect. The skin or hair colour may vary, but look at how much we are all the same!

I'm not saying that you should pretend everyone has the same skin, hair, or eye colour. Nor should you pretend we are all the same gender. What I'm saying is that it is okay to recognize differences without the attitude that the differences are bad. God made each one of us! He chose our parents. He knew what our culture, family size, stature, and colouring would be. We are each His creation!

In Acts, the Apostle Peter learned this principle and tried to teach it. Peter realized that God had called him to preach to the Gentiles as well as the Jews. He told the Jews that God *"knows the heart,"* and *"made no distinction between us and them"* (Acts 15:9). Peter's question was, *"Now then, why do you try to test God…?"* (Acts 15:10)

In Matthew 28:19–20, Jesus instructed,

Therefore go and make disciples of all nations, baptizing them in the name of the Father and of the Son and of the Holy Spirit, and teaching them to obey everything I have commanded you.

He has called us to witness to *all* nations. It is not up to you or I to decide who deserves to know the Lord; it is up to the Lord Himself. Don't test Him!

SEPTEMBER 6

Safety

But let all who take refuge in you be glad; let them ever sing for joy. Spread your protection over them, that those who love your name may rejoice in you.
(Psalm 5:11)

Do you look for cars before you cross the street? Do you use oven mitts to take hot things out of the oven? Do you avoid dangerous areas? Do you read your Bible and spend time regularly with God?

Why would anyone be concerned about protecting their physical bodies and not be concerned about their spiritual wellbeing? Why would you caution others (perhaps your children) in areas of physical safety and not do the same for their spiritual safety? What good is a healthy physical body, which is temporary, compared to eternal health with Jesus?

Suppose you sit your child down and teach them all about road safety. They listen to you, read books, and watch video clips. Then you send them out to play, and the first thing they do is run out into the street in front of a car. All those lessons were well-intended, but if the child does not practise what he has learned, they are of no value. He is not protected simply by being instructed.

The fact that you are even reading this devotion tells me that you have some concern for learning more and developing your spiritual understanding. It is quite likely that you also do a number of other things to develop your spiritual health. However, like the child mentioned above, when you go out into the world, do you use what you have learned?

Suppose that child looks carefully before crossing the street safely, and then runs out in front of a car in a parking lot. The results are just as devastating! I would encourage you to be spiritually aware of all things. It's not necessarily just man you need to be on guard from, but also *"the spiritual forces of evil in the heavenly realms"* (Ephesians 6:12). Be safe under the Lord's protection.

SEPTEMBER 7

Plan vs. Purposes (Part One)

But the plans of the Lord stand firm forever, the purposes of his heart through all generations.
(Psalm 33:11)

Are our whole lives planned out before us? Yes, the Bible tells us that God has plans for us. Does that mean everything we do is predetermined? No, I don't believe that every choice we make, everything we say or do, is planned and unchangeable. God gave us a free will.

Does that mean we can mess up God's plans? I don't think so. Although we sometimes say things like a pregnancy was a "mistake," God is not caught off-guard by it. It's not like when someone is born God says, "Oh! What am I supposed to do with that one?" He knows the exact timing of each conception and birth from the beginning of time until the end.

So what happens when we choose a career, house, or spouse? What if it is not the one God planned? He's not going to think, "Oh! I planned such-and-such for that person! Now what am I going to do?" God has plans for every Christian in every situation. He does not dictate, and may not even reveal ahead of time, the exact choice you are to make. You have free will. If you ask, He will guide through the Holy Spirit and give you peace when you carefully and prayerfully make your choices.

If someone chooses to live outside the will of God, and for example leads an immoral lifestyle (such as a criminal career), they should not expect to be fulfilling their purpose. However, even then, if they chose to receive Jesus as their Lord and Saviour, and repent and follow Him, it is not too late. God knew they would take a wrong turn, but He can use their lives to fulfill His purpose for them.

No matter what choices we make, God already knew about them, and He has a purpose for each of us.

SEPTEMBER 8

Plan vs. Purposes (Part Two)

May he give you the desire of your heart and make all your plans succeed. (Psalm 20:4)

Yesterday we talked about God having a purpose for each of our lives. Today I want to discuss "plans." This can be a topic of great debate and discussion. I propose to present some ideas, and hope you and your spouse will continue to contemplate your own understanding together.

To be a Christian is to know Jesus. If you really know Jesus, I would say that out of your love for Him, it would be your desire to please Him and be in alignment with His will. Therefore, when the Bible refers to the desires of your heart, as in today's verse, I would say those desires would be for God's purpose. With that in mind, your plans should enable you to be more Christ-like and fulfill the calling (or purpose) God has for you.

Okay then, let's look at an example. Let's look again at choosing a job or career. Should you be a teacher or a business person? Well, what do you like to do? Don't you think God can use teachers and business people? Say you choose to be a teacher. Should you teach preschool, high school, university, or even teach in the private sector? Which one do you think God can use? Do you see my point yet? Even if you change your mind and decide after a while that you would rather do some other job, God already knew that. As long as the desire of your heart is still love for Him, God can use any job to fulfill His purpose for your life. He can and will *"make [those] plans succeed."*

"Well, wait a minute! Then why didn't I get that job I applied for, or why did I get laid off?" I can't tell you that. Perhaps God knows there's something better out there for you. Something you didn't even notice, or would not have looked for. Perhaps it was Satan's attempt to derail you, but our God is greater! His plan is for you is success. Praise God!

SEPTEMBER 9

Authority Over Evil

Away from me, all you who do evil, for the Lord has heard my weeping. (Psalm 6:8)

I don't like to give Satan too much attention so as to build him up. However, I also don't like to ignore him and allow him to continue to scheme, manipulate, and do his work. It is true that we should keep our eyes on Jesus, for where His light shines, darkness cannot exist. We must remember, though, that we live in a world where darkness and spiritual forces of evil do exist.

Through sins, generational curses, and exposure to the world around us, we may allow Satan's demons to enter into our lives and bind us. We know it is important to continually confess our sins, repent, and invite the Holy Spirit to fill our lives. It is also important to ask God to reveal to us any area where Satan's demons have wormed their way in, taking from us the authority we have been given. We must address them and declare. *"Away from me, all you who do evil"!*

We are so fortunate that our God is a god of second chances. Many times, the Bible tells us that if we sin, but then turn back, God will hear us (see 2 Chronicles 7:14, Proverbs 28:13, and 1 John 1:9 for three examples). There is power in verbal confessions. The Bible also tells us that we can be freed from generational curses (see Jeremiah 31:29–30 and Exodus 18:2–3). The most empowering thing, though, is that the Bible tells us we have the power in the name of Jesus to take authority over evil. Jesus told us, *"And these signs will accompany those who believe: In my name they will drive out demons"* (Mark 16:17). Satan knows we mean business and he knows we have been given authority.

Pray that God will reveal truths to you and your spouse. Pray that neither of you will be blinded by the enemy. Ask God for His wisdom to avoid evil. Praise God for your healing, deliverance, and protection.

SEPTEMBER 10

Do They Know?

I will praise you, O Lord, with all my heart; I will tell of all your wonders. (Psalm 9:1)

I recently heard a story of two people who had worked together for a number of years. One Sunday, they both showed up at the same church. Both of their reactions were, "Wow! I didn't know you were a Christian!" Ouch! How could that be?

Then I started wondering about my own life. Many people know that I'm a Christian, but would anyone be surprised to find out? Is there enough evidence in my daily life to show that I'm a Christian? When I leave this world, will I hear Jesus say, *"I never knew you"* (Matthew 7:23) or *"Well done, good and faithful servant"* (Matthew 25:21)? I sure hope there won't be anyone in heaven saying "Wow! I didn't know you would be here!"

What about you? Do you share what God has done, and is doing, in your lives? If you don't tell others, how will they know? Do you praise God outside the church building? Do you praise God in front of people even if you don't know if they are Christians? Do you rejoice in the things of the Lord and let others know where your joy, peace, and strength come from?

When someone gets in your car or enters your home, what music might they hear? Do you quickly change the radio station or CD from Christian music to something else when someone is near? What books might people see you reading? Do you hide your Bible or Christian books?

Do you actually recognize the blessings God pours upon you? Do you thank Him and give Him praise? Share the wealth of all you have in the name of Jesus.

Sing praises to the Lord, enthroned in Zion; proclaim among the nations what he has done. (Psalm 9:11)

SEPTEMBER 11

Renewing of Your Mind

Do not conform any longer to the pattern of this world, but be transformed by the renewing of your mind. Then you will be able to test and approve what God's will is—his good, pleasing and perfect will.
(Romans 12:2)

Have you ever had a troubling time when you prepared a conversation ahead of time? "I'll say this. Then, if he says that, I'll say this." Does that really help? What if he or she doesn't say what you planned for them to say? What if they have an entirely different reaction than the one you prepared for? All you're doing is allowing yourself to become worked up over something that might not even happen!

Instead, take control of your mind and emotions. Do not entertain just any thought. When disruptive thoughts come to mind, take them captive. *"We demolish arguments and every pretension that sets itself up against the knowledge of God, and we take captive every thought to make it obedient to Christ"* (2 Corinthians 10:5). By knowing God and His word, you will be able to stop the lies and deception of the enemy and replace those thoughts with the edifying word of God.

Ask God for His wisdom about what you allow into your mind. Ask for His peace. Ask Him to reveal anything to you that you need to recognize in your own attitude. Trust that the Holy Spirit is with you and will give you the words to speak when you need them. Trust that the Holy Spirit will guide your reactions and emotions. Pray that it will not be a matter of self-control, but God-control. Prepare to be amazed as you look back on the situation and realize how calm and peaceful the encounter was, how you had just the right words and no more to reach an understanding.

May God's *"good, pleasing and perfect will"* be done. Amen.

SEPTEMBER 12

Where's Peace?

Finally, brothers, whatever is true, whatever is noble, whatever is right, whatever is pure, whatever is lovely, whatever is admirable—if anything is excellent or praiseworthy—think about such things.
(Philippians 4:8)

True peace comes from God only. You come to *feel* peace by receiving His Spirit of peace, allowing it to mould your mind and emotions. You do have a choice about where your thoughts go. When anything enters your mind that isn't edifying, stop! Choose to replace those thoughts with edifying, God-pleasing thoughts.

Ask God to fill you with His Spirit of peace regularly. Pray that He would free you from confusion and bring you clarity of mind. Where any of your thoughts are out of alignment with His will, ask Him to reveal them. Ask Him to reveal to you any rebellion you may be entertaining, and convict you to repent. Where you have anxiety, ask Him for peace. When you have sadness, ask for His joy. Where you have insecurity, ask for His confidence.

I realize that there will be times in your life when you find this more difficult. However, God's peace is always available and worth seeking, no matter what your circumstances are. As you receive the peace of God, choose to maintain that peace by conforming your mind to His will. As today's verse instructs, choose to think about whatever is good. Choose not to dwell on hurts, pain, sorrow, or injustices. Our God is a good god, and He wants what is good for you.

So where is peace? It is in allowing God to do His work in you and choosing to allow Him to fill you with His Spirit of peace.

The Lord gives strength to his people; the Lord blesses his people with peace.
(Psalm 29:11)

SEPTEMBER 13

How to be a Great Leader

Now that I, your Lord and Teacher, have washed your feet, you also should wash one another's feet.
(John 13:14)

There is no better example of great leadership than Jesus Christ Himself. The account we read in John 13 is Jesus' lesson on how to be a great leader. The disciples, and in fact many people, misunderstand the definition of leadership. Leadership does not mean attaining power and status. To be a leader is to be one who guides or directs others. If nobody is following, you are not actually leading! You attain leadership by serving those whom you desire to follow you.

Men, to be the leader in your household, you need to serve the needs of your spouse and children. You do not attain respect by demanding it; rather you are *given* respect by the loving admiration of your family. Women, you too will attain leadership by serving the needs of your family and those around you. It's not about being in charge; it's about being a good leader.

In John 13, Jesus was also teaching the disciples about forgiveness. Jesus has made the ultimate sacrifice for you and me before either of us was even born. He paid the price by dying on the cross for all our sins. He forgave us. When Peter asked Jesus to wash his whole body, Jesus told him that was not necessary. Jesus has already forgiven us. When we sin again, we do not need to start all over; just confess that sin and receive His forgiveness to be clean once more.

Jesus then told the disciples *"Now that I, your Lord and Teacher, have washed your feet, you also should wash one another's feet"* (John 13:14). He has forgiven us entirely. When we fall into sin again, simply confess and repent and He forgives us again. We also are called to forgive one another, serve one another, and strive to meet one another's needs. That is how we become great leaders.

SEPTEMBER 14

Success

May the favor of the Lord our God rest upon us; establish the work of our hands for us—yes, establish the work of our hands.
(Psalm 90:17)

What a great blessing it is to have the Lord *"establish the work of our hands."* It is wonderful to know that we have God's blessing in all we do, and that He will give us success. We serve a great god who wants only good things for us. Of course He would delight in prospering us.

Does that mean we can do anything we want and God will make us successful? As a parent, or even a spouse, we desire our children and spouse to be successful. However, if we find they are involved in things that are harmful to themselves or others, we would not be willing to support that. Likewise, if God sees us doing things that are self-destructive, illegal, or immoral, He will not bless it.

If you love the Lord, choose to do only those things that please Him. If you put your time, energy, and finances into a career, ministry, or other endeavour that is pleasing to God, He will bless your work.

If you remain in me and my words remain in you, ask whatever you wish, and it will be given you. (John 15:7)

In Matthew 7, we are told that the Lord will give to us all we ask. Romans 8:31–32 tells us that God is so gracious to us that He didn't even spare His own son for us. Luke 11:8 tells us to ask *boldly.*

When you ask, you do not receive, because you ask with wrong motives, that you may spend what you get on your pleasures. (James 4:3)

Therefore, I would encourage you to check your motives, ask the Lord to bless whatever it is you endeavour to do, and receive His blessings. May you be successful at all you do.

SEPTEMBER 15

Mentorship

He began to speak boldly in the synagogue. When Priscilla and Aquila heard him, they invited him to their home and explained to him the way of God more adequately.
(Acts 18:26)

You are doing a great thing by continuing to come together with your spouse to further study God's word. It is right that each of you should seek to continue to grow spiritually. No matter if you are a fairly new Christian, or if you have been a Christian since childhood and are now a church leader, we all have more to learn. Even Jesus spent His time here on earth endeavouring to know exactly what the Father was saying to Him, and what the Father would have Him say and do.

It is also important that we help each other along the way. Priscilla and Aquila recognized that Apollos had a heart for God. They also realized that he was continuing to develop his understanding of the ways of God even as he taught others. Since they knew they had some additional understanding, they offered Apollos their support.

Notice that they didn't go up to Apollos in public and start berating him for not knowing enough about what he was teaching. Instead, *"they invited him to their home."* They loved him and encouraged him. They gracefully *"explained to him the way of God more adequately."* Then they encouraged Apollos to continue on with the good work he was doing.

Look around you. Who might you teach and encourage? Do you need to open your home for a Bible study? You don't have to know it all; just be willing to discuss the Bible with other people. I'm sure you will all have something to learn from one another. Perhaps there is another married couple or young adult you could mentor. Ask God to whom He is calling you and then keep your ears and eyes open for His answer. Keep on seeking God.

SEPTEMBER 16

Pay It Forward

You then, my son, be strong in the grace that is in Christ Jesus. And the things you have heard me say in the presence of many witnesses entrust to reliable men who will also be qualified to teach others.
(2 Timothy 2:1–2)

There was a movie a few years ago about a young boy who did something nice for someone. When the person wanted to repay him, he refused it. Instead he asked that person to pay the favour forward. Well as the story continued, each person who blessed another denied repayment and instead encouraged the next person to pay it forward. That is actually a very Biblical act. In Luke 14, Jesus told His host not to invite his friends and family to his banquet. Instead, Jesus said that he would be blessed if he invited the needy because they couldn't pay him back (Luke 14:14). The host would be rewarded at the resurrection. (I'm sure it is okay with Jesus if we share a meal with a friend. It is just not considered an act of ministry for which we should expect to be rewarded.)

Getting back to today's verse, we are told to take the things of God we are learning and teach them to others. It's not enough to go to church, study the word, and gain our own knowledge of God. It's not enough to encourage someone to find their own teaching. We need to be willing to share what we know. Provide opportunities for others to further develop their spirituality.

You may be surprised at the opportunities you have to enlighten others by what you learn. I remember when someone I knew first received Jesus Christ as His Saviour. The news was shared with great joy! It was interesting to hear someone say, "I thought he was already a Christian." Being a nice person and getting married or buried in a church service doesn't make you a Christian. It's not enough for people to know about Jesus; they need to *know Him*. God bless you as you continue to seek Him, and pay it forward.

SEPTEMBER 17

Now I Get It

I have much more to say to you, more than you can now bear. But when he, the Spirit of truth, comes, he will guide you into all truth. He will not speak on his own; he will speak only what he hears, and he will tell you what is yet to come.
(John 16:12–13)

Have you ever wondered why when you read a verse or section of the Bible, you suddenly understand something more than you did on all your previous readings of it? You know the words haven't changed, yet a light bulb goes on this time. There are a variety of reasons. You might have been slightly distracted on previous readings. You are going through different life experiences now. I would suggest that it is something more.

Jesus was preparing His disciples for His upcoming separation from them when He would return to heaven. At this point Jesus, knew they would not be able to *"bear"* hearing about His death and separation from them. It was not time. Jesus promised that *"the Spirit of truth"* would come to them and guide them. That Spirit also comes to us to guide our spiritual development. We cannot absorb everything God would have us understand at once. It is a process.

This works a little differently than we would expect. If, for example, I want to learn how to make a dress, I take sewing lessons. I learn all the steps, but the end goal is to have a new dress. Spiritually, however, we will never be God. We are to continually seek God and further our understanding. There will always be more. Understanding Him is in the process, not some final result.

We know also that the Son of God has come and has given us understanding, so that we may know him who is true. And we are in him who is true—even in his Son Jesus Christ. He is the true God and eternal life. (1 John 5:20)

SEPTEMBER 18

God's Love

And hope does not disappoint us, because God has poured out his love into our hearts by the Holy Spirit, whom he has given us.
(Romans 5:5)

Doesn't it feel great to be loved? To know someone thinks you are special and loveable? Think of how much your spouse loves you. Think of how much you love your spouse. Now try to imagine that God loves your spouse more than you do. That's how much God loves you, too! It's too much for us to get our heads around. Thank God for His unconditional love and blessing you with the Holy Spirit!

Receiving all that love is wonderful, but God doesn't intend for it to stop there. If it does, it will go stagnant, like a pond with no exit. The water (love) is there, but it is not good (useful). Instead, God would desire that you allow the Holy Spirit to fill you so much with His love that it overflows to those around you. It's not like if you give God's love away to others you won't have any left for yourself! Do you remember the song that goes, "Love is like a penny. If you give it away, you end up having more."

In Mark 12:29–31, Jesus told us that the most important command is to love God, and secondly to love your neighbour. In Matthew 5:44–45, Jesus goes further to say, *"Love your enemies and pray for those who persecute you, that you may be sons of your Father in heaven."* That's right; we are to show God's love to everyone, even those who aren't nice to us. (When you pray for your enemies, it doesn't mean you ask God to make them smarten up and see things your way. That's not a loving attitude.) Pray that God's will would be done. Ask God to show you, through the Holy Spirit, how to love those around you in His name.

Freely you have received, freely give. (Matthew 10:8)

SEPTEMBER 19

Check the Motives

The assembly was in confusion: Some were shouting one thing, some another. Most of the people did not even know why they were there. (Acts 19:32)

It is alarming how quickly peoples' opinions can be swayed. Ask anybody in politics or other types of public work, and they can tell you how easy you can be "tried by media," or other organized groups or individuals, without having the opportunity to present the real facts. It's okay to have different opinions, but it's not okay to make judgements without knowing all the facts.

In Acts 19, Demetrius, a silversmith, was motivated by greed. His business suffered because people were beginning to understand the truth and stopped buying the idols he was making. Instead of putting his talents to more honest endeavours, Demetrius began to rile up the craftsmen. He presented the Apostle Paul as an enemy who was out to ruin his business.

The mob mentality took over. Today's verse tells us that *"the people did not even know why they were there."* They didn't have the facts, but they had been convinced to participate in the protest. Fortunately, God used a city clerk (Acts 19:35) to provide the voice of reason and show favour upon Paul. The clerk warned the people that they were out of line, that they were in fact in danger of being charged themselves. Oops! Maybe they had better find out what was really happening!

There are many good things to stand up for, and bad things to stand against. However, I would suggest that you use great discernment and check out how those issues line up with God's word before being swept away. Check the motives. I would also suggest that you ask God how He would direct you to respond in a godly manner.

In any battle, I want to be on God's side.

SEPTEMBER 20

Life's Manual

The law of the Lord is perfect, reviving the soul. The statutes of the Lord are trustworthy, making wise the simple.
(Psalm 19:7)

Manuals don't ever seem to be "hard to put down" kind of books. How often do we get something new, and in our excitement just tear right into the packaging and start trying to use it right away? Well, that might work for simple things, but oftentimes we eventually get bogged down and have to resort to finding the manual and reading it to find out how to put the new item together and use it properly.

God is perfection. He wants what is good for those who choose to follow Him. In fact, He wants us all to follow Him and receive His many blessings, including eternal life with Him. I choose to trust that all the instructions the Lord has provided us in the Bible are for our good.

Psalm 19 tells us that if we do things His way, our very souls will be revived—that is, to be brought back to life, refreshed! This psalm goes on to tell us that by following the Lord's direction, we will have joy, understanding, and righteousness. In verse 10, we are told that the Lord's ways are *"more precious than gold"* and *"sweeter than honey."* He has given us the manual for life, the Bible, to warn us so that we may have *"great reward"* (Psalm 19:11).

I don't know about you, but this is one manual I want to read completely! Life is not simple. I want to know everything I can about how God would have me live this life! I want all the knowledge and wisdom I can get about what we are capable of and meant to do.

The Bible is one manual that's worth reading cover to cover! It is a "hard to put down" book!

SEPTEMBER 21

Keep Watch

Keep watch over yourselves and all the flock of which the Holy Spirit has made you overseers. Be shepherds of the church of God, which he bought with his own blood.
(Acts 20:28)

We may not all have a church to watch over, but each one of us has our own circle of influence. Notice that the Apostle Paul first directed the leaders of the Ephesian church, *"Keep watch over yourselves."* Paul knew that they would face spiritual battles. We all do. If we are not continually alert, we permit an opening for Satan to sneak in and mislead or ambush us. If we do not guard our own spiritual lives, we will not be able to watch over others. It's like the mother who keeps running to meet the needs of everyone else, and then finds her own health giving out.

So, our first responsibility is to keep our own spiritual lives in check. Why? For our own benefit and so that we can help watch over the *"flock of which the Holy Spirit"* has given us influence. That may be our spouse, family, friends, fellow church members, neighbours, colleagues, or others. Keep in mind that in God's world, being a leader means being servant-hearted. We are to help keep each other accountable to God in a Christ-loving manner. We are not able to control the will of others; even God doesn't choose to do that. However, we are accountable for the insights and opportunities God provides us, to keep each other in God's will.

Sometimes that may mean an actual confrontation. As much as I hate confrontation, I would hope a friend in Jesus would risk being uncomfortable for the short time, to prevent me from making eternal mistakes. Sometimes they may encourage me to continue seeking and rejoicing in the Lord. It might be a reminder of all the great things God has done for us, not the least of which is buying us *"with his own blood."*

SEPTEMBER 22

In God's Hands

Now I commit you to God and to the word of his grace, which can build you up and give you an inheritance among all those who are sanctified. (Acts 20:32)

Praise God! What a wonderful blessing the Apostle Paul gave his Ephesian friends as they parted. He had instructed them in the ways of God, and then he surrendered them into the hands of God to receive their inheritance.

It is like raising children. As our children grow, we do our best to teach them all the things they need to know to become mature, well-adjusted adults—spiritually, emotionally, and physically. What would be the point of doing all that if we never encouraged them to step out on their own and use what they have learned?

It would be like buying a beautiful new car and parking it in a garage forever so it won't get damaged. Or like making a special cake and beautifully decorating it, but only letting people look at it rather than eating it. Neither will have served the purpose for which they were intended. Parts of the car will begin to break down, and the cake will go mouldy and deteriorate. How much better it would be if they had had the opportunity to serve their purpose!

Whether it is our own children or those we have had an opportunity to mentor spiritually, eventually we must encourage them to step out in their own faith. We must surrender them into the safest place possible: God's hands. Fortunately, unlike the Apostle Paul, that doesn't necessarily mean we will never see them again. We are usually still able to walk beside them, encourage them, and help them up when they fall. Although in some situations it might be hard to release them, there will be great joy when they successfully begin to walk in their own faith.

May God give you wisdom to know when and how to release your charges.

SEPTEMBER 23

It's All His!

The earth is the Lord's, and everything in it, the world, and all who live in it.
(Psalm 24:1)

I'm not entirely sure what it will be like when I meet the Lord after leaving my earthly body, but I will have a few questions for Him. I certainly appreciate the beauty of His creations, but there are a few I just don't get. What is the upside of a mosquito, for example? Then there is the weather. I love a beautiful sunset or sunrise, even an amazing rainbow, but what's with devastating tornados or tsunamis?

Then we come to people. I'm a people person and love to be around a variety of people. I celebrate each of our unique attributes. The Lord has blessed me with a large family, some very special friendships, and many more other friends and acquaintances. I am grateful for each of them.

Confession time. There are some people I just don't understand. I can't imagine how terrible it would be to have so much hate and evil inside that they are able to commit horrible acts against other human beings. What's with that? If we all belong to God, why isn't everything perfectly ordered, as God would have it be? Well, this discussion would take more space than I have room to write about today. In fact, as long as we live in our earthly bodies, we will not have all the answers. Suffice to say, it involves Satan's fall from heaven, and Adam and Eve's original sin.

The point I would like to make today is that *everything*, lovely or not, belongs to God. God didn't make any mistakes, nor is He wasteful. No one is beyond deserving to know Jesus. No one is beyond God's reach. No one is pointless to pray for. If there is someone in your life who doesn't know Jesus, or has fallen away, do not give up hope or praying for them. They belong to Jesus!

SEPTEMBER 24

Life Is Good

Surely goodness and love will follow me all the days of my life, and I will dwell in the house of the Lord forever.
(Psalm 23:6)

There are days that don't seem so wonderful. We have all gone through such times, and I'm sure there will be more to come. Psalm 23 is a well-known chapter to turn to when you need comforting. Today's verse is the concluding verse to this chapter. God is good and loves beyond what we can comprehend. As Christians, we can rest assured that we will live in eternity with the Lord Himself. What could be better? There is nothing any of us can go through today that is not worth it for such a great promise.

God loves at all times. He may not always love our choices, but He always loves us. He is always with us. God wants good things for us! He wants to bless us. He wants to supply all our needs. He wants to encourage us. We can't earn His love or blessings. He freely offers them to us.

King David, the author of today's verse, certainly had times of trouble. He even made some big mistakes. However, David knew that God still loved him. He recognized God's great mercy and grace. King David knew that we are not smiled upon and loved by God only when we are being good. Nor is God's love a fickle or temporary thing. It is unchangeable, unshakable, and permanent!

Bask in His love. Receive all His goodness. Admire His beauty all around you. Enjoy each day He has provided you. Choose to live in His light always.

Rejoice in His promise to receive us into His house for all eternity.

SEPTEMBER 25

By His Spirit

"Not by might nor by power, but by my Spirit," says the Lord Almighty. (Zechariah 4:6)

Whew! What a relief it is that I don't have to do all things on my own! I just can't do it! God has blessed each of us with various talents, gifts, and knowledge. However, He did not supply everyone with everything. In other words, He did not make a bunch of little gods. We are created to be interdependent on each other, and totally dependent on Him.

Today I am not addressing those things that we have been given the ability and direction to do, in the will of God. Today I am talking about those *"mighty mountain[s]"* (Zechariah 4:7) you will have occasion to face. There are times when you are not called to rely on your own strength or human resources. This is the time to call on God's grace as an act of faith. This is the time to admit that the solution is beyond ourselves, but never beyond what God can do.

It is reassuring to know that the Lord has everything under His control. Confess your need to Him. Pray for His intervention. Take time to listen for what He would say to you. Watch intently for His answer. Trust that His answer is best, even when it is not what you might expect.

Remember that when we read about answers to prayer in the Bible, there is often a waiting period. We might read about the answer in the next verse or chapter, but in real-time there may be months or years in between. Sarah and Abraham were promised a child. It was many years later (even though Sarah was well beyond child-bearing years) when Sarah became pregnant and gave birth to Isaac. Other times, the answer may come very quickly.

Trust in the wisdom and timing of the Lord. Remember: *"Be joyful always; pray continually; give thanks in all circumstances, for this is God's will for you in Christ Jesus"* (1 Thessalonians 5:16–18).

SEPTEMBER 26

Praising the Lord Together

I will extol the Lord at all times; his praise will always be on my lips. My soul will boast in the Lord; let the afflicted hear and rejoice. Glorify the Lord with me; let us exalt his name together.
(Psalm 34:1–3)

Today, my husband returns home after having been away on the missions field. I have missed him very much and I am very excited to pick him up from the airport. I also look forward with great anticipation to hearing the stories of all the things the Lord has done for the team, and through their work. Knowing that the Lord has touched the lives of so many needy people is encouraging enough, but it is exciting and encouraging to hear individual stories.

God is good and His provision is amazing! I can't imagine keeping to myself all the marvellous blessings He has provided. In fact, I believe that if I did, He would no longer have a purpose in revealing His mighty hand to me.

Even in those times when life does not appear perfect in my eyes, I know that the Lord exists and He is good. The encouragement of shared blessings helps me to remember this *"at all times."* Attending church, Bible studies, prayer meetings, and other forms of Christian fellowship provides opportunities to praise the Lord with others. It is an amazing experience to sing worship songs to the Lord together, share answers to prayer, and just stand together seeking Him.

It is not always possible to join together with others. In fact, it is very good to spend time alone with the Lord as well. When I bubble over with joy in the Lord, or when I need encouragement to praise Him and nobody is around, I seek out a Christian radio or TV program or call a friend. Don't hide His light!

SEPTEMBER 27

Calming the Storm

A gentle answer turns away wrath, but a harsh word stirs up anger. (Proverbs 15:1)

Nobody likes to be snapped at or be put down. A harsh word can very quickly exacerbate a situation from seemingly nothing to an all-out screaming match. In fact, not the actual event, but hurts and misunderstandings from the past often fuel new confrontations. Once the focus is lost, it is hard to recover and repair the damage. If not handled well, this new conflict can in turn fuel yet another attack.

Remember that a *"gentle answer turns away wrath."* I'm not talking about the passive aggressive, controlling type of calm answer. That does not lead to a peaceful resolution, rather a feeling of power or helplessness. This *"gentle answer"* is calm and loving, in fitting with 1 Corinthians 13. This answer says, "I see you are upset and I am concerned for you."

Discuss which type of person you think Jesus would be. Which type of person do you think God would have you be? Can you think of any situations you handled well with a gentle answer, and thus defused anger? Can you recall a situation when you spoke harshly or responded in anger to someone else's harsh words? If the poorly handled situation involved your spouse, take the time right now to repent and forgive one another.

"A hot-tempered man stirs up dissension, but a patient man calms a quarrel" (Proverbs 15:18). It is not as simple as deciding not to be harsh or hot-tempered, or to be gentle and patient. Along with that conviction, you must ask God to do His work in your through the Holy Spirit. Ask your spouse to pray with you. If you have a particular person or environment you find difficult to remain gentle in, ask your spouse to pray with you specifically for that situation. There is power in the cord of three.

SEPTEMBER 28

Run!

The prudent see danger and take refuge, but the simple keep going and suffer for it.
(Proverbs 27:12)

If a tree was falling on you, would you stand there and just pray for God to make it fall in a different direction, or maybe return it to its upright position? If you saw a truck losing control and heading for you, would you just continue walking and assume the Lord will protect you from its path? No! You would run for cover!

This verse encourages us to do the same when we see the danger of sin. Run! Take refuge! Whether it's pride of life, lust of the flesh, or lust of the eyes, be alert to the risk factors of sin. Just don't go there! Run away!

When my children were young, we had a book series on life skills which came complete with tapes, songs, and puppets. One of its lesson songs was about "garbage in, garbage out." That principle applies well to our food intake and how our body performs. It also applies to our minds, in how we can govern our thoughts through what we read, watch, or listen to. It involves our spirits as well, in our choice on whether we allow the Holy Spirit to guide us or expose ourselves to the influence of the evil one.

The most obvious lesson here is to purposefully avoid those things that you know will tempt you to sin. I would suggest you seek to go further into that refuge. Fill yourselves with *"whatever is true, whatever is noble, whatever is right, whatever is pure, whatever is lovely, whatever is admirable"* (Philippians 4:8). Remember, where there is light, darkness cannot exist!

Ask the Lord to reveal to you any area of sin in your life you might not be aware of. Invite the Holy Spirit to give you wisdom and discernment in regards to your areas of weakness. Ask your spouse—or, if not appropriate, a trusted Christian friend—to help keep you accountable. Do whatever it takes to protect yourself from Satan's grip!

SEPTEMBER 29

Loving Obedience

Sacrifice and offering you did not desire, but my ears you have pierced; burnt offerings and sin offerings you did not require.
(Psalm 40:6)

"God, if I do this or that, will You still accept me?" How many times do we find ourselves slipping into this worldly way of thinking? We know that we don't earn our salvation, but that we have received it by grace. Jesus did not die for those who were "good enough." None of us are worthy in ourselves. We do not *earn* God's blessings or answers to prayer.

It all comes back to our motivation. If you do things to earn your spot in God's realm, rather than as a desire to express obedience out of your love for Him, you have missed the mark. The phrase *"my ears you have pierced"* refers to the custom of piercing a servant's ear as a sign of his voluntary perpetual service to his master.

If you find yourself participating in a ministry just because we all have to do our part, or because you think nobody else will do it, then I suggest you re-evaluate your role in that ministry. We are called to fast and pray in some circumstances. However, if you are fasting as a way of earning God's attention to your cause, again I would suggest you re-evaluate. If you read your Bible regularly, pray, go to church, or do any other religious activity because you are supposed to, I suggest you re-evaluate.

Any type of sacrifice or offering done out of your desire to love the Lord and be obedient to Him is good. It will please God, not indebt Him to pay you back in some way. However, nothing you give will be able to out-give God. When you voluntarily give Him your heart, He will pour His blessings upon you out of His love for you.

May your prayer be, *"I desire to do your will, O my God; your law is within my heart"* (Psalm 40:8).

SEPTEMBER 30

The Lord's Protection

Do not withhold your mercy from me, O Lord; may your love and your truth always protect me.
(Psalm 40:11)

Satan looks for every opportunity to deceive us and sidetrack us from keeping our hearts and eyes fully on God. God knows that. Jesus Himself spent forty days in the wilderness resisting the temptations of the devil. He was tempted in the flesh (hunger), His pride was challenged (to prove God's provision), and His ego was challenged (through Satan's offer for Jesus to reign over the world) (see Matthew 4 and Luke 4).

We, too, face temptations. We struggle with the lust of the flesh, coveting things we see in the media or things that others have. We struggle with pride, building ourselves up too much or criticising ourselves. We struggle with lust of the eyes, wanting control over things big or small. Unlike Jesus, who was free of sin, every one of us is sinful.

We must allow God to pour His mercy on us. We need to rely on His love and truth to protect us. We need these for ourselves and for others. When God reveals sin in our lives, it is important to repent, then receive His merciful forgiveness. Don't keep bringing it back up and flogging yourself with your past! Similarly, when someone you know has sinned and *repented*, you too should be forgiving. Don't keep bringing their transgression up and flogging them with it.

Let us rely on God's love and truth for our protection. The closer you are to God, the better you will know His ways. The better you know God's truth, the less susceptible you will be to the devil's lies. As you seek God's truths, He will reveal them to you.

Thank the Lord for His love and mercy for you, and through you to others. There is no greater protection than the Lord's!

OCTOBER 1

Recipe for Joy

You love righteousness and hate wickedness; therefore God, your God, has set you above your companions by anointing you with the oil of joy. (Psalm 45:7)

I feel sorry for people I have known who are always angry and bitter. These people dwell on offences in the past, feel unfairly treated, and think like victims. It must be miserable to always be in such a negative state. What a life!

Do you want to be joyful? Today's verse sums it up: *"love righteousness and hate wickedness"*! Firstly, you are to set your heart on those things that are righteous, those things which you know are of God and are pleasing to Him. This is where you are to focus and spend your energy, time, and money. Secondly, you are to *"hate wickedness."* Do not participate or give your attention to those things which you know are evil.

Will you always feel joyful? Probably not. Life happens, and you will allow yourself to glance away at times. You might, for example, allow yourself to get angry at a person who steals from you, but you can choose not to stay focused on the offence. What they did was wrong and wicked. Yes, you have to deal with the results, but the choice is yours whether to stay in that state of anger or hurt or turn your eyes back to righteous things.

I'm not talking about the notion of mind over matter. I'm not talking about determining to use your willpower to stay happy. I'm talking about real *joy*, that type of joy that only comes from a relationship with God. It is important to choose to be positive, but do so by keeping your focus of the things of God, not living in denial. Allow Him to fill you with His joy.

You have a choice about what you read, watch, participate in, and talk about. You have a choice to live in and spread God's joy or to wallow in the mud of negativism and wickedness. If you choose righteousness, the promise is that God will anoint *"you with the oil of joy."*

OCTOBER 2

Is It Important to Eternity?

Don't have anything to do with foolish and stupid arguments, because you know they produce quarrels.
(2 Timothy 2:23)

This verse contains very wise advice from the Apostle Paul to his spiritual son, Timothy. As you read through the New Testament, notice how Jesus handled quarrels. For the most part, Jesus would answer with words to make those involved really think about their heart attitude. There were times, however, when Jesus took a stand—for example, when He turned over the tables of the people who were cheating others right inside the temple.

When trying to assess how important an issue is to pursue, think first in terms of eternity. Will this make a difference in the big picture? When you come face to face with Jesus, will you feel confident that you made the right decision in conceding or pursuing an issue?

When a disagreement involves your spouse, consider also if the issue is really worth damaging your relationship. Ask yourself if your stand is the only right one. Are you holding your ground for God's purpose or for your own ego? Could you be misunderstanding your spouse's intentions? In a loving relationship, one does not intentionally harm another.

Please do not think that I'm promoting lack of communication. Nor am I suggesting that you just take what you perceive as abuse without question. Not only is there nothing wrong with telling your spouse that your feelings are hurt or that something they said or did irritated you, it is good to be honest with each other. However, I would caution you to check your own attitude first, and then carefully choose to use loving words in wise timing. Clarify your concerns and understanding. Your unity is important now and for eternity.

OCTOBER 3

God Help!

God is our refuge and strength, an ever-present help in trouble.
(Psalm 46:1)

What's the first thing you do when you find yourself in a difficult situation? Many people try to bail themselves out. There's nothing wrong with using the intelligence and skills the Lord has given us if it is for good purposes.

Suppose this situation is beyond you. You may think of who you can call upon for help. You may think of your spouse, parent, adult child, or friend. There's nothing wrong with that. We are supposed to support one another and carry each other's burdens. I certainly don't mind helping someone out in a pinch if it's within my power to do so.

Suppose nobody can help out in this circumstance. Now what? Oh! When all the human strength and safety nets are exhausted, people turn to God. This very human way of approaching life is out of alignment with God's will.

As the verse says, *"God is our refuge and strength."* He is always available! When you call on God, you don't get a busy signal or a recorded message saying, "Please leave a message. I'll get back to you when I can." He is ever-present. According to Psalm 46:11, *"The Lord Almighty is with us; the God of Jacob is our fortress."* Why waste time? Go to the Lord first! He's already there and He is your fortress, or secure place.

When you call on God, trust in Him to answer. Through the Holy Spirit, He may place a thought in your mind. He may bring someone else to help you (you may know this person or you may not), or He may miraculously change the circumstances. No matter how He answers, trust that His way is best.

Are you facing troubling times? Then call out, "God, help!" Listen for His answer in His timing.

OCTOBER 4

The Sacrifice God Is Looking For

The sacrifices of God are a broken spirit; a broken and contrite heart, O God, you will not despise.
(Psalm 51:17)

This psalm was written by King David after he had committed adultery with Bathsheba. Nathan, the prophet, came to David and revealed God's awareness of David's sin (1 Samuel 12). King David had really blown it. He had given in to the temptation of lust. He had used his power to get what he wanted. He had committed adultery. Then, instead of repenting that sin, he added to it by lying, manipulating, and ordering a man murdered to cover his own mistakes. How foolish he was to think he could hide anything from God, or erase his sin on his own!

David isn't the only one who tried to cover up sin. Adam and Eve also tried to cover up their sins in the Garden of Eden. They tried to hide what they had done from God. When they were discovered, they started making excuses. How human it is to try to hide or excuse sin.

God knew the truth for Adam and Eve, as well as King David, and He knows the truth for each one of us. He does not ask us to pay for our sins (although there may be earthly consequences). Jesus did that for us already. What the Lord desires is our *"broken spirit."* He wants us to acknowledge our sins with a *"contrite heart,"* to be sorrowful of our mistakes, repentant, willing to confess our wrongdoings, and take ownership.

As God forgave Adam and Eve and King David, He will forgive you and me. He *"will not despise"* you, no matter your sin. It is the sin itself that He despises. God loves you and will be pleased with you for your confession to Him.

So, drop the excuses and confess all to our loving Father in heaven. Receive His love and forgiveness. Invite the Holy Spirit to direct you by changing your heart and creating a new spirit within you. Give God the sacrifice He desires. Give Him thanks with a grateful heart.

OCTOBER 5

Standing in the Gap

I looked for a man among them who would build up the wall and stand before me in the gap on behalf of the land so I would not have to destroy it, but I found none.
(Ezekiel 22:30)

The gap God is speaking about in this verse is between God and man. The man (person) is the intercessor who prays on behalf of another. God promises that if even one person steps in to pray for another, He will hear them and not destroy the guilty. That prayer helps build a protective wall around the person when they have allowed a breach, or committed a sin (broken their relationship with God).

There is nobody closer to me than my spouse. Apart from God, no one knows me as well as my husband. When we became married, we became as one: *"'and the two will become one flesh.' So they are no longer two, but one"* (Mark 10:8). Therefore, my husband has a very important stake in my relationship with God. I'm grateful for the prayers my husband makes on my behalf, and I pray for him daily. I trust that my husband will lovingly confront me if he recognizes ongoing sin in my life. I also trust that I can confess my sins to him for his prayer support and accountability.

Therefore confess your sins to each other and pray for each other so that you may be healed. The prayer of a righteous man is powerful and effective.
(James 5:16)

I know my husband would want me free of anything that separates me from God and allows the enemy into my life. My husband is a righteous man, so I know he is *"powerful and effective"* in his prayers.

How fortunate we are that God has blessed us with loving Christian spouses! How blessed we are to be able to lift each other up in prayer. Thank God that He has provided a third strand (our spouse) to fill the gap and keep us firmly attached to the centre strand (Jesus).

A cord of three strands is not quickly broken (Ecclesiastes 4:12)

OCTOBER 6

Make It Count

Teach us to number our days aright, that we may gain a heart of wisdom. (Psalm 90:12)

In my email today, I received one of those forwarded messages. It talks about contemplating what you would do if you received $86,400 a day in your bank account. The restrictions are that you must spend it each day or lose what's left, and you cannot simply transfer to another account. The other catch is that it will stop at some point, but you have no idea when that might be.

Just imagine! At first, it would be easy for most people to spend all the money, but after a while it would take more thought to find ways to use it up. You don't want to waste any of it!

Now, the punchline: it's not money, but seconds in the day. Each day you receive 86,400 seconds. No more, and no less. You cannot transfer it to the next day. What you don't use wisely is gone forever. Each day, you get a new 86,400 seconds. It will stop at some point without warning. Will you have accomplished the important things?

It is too easy to take for granted that you will have a tomorrow. "I'll spend more time with my family when we go on vacation or when I retire. I'll volunteer more, be more involved in missions, or help out my neighbour or the needy when I finish what I'm doing now."

Do you get my point? God has given each one of us a set amount of time. You don't get more or less if you work harder or procrastinate more. With God's wisdom, we need to *"number our days aright."* What balance do you need to find? It's similar to budgeting your finances. You need to recognize the amount of time you have and re-evaluate how you spend it regularly. What was balanced for one season of your life is not necessarily balanced in another season. Enjoy your supply and use it wisely!

OCTOBER 7

Hidden Treasure

...then you will understand the fear of the Lord and find the knowledge of God.
(Proverbs 2:5)

Fear of the Lord is a good thing. This "fear" doesn't refer to a feeling of dread, but rather of awe or reverence. It is not that we have a mean master from whom we tremble. We revere (have great respect for) the Lord and seek *"the knowledge of God."*

Proverbs 2 encourages us to accept the words of God. We are to listen to God and seek to understand what He is saying. God tells us through this verse to seek to understand His word as we would hidden treasure. Then we will understand His reverence and His ways. The thing about this hidden treasure is that we are sure it exists and there is plenty for all! Our treasure map is His word.

Unlike most treasure maps, we start from the "x" rather than working towards it. Our treasure is God Himself, given to us through the sacrifice of Jesus. It is He who enlightens us as to how to walk out our lives. Typical treasure maps start from some random point and hide the clues to make the final goal difficult to reach. Our treasure is available to all who want it; typical treasure is only for the person who manages to find it. Our treasure is meant to be shared and multiplied; typical treasure can be used up and usually promotes greed and hoarding. Our treasure brings peace, love, and joy; typical treasure brings deception and separation.

If we seek to understand God, He promises us His wisdom, knowledge, understanding, discernment, and protection from evil. The more wisdom of God we attain, the less Satan is able to deceive or tempt us.

Which treasure do you really want?

Teach me your way, O Lord... (Psalm 86:11)

OCTOBER 8

Sex

The wife's body does not belong to her alone but also to her husband. In the same way, the husband's body does not belong to him alone but also to his wife. Do not deprive each other except by mutual consent and for a time, so that you may devote yourselves to prayer.
(1 Corinthians 7:4–5)

Today's title likely got your attention—some people with great intrigue, other people with shock. We as a human race have really done a bad job on this topic.

God created man and woman. He created us in such a way that necessitated intimate sexual relationships to create new life and sustain our race. God made sex, in a loving relationship, to be pleasurable. Sex in and of itself is not a shameful, nor an embarrassing thing. In the proper context of a monogamous marriage, sex is a gift of God. It is the most intimate act possible between two human beings. We are to be willing to share our bodies with our spouse in this intimate act to meet each other's sexual needs. The only exception for depriving one another is *"by mutual consent and for a time, so that you may devote yourselves to prayer."* Only your relationship with God should come before that with your spouse.

Unfortunately, the evil in this world has taken this gift and twisted it. I'm sure you do not need me to list the many ways sexuality has been perverted. Satan has taken this blessing and turned it into something shameful, embarrassing, dirty, lustful, and guilt-producing. It is used as the most horrific, offensive act possible. Compromising someone's sexual purity by force has become the ultimate act of degradation.

Healthy sexuality in marriage is a gift from God. God only gives good gifts. What we do with this gift is up to us. We can misuse it, abuse it, or enjoy it.

OCTOBER 9

Out with the Bad

Create in me a pure heart, O God, and renew a steadfast spirit within me. (Psalm 51:10)

I recently heard someone say that you don't become pure by adding more pureness; you become pure by removing the impurity. I realized how true this is. If you take a container of contaminated water and add more clean water, all the water is contaminated. If you put a rotten apple in with a bunch of good apples, the rotten apple does not become good; in fact, it makes the good apples rot.

As we seek to draw closer to God, we often think of adding more of Him to our lives in order to become more Christ-like (Christian). Jesus was, is, and always will be sinless. To become more Christ-like, we really need to remove sin from our lives. We need to remove sin to protect the goodness within ourselves which we received when we invited Jesus into our lives. To ignore sin is to allow our goodness to be contaminated.

How do you remove the sin? First, you need to be aware of it. Ask the Lord to reveal any sin in your life. Next, you must be willing to give it up. There is no point going to God and asking Him to make you pure if you aren't willing to give up that which is sinful. In John 5:14, when Jesus healed the sick, He told them to stop sinning. They could not remain cleansed if they continued in their sin. (Jesus also clearly stated in John 9 that illness was not always a direct result of sin.) Finally, ask the Lord to continue to work in your life *"and renew a steadfast spirit within [you]."*

We are sinful creatures by nature, and this will have to be an ongoing process. God will not get tired of us coming to Him time and again asking for forgiveness and helping to make our lives purer. It is His pleasure to help us walk through our lives with our hearts intent on purity in His sight.

OCTOBER 10

Enjoy the Journey

That everyone may eat and drink, and find satisfaction in all his toil— this is the gift of God.
(Ecclesiastes 3:13)

Our Father in heaven loves us. He gives us good gifts and wants us to enjoy them. We may not always understand His ways or the plans He has for us, but we must resolve to do our best to do good. It's okay; we are allowed and even encouraged to enjoy the good gifts He gives us.

We have been given this opportunity to live in the time and place God selected just for us. It was meant as a blessing, not a trial. God would have us enjoy our journey through life here on earth. Yes, there is work to be done, but God would have us *"accept [our] lot and be happy in [our] work"* (Ecclesiastes 5:19). It was never God's intention for us to just survive through each day. As the Apostle Paul reminded the church in Colossae: *"Whatever you do, work at it with all your heart, as working for the Lord, not for men"* (Colossians 3:23).

Look around you at God's beauty. My husband is a wonderful role model to me in this regard. I can sometimes get my head down into the task at hand and miss just being in the moment. My husband will stop me and point out the sunset, a beautiful butterfly, or an interesting bird. He has even phoned me from work, telling me to look out the window at the beautiful sunrise. Has God provided you with a job? Praise God! Has He provided you with a time of rest? Praise God! Has He blessed you with loving family and friends? Praise God!

God has blessed me so abundantly that it is hard to know where to begin to give thanks. As a Christian, no matter what your situation is, you too can list the many ways in which God has blessed you. Enjoy your life! It is a gift from God.

OCTOBER 11

Reconciliation

Not only is this so, but we also rejoice in God through our Lord Jesus Christ, through whom we have now received reconciliation.
(Romans 5:11)

Reconciliation is the result of conflict, struggles, and finally forgiveness and a change of heart. I know of many broken relationships or separations that have fortunately been reconciled. A son had completely removed himself from his family for almost a year, and then, like the prodigal son (Luke 15), he returned with some anxiety, but was welcomed back into relationship and was reconciled to his family. Another son struggled with drug addiction, but eventually chose his family over the drugs. I know of a couple whose marriage relationship broke down and they separated ways. Five years later, they were reconciled and continue to live as a married couple to this day. Unfortunately, I also know of many conflicts that have not been resolved and have not yet been reconciled.

What a blessing we have in Jesus Christ! *"For God so loved the world that he gave his one and only Son…"* (John 3:16). Through this son, Jesus Christ, we have *"received reconciliation"* to God. Jesus *"justified"* us by His blood (Romans 5:9), choosing to intervene and sacrificing His very life to bring about our reconciliation with God. We have the opportunity to have a relationship with God because our sins are no longer counted against us.

It is God's desire that we should all be reconciled to Him. We have been blessed with this reconciliation and now are charged with bringing the message of God's grace to others.

We are therefore Christ's ambassadors, as though God were making his appeal through us. We implore you on Christ's behalf: Be reconciled to God. (2 Corinthians 5:20)

Rejoice in God for His great mercy in reconciling with us while we were yet sinners! How are you using your *"ministry of reconciliation"* (2 Corinthians 5:18)?

OCTOBER 12

You Do Affect Others

For just as through the disobedience of the one man the many were made sinners, so also through the obedience of the one man the many will be made righteous.
(Romans 5:19)

You don't have a choice. Every word you speak to others, every action you take or fail to take, affects others. I've heard of people who failed at a marriage relationship and then claimed that their actions have no effect on the children. I've heard of people who chose to take illicit drugs and then claimed that it was none of their family's business. I've heard of people who rejected Jesus, claiming it has no effect on their Christian loved ones. Whether it is denial, ignorance, or justification, none of these examples ring true.

What do you suppose Adam was thinking when he disobeyed God? Do you think he knew or thought about the effect it would have on all mankind? It appears he was only concerned about *his* present lust. How different is that from the poor choices we make? Then there is the obedience of Jesus. He was obedient to God even to death for the benefit of all. We, too, can have a positive effect on others when we are obedient to God.

What you say and do may not affect all mankind forever, but it will have a greater effect than you realize. How your words or behaviour affect one person for God's glory radiates out through their lives to others, and for generations to come. None of us are perfect, but our goal should be to be obedient to God at all times.

Our prayer should be that we are in alignment with God's will and that we are obedient to Him. Our desire should be to know His will and bring glory to His name. We should desire to be used to direct others to Jesus for forgiveness, reconciliation, healing, and salvation. May God forgive our poor choices and failures. May He prevent our actions from damaging anyone else's relationship with Him.

OCTOBER 13

Unknown Spouse

For as I walked around and looked carefully at your objects of worship, I even found an altar with this inscription: to an unknown god.
(Acts 17:23)

Suppose, as a single person, that you contemplated whom you would marry. There appeared to be a few possibilities. You were not confident enough in your ability to choose the right person, so you covered your bases and married several people. You married each person in different ceremonies in different faiths. That should do it, right? Of course not.

I can't even imagine the complications of having more than one spouse, let alone each one having a different set of values and beliefs. Then throw in trying to manage and support a household big enough to respect all the various personalities and needs. How loved and devoted to you do you think each one would be, knowing that you weren't entirely sure if they are what you want? Do you think they would each be completely devoted to you? Do you think you would be their primary concern?

The people of Athens failed at making a decision as to which god they were to honour. They foolishly thought they could cover their bases by worshiping all the gods to which they were introduced. As Christians, you already know that you cannot worship the one true God and a few others just in case. You know the importance of keeping your focus on God and not the distractions of other idols (money, work, ego, etc.). How blessed you are for making that decision and commitment!

As a spouse, I would encourage you to also value the companion you have chosen. Avoid crowding so many other things into your life that your spouse becomes only one of many interests. How blessed each of you will be when you devote yourselves to one another! Know your spouse!

OCTOBER 14

How Do You Treat Your Gift?

Do not offer the parts of your body to sin, as instruments of wickedness, but rather offer yourselves to God, as those who have been brought from death to life; and offer the parts of your body to him as instruments of righteousness.
(Romans 6:13)

How exciting it is to think that God will continue to use me to glorify Him! I think it is fairly safe to say that anyone reading this would agree that it is definitely preferable to offer ourselves to God as *"instruments of righteousness,"* than to sin as *"instruments of wickedness."*

Imagine you are going to give a gift to someone special in your life. Do you just pick up any old tattered thing and toss it at them? More likely, you will carefully select something you consider very precious and/or thoughtful especially for that person. You might even take extra care to wrap it in beautiful decorative wrappings. Then, when you present it, you'll want to have their attention and offer it to them lovingly. You will probably wait in anticipation as they open the gift to see the joy it brings to them.

What about your gift to God? Is your attitude, "Take me as I am, like it or not"? Or do you think, "Here's what's left of me after I finish everything else"?

God should be the most important relationship in your life. If that is so, you should desire to offer Him the most perfect "you." Do you give Him your best time, energy, and attention? Do you take care of the person He has made you? What about your spiritual being, your emotional being, your physical being?

Do you not know that your body is a temple of the Holy Spirit, who is in you, whom you have received from God? You are not your own; you were bought at a price. Therefore honor God with your body. (1 Corinthians 6:19–20)

May God be pleased with His instrument.

OCTOBER 15

Do You Remember?

We will not hide them from their children; we will tell the next generation the praiseworthy deeds of the Lord, his power, and the wonders he has done.
(Psalm 78:4)

Can you believe those Israelites? God did so much for them and performed many miracles, but they kept turning away from Him! He brought them out of slavery in Egypt, He protected them, He provided food and water for them in the wilderness, He brought them to the Promised Land and gave it to them, and He provided leadership for them. How could they forget? How could they turn away from His ways?

Are you and I any different? What has God done for us? The most obvious is that He sent Jesus to take on our sins and die for us, thus providing us with complete pardon and eternal life. We'll get more specific. Like the manna and water He provided for the Israelites in the desert, what concrete things has He provided for you? I could list some of the blessings and provision in my life, but I would challenge you to really think about what God has done for you. What times can you look back on when you knew God was with you, when He went before you and provided for you? What specific answers to prayer have you experienced? What things have happened that you know were only possible through God?

Don't hide what God has done! This verse isn't addressing just biological children, but also other spiritual children. By sharing the *"praiseworthy deeds of the Lord,"* we not only pass on a teaching, but refresh our own memories. It makes us reflect and acknowledge the power of God and *"the wonders he has done."* We must never take His blessings for granted. As well as enlightening others, telling others about how God has worked, and is working, in our own lives helps us not to forget. It helps us to maintain our focus, so we won't get distracted or find that we've turned away from God, for that is a very dangerous place to be!

OCTOBER 16

How to Honour God

...that all may honor the Son just as they honor the Father. He who does not honor the Son does not honor the Father, who sent him.
(John 5:23)

What does it mean to honour someone? We use this word as a respectful title, as in addressing a person in a certain profession, such as a judge. We talk about honouring someone when they have accomplished a particular goal, as in a graduation ceremony. We honour people by attributing them glory, distinction, or fame. So, how do we honour God?

My son, give glory to the Lord, the God of Israel, and give him the praise. Tell me what you have done; do not hide it from me. (Joshua 7:19)

Tell Him the truth! Be honest with God! Just as it would not be appropriate to lie or stretch the truth before a judge, it is not honouring to God to be anything less than completely honest to Him. As John 14:15 says, *"If you love me, you will obey what I command."* Be obedient to God. Man's laws (enforced by judges) are meant to be for the good of all. More so, the things God instructs us to do are for our good. Respect Him by obeying His word without arguing or complaining.

You can show honour to God by worshipping and praising Him. God created the world! God sent His son to die for us, and sent the Holy Spirit to be our counsellor! Those are only a few of the amazing things God has done that are worth acknowledging. He is worthy of praise! Honour God by spreading the word. Tell others about Him: *"Therefore go and make disciples of all nations"* (Matthew 28:19). He is glorious and famous!

What things in your life demonstrate your honour to God? Are there any areas in which you are showing disrespect or contempt towards God?

Those who honor me I will honor, but those who despise me will be disdained. (1 Samuel 2:30)

OCTOBER 17

You Are Not Alone

As I was with Moses, so I will be with you; I will never leave you nor forsake you.
(Joshua 1:5)

God is with us at all times. During the good times and healthy times, that's great! We enjoy our relationship with God and rejoice in Him and give Him glory. But what about the not-so-good times? What about when disaster hits, our health fails, or things just aren't working out the way we would wish?

God is with us then, too! He has promised that He *"will never leave [us] nor forsake [us]."* No matter the reason we face difficulties or feel all alone, God is with us. He may not miraculously transport us to a better place, but He will walk us through the situation.

Things certainly weren't always rosy for Moses! Moses was given a big responsibility. At times, he felt overwhelmed and would have preferred a different assignment from God. Moses' prayers were not always answered immediately or in the way he would have liked. Moses wandered around the desert for forty years with a bunch of rebellious people for whom he was responsible! Did God give up and leave Moses and the Israelites? Of course not! Did Moses give up on God? No, he needed God all the more.

Does that mean that we are faithless failures when we feel all alone? No. Even Jesus felt unable to bear His circumstances alone and feared that the Father had deserted Him for a time on the cross. Jesus cried out, *"My God, my God, why have you forsaken me?"* (Matthew 27:46) God of course had not deserted Him, but had to allow Jesus' death. By dying and then rising from the dead, Jesus broke the hold of death for all time. With the Father, Jesus accomplished eternal life for all who choose to follow Him. Take comfort in knowing God is with you, too. You are not alone. He has a purpose for you.

OCTOBER 18

Choice of Spouse

The Lord, the God of heaven, who brought me out of my father's household and my native land and who spoke to me and promised me on oath, saying, "To your offspring I will give this land"—he will send his angel before you so that you can get a wife for my son from there.
(Genesis 24:7)

Abraham spoke with God about a wife for his son. In Genesis 24, Abraham sent his servant out to find a woman who knew the one true God, to become the wife of his son, Isaac. Our North American society doesn't practise the tradition of parents choosing spouses for their children. However, as Christians, we should certainly be talking to God about it! I have been praying since my children were young that God would direct them to godly women to be their wives. He has answered that prayer for one of them already!

Did someone pray for your future spouse before you married? Some of you will be able to immediately respond to that question positively. Others may not be aware of the prayers that were sent out on your behalf. I will assume that if you're reading this devotional, God has blessed you with a Christian spouse.

If you have unmarried children, are you praying for their future spouses? How about your nieces, nephews, or unmarried friends? Are you talking to God about blessing them with a Christian spouse? It is never too early.

Is there only one right person for each of us to marry? That is a topic of great debate. We do have Biblical direction, including, *"Do not be yoked together with unbelievers"* (2 Corinthians 6:14). That is because God wants only what is good for us. The unbeliever *may* accept Christ at a later date, but there will be conflict and risk that the believer will be led astray.

Pray that the people in your circle of influence would choose their spouses wisely.

OCTOBER 19

Thank God for Your Purpose

It does not, therefore, depend on man's desire or effort, but on God's mercy. (Romans 9:16)

I know so many wonderful men and women of God! I know several great speakers who are able to instruct others in the word of God in very effective ways. I know of people God has used to heal others in need. I know of people who have given up careers that they trained for and invested in to follow God's will for their lives in entirely different directions than they had planned. I know people who are constantly serving others in a quiet "behind the scenes" manner. Although I may admire their faithfulness, and rejoice in their fruitfulness, it is not up to me to determine to be just like any one of them.

God has very definite purposes for each one of our lives. There is no point in any of us coveting the desire for God to use us like someone else. Rather, our desires and prayers should be that God would direct our paths and use us for the purposes He created us for.

But who are you, O man, to talk back to God? "Shall what is formed say to him who formed it, 'Why did you make me like this?'" (Romans 9:20)

We cannot earn our righteousness. We are not entitled to blessings. Those who try to deserve God's blessings through work will be sorely disappointed. As Romans 9:32 tells us, we must pursue righteousness by faith so as not to stumble over the *"stumbling stone."*

Thank God that He created us perfectly for what He purposes us to be. Thank God for His patience when we don't get it right. Thank God for His mercy in that He is a God of second chances when we set our hearts upon Him.

This definitely doesn't mean we are to sit back and let the world happen. Our desire needs to be that we be used by God for His glory. We are to be willing to put effort into the things He directs us to do.

Not sure of your purpose? Ask your creator.

OCTOBER 20

A Love Like God's

I will declare that your love stands firm forever, that you established your faithfulness in heaven itself.
(Psalm 89:2)

In a world of self-centredness and fickleness, it is comforting to know that the love of God is permanent—not permanent *for now* or until it is no longer convenient, but permanent as in never-ever wavering. God's love is not dependent on how well we do or how deserving we are. God's love is *"established [in his] faithfulness in heaven itself"*!

Nothing else in this world is certain. Jobs change, friends change, health changes, and circumstances are always changing. God's love never changes. What an encouraging thing to share with others! What a comforting word to remind ourselves! What a great principle to base our marriage relationships on!

As God's love for us *"stands firm forever,"* so should we determine to love our spouses with unwavering faithfulness. God will never look at us and say, "Oh! You aren't what I expected. I've changed my mind. Erase. Erase. Erase." I have never heard a marriage vow yet that goes, "I'll love you as long as you still look good, or as long as you are a good provider, or as long as you don't mess up."

God loves us at all times and through everything! Is it your intent to love your spouse faithfully at all times and through everything? God didn't wait to see how well we loved Him before He invested His love in us. Are you willing to love your spouse regardless of how good a job they appear to be doing of loving you?

If you each choose to remain in God, basing your marriage relationship on His firm foundation, you are yet to be amazed at how much deeper your love for one another will grow. You will continually be amazed at how permanent and secure that love will be.

OCTOBER 21

Satan Can't Touch Me!

Indeed, our shield belongs to the Lord...
(Psalm 89:18)

Hallelujah! If we have the Lord's shield, we should be safe from all harm! Ephesians 6:16 tells us that we can *"extinguish all the flaming arrows"* of the enemy with *"the shield of faith."* Throughout Psalms and Proverbs, we are told that God is our shield and place of refuge. We are safe, then, for what can penetrate the shield of God?

Well, reality tells us differently. We are attacked by the enemy continuously. Sometimes those arrows manage to get through. What's with that? Is the Lord's shield impenetrable or not? Yes, of course it is. We know that our Lord is the victor.

What happens then? When we do not hold that shield in place, the enemy can reach us. When we give up seeking God, or put Him aside while we do our own thing, we become vulnerable.

Imagine the child who sneaks out to play with fire even though he knows he shouldn't. When he gets burned, he runs back to his parents for help. Could the parents have stopped the burn? Can they take away the burn? No. The parents can, however, provide whatever medical help they can and comfort the child to assist in the healing process. The parents can also use that circumstance as a teaching opportunity. God, too, will love us and help us through the healing process, even when we are damaged because we chose to step outside of His protection. He may not take away the consequences. He may use the circumstances as a teaching opportunity.

So how do we remain safe from the enemy?

He holds victory in store for the upright, he is a shield to those whose walk is blameless... (Proverbs 2:7)

Every word of God is flawless; he is a shield to those who take refuge in him. (Proverbs 30:5)

Be obedient to God and walk in His ways always.

OCTOBER 22

Freedom vs. Others

If your brother is distressed because of what you eat, you are no longer acting in love. Do not by your eating destroy your brother for whom Christ died.
(Romans 14:15)

I recently heard of a couple who put off hosting a neighbourhood gathering because of their belief in not drinking alcohol. After many years of struggling with their decision, they decided to go ahead and invite their neighbours anyway. They provided other choices of beverages, and much food and friendship. Some neighbours brought alcohol of their own and drank a bit. In the end, the hosts realized that it was not really such a big deal compared to the opportunity they had to develop relationships in their neighbourhood. This was all accomplished without compromising their own morals.

Would it have been better for the neighbours to abstain from alcohol for the sake of this good couple? Yes. However, they were not necessarily Christians yet, and in fact may not have even known the hosts well enough to know that it was a concern for them. One would hope that in the future alcohol could be denied out of respect for those who are distressed by its consumption.

So, too, should we consider all our actions, attitudes, and words. We should be especially cognizant of how our choices affect our spouses. First of all, we should desire to be righteous in God's eyes. Secondly, even when we consider ourselves free in Christ, it is incumbent on us to put aside our rights to prevent conflict within our spouses or others.

Which is more important—your rights or another's eternal life? Which is more loving—arguing and demanding your freedom, or extending grace to others? What could you possibly sacrifice in comparison to what Jesus Christ has sacrificed for you? As Jesus said, *"Love one another"* (John 13:34).

OCTOBER 23

As One

As a young man marries a maiden, so will your sons marry you; as a bridegroom rejoices over his bride, so will your God rejoice over you. (Isaiah 62:5)

The Bible refers to Christians as being the bride of Jesus Christ (Matthew 9). In Ephesians 5, we are given the example of how husband and wife relationships compare to Jesus' relationship to Christians. Jesus does not consider us like siblings, and neither should we consider our spouses that way. If our attitudes are about "fairness," that resounds of a sibling mentality. "If you get to do such and such, then I should get to do this! If you spent money, I should get to spend the same amount!" Nor does Jesus consider us roommates. Our spouses are not mere roommates. "I did such and such chore, so you have to do such and such. If I put in this money, you have to put in the same amount."

A healthier attitude is one of two independent beings choosing to be united and interdependent. Jesus did not die on the cross for us out of obligation, nor was He resentful. He freely chose to sacrifice His position in heaven with the Father for our sakes. He didn't choose to do this for a day, a month, or a few years. Jesus sacrificed for us until the death of His human body. He then sent the Holy Spirit that we could be united with Him for eternity. It is as permanent as we should consider our marriages.

It is not important how you choose to divide responsibilities for work or money. Your attitude is what's important. You should be willing to do what is necessary to benefit the marriage as one unit, not one or the other person. You should be pleased to sacrifice for or serve one another as Jesus did for you. You should feel pleasure honouring and bringing joy to the other spouse. I'm not referring to disgruntled willpower. If you are struggling in this area, I would encourage you to ask the Lord to create in you a new heart attitude through the Holy Spirit. Rejoice over your spouse.

OCTOBER 24

Joyful Worship

Worship the Lord with gladness; come before him with joyful songs.
(Psalm 100:2)

How do you worship the Lord? Worship means honouring, respecting, and being devoted to someone. Creating music is one method often referred to in the Bible. There are many other ways to worship, which you can discuss with your spouse.

The aspects I wish to point out in today's verse are the words "gladness" and "joyful." Do you only sing to the Lord when it is required, such as during a church service? When you do sing, is it with reverence to the Lord, or is your mind wandering to other areas of your life? Are you going through the motions, or are you dedicating the music to your Lord?

Regardless of which method of worship you choose, let us look at the attitude. Are you grateful for the Lord? Does the joy of the Lord well up inside you and spill out?

I'm not suggesting you purpose to worship on a particular day or at a particular time of day only. I'm not suggesting that you worship God only when you feel good. I am suggesting that your desire to worship the Lord be an ever-present part of your very being. You may not be glad or joyful about your current situation, but you should be glad and joyful towards your Lord always! In fact, that joyfulness will bring lightness during heavy times.

So how do you do that? First, you pray that the Lord will give you the right heart attitude. Ask Him to reveal to you anything that would interfere with that attitude so that you may address it. Talk with your spouse about suggestions for ways you could promote an attitude of gladness and joy towards the Lord.

How will you celebrate the Lord today?

OCTOBER 25

God Is Not Angry with You

For forty years I was angry with that generation; I said, "They are a people whose hearts go astray, and they have not known my ways."
(Psalm 95:10)

As of 2008, the average Canadian's lifespan is eighty-one years.[11] Let us say for the sake of argument that the first twenty years are childhood. That would leave, on average, sixty-one years of adulthood. Now suppose God was angry with you for forty of those years. That is half a lifetime, or two-thirds of an average adulthood. Ouch! I wouldn't want Him to be angry for even a minute, let alone forty years!

That is exactly what happened to the Israelites. They were hard-hearted and rebellious. They wanted all the blessings of the Lord without any responsibility or accountability. Instead of entering the Promised Land and all God had planned for them, they spent forty extra years wandering around in the dessert until an entire generation had died. Life was not easy. Today's psalm was given as a warning to the then-current generation to avoid the unbelief of their forefathers.

Through faith in Jesus Christ, we have the opportunity to enter the rest that the Lord spoke of in Psalm 95:11—*"So I declared on oath in my anger, 'They shall never enter my rest.'"* Hebrews 4 reveals that promise. Through faith in Jesus, we have been forgiven for the sins of which we have repented: *"let us hold firmly to the faith we profess. For we do not have a high priest who is unable to sympathize with our weaknesses..."* (Hebrews 4:14–15)

Thankfully, the Lord is no longer angry with us. However, we are to seek to be obedient to God and surrender to His will, for He has good plans for each one of us.

---

[11] "Live expectancy, at birth at and at 65, by sex and by province and territory," *Stats Canada*, May 31, 2012 (http://www.statcan.gc.ca/tables-tableaux/sum-som/l01/cst01/health72a-eng.htm).

OCTOBER 26

Life Is Short

As for man, his days are like grass, he flourishes like a flower of the field; the wind blows over it and it is gone, and its place remembers it no more. (Psalm 103:15–16)

When I was a child, the two months of summer vacation seemed like forever. My twelve years of grade school seemed like a long time, and were actually most of my lifetime at the point of graduation. Now I look back at my children, and their school years seem to have flown by! It's all in the perspective.

In Psalm 103, King David wrote about how short our lifespans are in comparison to eternity. God was there before creation, is still here today, and will always exist for eternity. He knew our parents, grandparents, great-grandparents, etc., from birth to death. He knows our generation, any children we already have, and all the generations that are yet to be born. He not only knows each one, He loves us.

But from everlasting to everlasting the Lord's love is with those who fear him, and his righteousness with their children's children... (Psalm 103:17)

Time is short. Life doesn't pass by like summer vacation; it's more like grass, as King David wrote. Is there anything you have been planning to do for God when you find the time? Is there something you feel God has been calling you to, but you haven't managed to fit into your busy schedule yet? God knows how many hours are in a day. God knows how many days He has assigned to each of us. If He is calling you, do you really think you should be putting it aside for later?

I would encourage you to pray alone and as a couple, asking God to direct your priorities. Here are a few more verses you may wish to consult for further study: Habakkuk 2:3, John 7:6, Psalm 75:2, Ephesians 2:10, Mark 13:33, Acts 1:7, Colossians 4:5, and Ephesians 5:16.

OCTOBER 27

The Lord's Works

May the glory of the Lord endure forever; may the Lord rejoice in his works.
(Psalm 104:31)

The Lord is amazing! He has created all of heaven and earth! He created every little aspect of the world and made it work together. Even this little corner of the universe we know as earth has been very carefully created and orchestrated. He has every right to *"rejoice in his works."*

Now, let me remind you of something. He created humans. He created you and your spouse. Yes, you are the work of His hands. He rejoices in each of you!

It is far too easy to focus at our failures. I know we aren't deserving even of His attention due to our own works, but we are worthy through Jesus! He loves us and takes joy in us. The Lord accepts us just as we are. He accepts us as flawed, but doesn't see our flaws. God desires that we each seek to draw nearer to Him. He desires to help us learn and grow in our spiritual maturity. He has not created us and then walked away. He continues to invest in us every day.

What a wonderful example this is for us in our relationships. Let us rejoice in the works of the Lord. Let us appreciate the marvels of His creation. Specifically, let us appreciate what the Lord has created in us. Let us appreciate what the Lord has created in our spouse, our children, and other people He has allowed us to be involved with. Rejoice in each of them.

Just as the Lord did not create us and then walk away, we too must not think of our wedding day as closing the book on our marriages. Rejoice in what the Lord has given you in your spouse. Don't focus on the faults in one another. You have been blessed with your spouse. Invest in and rejoice in one another. Now is a good time to share with one another some of those things you rejoice about in them.

OCTOBER 28

Stability and Security

Unless the Lord builds the house, its builders labor in vain. Unless the Lord watches over the city, the watchmen stand guard in vain.
(Psalm 127:1)

The joke in our family is that when we go to buy a new car, I ask about the colour. That's as far as my knowledge goes. Fortunately, my husband is a little more knowledgeable in this area and knows what questions to ask and what the answers mean. I would never try to purchase a car on my own. I could end up with a car that looks great in my driveway, but can't be used to get anywhere.

For all things, we must depend on God for what is best. We must seek to know God, rather than just seeking answers to our immediate wants. We need His guidance, not just verification of what we have already decided on. God knows what our needs are. Whether we're building a house, career, or ministry, it is important to do so with the Lord's wisdom and under His protection. What we see from our perspective is limited, but the Lord knows all there is to know about each decision we make. He knows the present and future results. Why waste your time and energy on things that will not be fruitful?

God's direction is based on His understanding of our motives, priorities, and methods. We have as much to learn from God about setting our hearts in alignment with His as we do about our personal needs and wants. I may want a BMW out of selfishness, but only need a bicycle. On the other hand, God may wish to bless me with a BMW, but I'm only looking at bicycles!

Our stability and security are found in God alone, not our own limited wisdom. Through the Holy Spirit, seek the Lord's wisdom, discernment, and protection.

Trust in the Lord for all things and in all things.

OCTOBER 29

Solid Foundation

Nevertheless, God's solid foundation stands firm, sealed with this inscription: "The Lord knows those who are his..."
(2 Timothy 2:19)

Tragedy comes in various forms, but eventually makes its way into all of our lives. Each person will handle grief in different ways. One thing I have noticed is that grief can drive people apart, or it can draw them together.

How do you protect your marriage and other relationships during these difficult times? Firstly, you need to be preventative! Each of you must make sure your own lives are solidly built on God's foundation. You will not know how to freely access God in a time of crisis if you have always depended on others before. "Remember me, God? I'm so-and-so's spouse (or child, or parent)." You must have confidence in your own faith in God. In addition, you must endeavour to keep your marriage built on that same solid foundation. Sharing these devotionals together is but one step in that process.

Secondly, when tragedy strikes, it is important to purposely decide that you will not allow division. It is important to allow each person to work through their own grief. You must purpose to allow extra grace during this process. Since you have purposed to build your marriage on the word of God, you will be in good standing as you weather the storms of life together. You will have what it takes to support one another.

Although tragedy and grief aren't pleasant to go through, there can be a reward at the end. Each experience can draw you closer than ever. As you successfully share life's hardships, there is a special camaraderie in not only surviving, but winning the battle together. Only you will ever know all the experiences that have woven you together to produce the strong bond you share in the end.

OCTOBER 30

Wise Faith

...so that your faith might not rest on men's wisdom, but on God's power. (1 Corinthians 2:5)

I have truly been blessed with very good spiritual leadership. I have been blessed by a minister who taught me that the Bible was more than stories and examples on how to be good. I have been attending my current church for over twenty years. I have received excellent teaching there under a senior pastor and various associate pastors. I have also had many opportunities to receive instruction from carefully selected speakers. In addition, I have learned from fellow Christians who have shared their understanding with me in Bible studies and in one-on-one situations.

Obviously, I value the wisdom of certain people who have spoken into my life. However, as today's Bible verse warns, my faith does *"not rest on men's wisdom, but on God's power."* First and foremost, I seek God's wisdom. I trust that God will provide my understanding of His word, be it through reading His word, praying, or various forms of study under other people He has supplied me with.

1 Corinthians 2:12 tells us, *"We have not received the spirit of the world but the Spirit who is from God, that we may understand what God has freely given us."* Only when we receive the Spirit from God will we have His wisdom. Have you ever wondered why some people cannot see the hand of God in their lives? They have not yet received that spirit of wisdom. Notice in Luke 24:45 that Jesus *"opened [the disciples'] minds so they could understand the Scriptures."* They could not find that godly understanding or wisdom in their own human strength.

I pray as the psalmist wrote: *"Let me understand the teaching of your precepts; then I will meditate on your wonders"* (Psalm 119:27). May God grant you wisdom for your faith. Thank God for those He uses to help you on your journey.

OCTOBER 31

Kingdom Power

For the kingdom of God is not a matter of talk but of power.
(1 Corinthians 4:20)

I recently returned to scuba-diving after a couple of scares. It had been a while since my last dive, which hadn't gone well. I had the security of the anchor line for orientation and ease of control of my descent. I also had my very patient husband descending with me and maintaining eye contact. I got to all of six feet in depth and just couldn't manage to equalize my ears. I was concerned about having difficulty and holding up my husband's dive and our other dive buddy who was with us. I was about to quit. It was great to have the security of the anchor line and my husband, but this time that wasn't enough. I prayed for God to help me!

What I didn't know was that my other friend was looking down at my bubbles from the boat. She could tell I was having trouble. She prayed for me that I would have peace, be safe, and have a good dive. I did descend and carry on with the dive, which turned out to be warm, calm, and safe. Prayer is powerful! Neither my friend nor I thought of our prayers as mere talk or wishful thinking. We were truly calling on the Lord. We were at that time joined together through the Holy Spirit in prayer: *"When I called, you answered me; you made me bold and stouthearted"* (Psalm 138:3).

It was a great encouragement when my friend shared with me about her prayer. It was rewarding to know that God had answered prayer on my behalf even when I didn't know the prayer had been offered up. Don't just hope or express concern for things to go well when you know others are struggling. That is *"a matter of talk."* Pray! May God reveal to you the fruit of your prayers.

NOVEMBER 1

Disagreements

The very fact that you have lawsuits among you means you have been completely defeated already. Why not rather be wronged?
(1 Corinthians 6:7)

A lawsuit is the result of a disagreement that two parties cannot resolve by themselves. The Apostle Paul told the Christians in Corinth that if they got as far as a lawsuit, they were *"completely defeated already."* His point was that it was not the perceived offence that was the problem; rather, it was the lack of harmony in the family of Christ. Paul told the Corinthian Christians that it would be better to be wronged and let it go than to be divided. Furthermore, going to court meant exposing the dispute to the pagan legal system.

How does this relate to married couples? Do not allow *any* disagreement to go unresolved. It is so important to address the little issues right from the beginning. Each perceived offence must be lovingly addressed or dismissed. Remember, it is better to be wronged and have peace. There should be no residual resentment or division at the conclusion. Don't allow issues or misunderstandings to build into major issues. If you are unable to forgive and move on, then consult a Christian friend or counsellor to assist you. Pretending everything is fine won't make the problem go away. By the time you get to a lawsuit or divorce, *"you have been completely defeated already."*

The divorce rate in North America is staggering. The divorce rate in Christian marriages is amazingly high as well. What does that witness to the world? What does your marriage disagreement witness to your circle of influence? What damage does your disagreement cause not only to yourselves, but to others?

By keeping your marriage Christ-centred, you will keep it loving, peaceful, and pure. That's a much better way to bring glory to God and show the world that God's way is good.

NOVEMBER 2

Women Called to Action

Likewise, teach the older women to be reverent in the way they live, not to be slanderers or addicted to much wine, but to teach what is good. Then they can train the younger women to love their husbands and children, to be self-controlled and pure, to be busy at home, to be kind, and to be subject to their husbands, so that no one will malign the word of God. (Titus 2:3–5)

Wives, you have been called to action! The Apostle Paul wrote the above verse to Titus when directing him on how the church was to operate amongst themselves as Christ-like models to the world.

Consistently throughout God's word we are encouraged to use our blessings to bless others. Women, if you are reading this devotional, you likely have been blessed with a loving husband. It is time to be proactive. In what way does your heart attitude towards your husband encourage other women to act towards their spouses? Do you always speak respectfully of him? Do you express joy to others for the opportunities you have to partner with him? Do you honour your husband in the way you dress, the things you say, and in your behaviour? If you have children, do you encourage and instruct others when you have the opportunity in helping to raise them in a godly manner?

If you have been married for fifty, twenty-five, five, or even one year, you have enough experience and responsibility to pass on your wisdom to other young wives. You may decide to take on a specific mentoring situation in addition to modelling your everyday life to everyone who knows you.

Men, you also have a responsibility to others. I would encourage you both to read all of Titus 2.

NOVEMBER 3

Happily Ever After

Give thanks to the Lord, for he is good. "His love endures forever." (Psalm 136:1)

My husband I recently attended a wedding ceremony. It was a beautiful and romantic outdoor wedding. The weather was cooperative and the ocean glistened behind the young couple. As they looked into each other's eyes and said their vows, I prayed that they would have the happily-ever-after marriage they dreamed of.

Notice that I said "ever after," not "always after." Yes, I would wish them to have many happy times together. However, it just isn't realistic to always be happy. It wouldn't allow for times of growth and a deepening of the relationship. If you only had health and never an illness, only experienced good and rich times and never any struggles, you would have a superficial relationship.

I thank God that *"he is good"* and that *"his love endures forever."* No matter what happens, I am completely confident that God will always be good, and that He will always love me, in this life and eternity.

My prayer for this couple, and all married couples, is that they would have a love that endures. As they adjust to living together as one, I pray they would enjoy the good times and learn to love each other through their differences, learn to compromise, and accommodate the flaws and weaknesses they discover in their spouses. As they discover their weaknesses, I pray they endeavour to be one another's strength and encouragement.

Most importantly, I pray that they would develop a cord of three, for when two strands pull on one another, they create stress and may break. I pray that they would determine to build their marriage on the strong foundation of Jesus Christ.

Are you choosing to live in a happily-ever-after marriage?

NOVEMBER 4

Significance

He determines the number of the stars and calls them each by name. (Psalm 147:4)

Have you ever just lay on your back on a clear summer night and looked up into the sky? My husband and I recently returned from a summer vacation in which we were blessed with just such an opportunity. As we looked up into the sky, my husband began to point out the various lights, explaining the differences to me. Some were actually satellites, some were planets, some were stars, and others were just airplanes.

As we stared up into the night sky, more and more stars came into focus. It was so amazing! God created each and every one of those stars! They were beyond numbering! He placed each one of them in their perfect place and created their function in the existence of the whole universe. They were not there just that one night for my enjoyment, but they have a much bigger role to play than I will never understand.

It made me think of how small my world is. I, like so many others, busy myself with my life, managing my health, relationships, finances, and other daily routines. I function on this one little planet, mostly in this one little country, in my little community, in my home. Meanwhile, God has created and oversees the whole world! Everything is integrally connected. If even one planet were to fall out of place, or one star fall at the wrong time, every part of the world would be affected.

If God has a purpose for each of the innumerable stars, and calls them by name, then I know He knows me and has a purpose for my life, too. I thank God for where He has placed me right now and who He has created me to be.

He has determined your life as well, and He knows you by name. You are significant.

NOVEMBER 5

Supporting Spiritual Leaders

When Moses' hands grew tired, they took a stone and put it under him and he sat on it. Aaron and Hur held his hands up—one on one side, one on the other—so that his hands remained steady till sunset.
(Exodus 17:12)

Remember back to when the Lord called Moses into ministry from a burning bush. Moses was caught completely off-guard and felt incapable of doing what was asked of him. Moses was full of excuses as to why the Lord should not pick him. In the end, the Lord sent Aaron, Moses' brother, to help him.

Moses was still called by the Lord to lead his people out of Egypt and into the place the Lord had promised them. Moses was obedient, but was made stronger with the help of Aaron, Hur, and other people in his care. It would seem that if Moses had direct communication with the Lord, nobody else was needed. However, Moses had his moments of weakness and felt he needed the support of others.

No matter who your earthly spiritual leaders are, they will benefit by your support. They will have times of weariness and weakness. Sometimes we feel there are others who are more spiritual or knowledgeable than we are. The truth is, we can all do something to encourage or support those from whom we receive leadership and teaching. Sometimes it might be direct interactions or activities, and other times it may be those unseen but faithful actions of intercession.

Discuss with your spouse what it is you could do to support and encourage your leader. Invite Jesus to be part of your discussion. Once you have determined your method of support, share that with your spouse as a form of accountability. Do not allow Satan to plant doubts, cause distractions, or allow the passing of time to deter you.

Your support could make all the difference! We are not alone.

NOVEMBER 6

We are Free in Christ

"Everything is permissible"—but not everything is beneficial. "Everything is permissible"—but not everything is constructive.
(1 Corinthians 10:23)

God created us with our own wills. We are free to make our own decisions every second of every day. However, as Apostle Paul points out, although God allows us to make our own choices, not everything leads to a positive outcome. So, how do we decide what is righteous? In 1 Corinthians, Apostle Paul gave us a few guidelines for making our decisions.

Firstly, ask yourself if it is beneficial. Will your behaviour be beneficial in the long run, or will it enslave you to sin?, In 1 Corinthians 6:12 Apostle Paul says that even though he is permitted to do everything, he won't let anything master hm. Secondly, will it put a stumbling block in the way of anyone's spiritual growth? In 1 Corinthians 8:13 he states that he will not do anything to cause a brother to fall into sin. Thirdly, is it edifying? Apostle Paul directed us in 1 Corinthians 10:24 to seek the good of others rather than ourselves. Finally, will it glorify the LORD? Ultimately, in 1 Corinthians 10:31 we are directed to focus on glorifying God in all we do.

Now think about what you watch on television or at the theatres. Think about what sports or activities you do in your free time and how you participate in them. Think about how you deal with conflicts, gossip, and jokes. Are your choices beneficial or enslaving? Are your choices a stumbling block or edifying to other people's spiritual growth? Is God being glorified?

Take time to discuss some of your questionable with your spouse. Join together in prayer to ask God to speak into your lives. May your choices be beneficial, edifying, and give glory to God.

NOVEMBER 7

Interdependent

In the Lord, however, woman is not independent of man, nor is man independent of woman. For as woman came from man, so also man is born of woman. But everything comes from God.
(1 Corinthians 11:11–12)

God created the first man, Adam. He then determined that man needed a *"suitable helper"* (Genesis 2:20).

Then the Lord God made a woman from the rib he had taken out of the man, and he brought her to the man. (Genesis 2:22)

Although researchers in modern medicine are developing ways around it, God created humans in such a way that it would take a man and a woman to conceive a child. The woman would bear and give birth to the child. It's seems pretty clear that God intended for man and woman, as a species, to be interdependent.

God also intended for husband and wife to be interdependent (not independent or dependent). Matthew 19:6 says, *"So they are no longer two, but one. Therefore what God has joined together, let man not separate."* Your decisions, behaviours, and attitudes will have an effect on your spouse and therefore your marriage.

Certainly you will not spend every minute of every day doing exactly the same activities. Your season of life will have an influence on the type of shared interests and time you spend together. However, I've noticed that the couples who develop common interests and enjoy doing things together seem to be the ones who have happier, stronger, longer marriages. How many times have you heard a separated or divorced couple say, "It's not like we were fighting or anything; we just didn't have anything in common anymore"?

Sharing devotional time is one good way to stay connected. Now is a good time to discuss with your spouse what other things or interests you share at this point in your lives. What are your hopes and goals for your future? How will you stay interdependent?

NOVEMBER 8

Whose Plans Are They?

In his heart a man plans his course, but the Lord determines his steps. (Proverbs 16:9)

"Hey, hold on a minute! I had plans! They were good plans, too! I was preparing my ministry to do God's work! What do you mean it's not going to happen?" Have you ever had a situation like that? The idea was developed, the ball was rolling, and suddenly everything came to a screeching halt. What happened?

The answer will not be the same for every situation. It may be God's plan, Satan's ambush, or man's confusion. However, I choose to believe that God is omnipotent. If it is His will, He can make it happen through me or someone else. If it is not His will, I am grateful that He intervenes. I choose to believe that God is mightier than Satan and his legions. I know I am not always perfectly in alignment with God, but He is forgiving and is a God of second chances.

Think about some of these additional verses:

"For my thoughts are not your thoughts, neither are your ways my ways," declares the Lord. (Isaiah 55:8)

"For I know the plans I have for you," declares the Lord, "plans to prosper you and not to harm you, plans to give you hope and a future." (Jeremiah 29:11)

If the Lord delights in a man's way, he makes his steps firm; though he stumble, he will not fall, for the Lord upholds him with his hand. (Psalm 37:23–24)

"Don't be afraid," the prophet answered. "Those who are with us are more than those who are with them." (2 Kings 6:16)

Teach me your way, O Lord, and I will walk in your truth. (Psalm 86:11)

Show me your ways, O Lord, teach me your paths. (Psalm 25:4)

Take this time to join together with your spouse and seek God's will. His plans will have much better results than anything you or I can conceive.

NOVEMBER 9

What Are We Supposed To Do?

"Tell us by what authority you are doing these things," they said. "Who gave you this authority?"
(Luke 20:2)

It seems almost comical to me about two thousand years later to imagine the nerve of the chief priests and elders to question Jesus Christ's authority to do miracles, deliver healings, and teach God's word. However, I wonder how I would have reacted at the time, not having the benefit of God's written word and the presence of the Holy Spirit. After all, we are warned in the Bible to watch out for false teachers.

I recently was talking to a missionary who had the opportunity to go to an area where the people were fairly new in their faith. These people now go to a small church and are enthusiastically going about the work of God. People came to them to be prayed over in the name of Jesus. As a result, many miracles and healings happened. I'm not sure what was said, but one of these spiritual children turned to the missionaries and asked, "Isn't that what we're supposed to do?" They were seeking confirmation or correction! The missionaries smiled and assured them they were correct.

What authority did these people have to pray for, have faith for, and witness the miraculous hand of God in the lives of people? Jesus said, *"All authority in heaven and on earth has been given to me"* (Matthew 28:18). At this point, Jesus sent His followers out to all people. Luke 24:49 tells us that Jesus sends us *"power from on high."* Then, in Mark 16:17–18, we are told,

> *And these signs will accompany those who believe: In my name they will drive out demons… they will place their hands on sick people, and they will get well.*

Do you believe? Are you using the authority you have been given?

NOVEMBER 10

Beautiful Wife

Your beauty should not come from outward adornment, such as braided hair and the wearing of gold jewelry and fine clothes. Instead, it should be that of your inner self, the unfading beauty of a gentle and quiet spirit, which is of great worth in God's sight.
(1 Peter 3:3–4)

I don't believe the Apostle Peter was directing wives not to give any attention to their outward appearance. If that was the case, he would be promoting lack of personal grooming in combing and tending one's hair, and the lack of all jewellery and clothes! I believe his point was that someone's personality and inner self is more important than their outward appearance.

From just looking around at the beauty of the world, we know that God condones beauty. It is good to take care of the temple (our body) He has given us. It is a respectful thing to take time and care to clean and groom ourselves. We are to respect our husbands. One way to do that is to make ourselves pleasing to his eyes. Face it; don't we all enjoy being around sweet-smelling, clean, attractive people? Taking care of oneself says, "You are worthy of my efforts."

In addition, we need to tend to our inner self. That *"gentle and quiet spirit, which is of great worth in God's sight"* is also of great value to our husbands. It may be the outward appearance that catches his eye, but the inner beauty will capture and hold his heart. Without the inner beauty, the outward beauty is of little value.

So, where do we find that inner beauty? We find it in the Lord, by inviting and receiving the indwelling of the Holy Spirit. We find that beauty, peace, and joy by keeping our eyes on God alone. Wives, pray that the Lord would help you to recognise distractions and keep you focused. Husbands, your wife can always benefit from your support and encouragement. Continue to pray for your wife always.

NOVEMBER 11

He's in Your Boat

He replied, "You of little faith, why are you so afraid?" Then he got up and rebuked the winds and the waves, and it was completely calm.
(Matthew 8:26)

Matthew 8 tells of the occasion when the disciples were crossing the Lake of Galilee and a tremendous storm came up. The waves were overwhelming and the disciples thought they would all drown. They all went to Jesus, who was sleeping in the boat, and woke Him up. Jesus calmed the storm and they safely arrived at the shore. How fortunate they were to have Jesus with them.

Guess what? Jesus is in your boat, too! No matter what difficulties you might be facing, or how you got there, Jesus is always with you. He can calm all storms.

I am currently aware of a few marriage relationships that are having difficulties. Some are entering the storm while still trying to handle the problem on their own. Others are in the mist of the crisis and have turned to Jesus. I have witnessed relationships that seemed beyond hope, and therefore dead, and then were surrendered to God. I rejoiced with those couples as the storm calmed, bringing the restoration of their relationship.

Are you facing any storms, big or small, in your marriage relationship right now? Perhaps you know of other couples who might need your prayer support. Have faith! Matthew 8:24 that, *"Without warning, a furious storm came up."* The disciples weren't expecting the storm, but God knew about it. In the same way, God knew that these difficulties would arise in yours or your acquaintances' lives. He is able to calm the storm if He is asked. Pray for His help, and that He would see you safely to the other side. Know that the love of Jesus can restore broken hearts and heal wounds as completely as He can calm the storms.

NOVEMBER 12

How Is Your Home Doing?

The wise woman builds her house, but with her own hands the foolish one tears hers down.
(Proverbs 14:1)

Wives, are you women of wisdom in regards to your homes? There is an article that circulates now and again about how to prepare to be a good wife from a 1950s home economics textbook. It covers such things as having dinner prepared (made from scratch, of course), ensuring that you and the children are cleaned up, and making sure the house is calm and clean for when the husband arrives home from his Monday to Friday daytime job. It is meant as a good laugh to those with whom it is shared.

Joking aside, what does a wise woman do to care for her home? The information in the 1950s textbook was actually meant to be taken seriously in the time and culture in which it was written. The intent was to equip young women in how to run their homes. The Bible is able to instruct for all times and cultures. Proverbs 14:1 is one of many verses of instruction.

Wise wives (and husbands) are to build up their spouses and families, not tear them down. What is your attitude towards your spouse and family? Do you give encouraging words? Are you respectful? Is there joy? Laughter is good, if it doesn't come at the expense of someone else's feelings.

Is your home a place where you, your spouse, and your children, if you have any, want to be? Do you want to spend time together whether you are in the home or out? (Home is not just the building.) What do your actions, attitude, and words say to your family?

I would encourage both husband and wife to pray for each other and the whole family daily. Pray for God's blessings, wisdom, direction, and protection. Pray that He would reveal anything that you say or do that would tear down a family member. Pray for the grace to ask, and to give forgiveness when necessary.

NOVEMBER 13

Who Will Your Family Serve?

But if serving the Lord seems undesirable to you, then choose for yourselves this day whom you will serve… But as for me and my household, we will serve the Lord.
(Joshua 24:15)

Many years ago, I was given a plaque with the last part of this verse inscribed on it. I hung it on our kitchen wall, where it remained for many years. I wanted to serve the Lord and teach my family how to do the same.

I continue to pray for myself and my family that we would each continue to grow closer to God day by day. I pray that each one of us desire to know God's will and purpose for our lives. I pray protection from the enemy over each of us.

What happened to that plaque? When our youngest son moved out on his own, it just seemed right to take the plaque down and give it to him. It was an important aspect of our family life that we wished to continue to bless his adult life with. Although he didn't have a wife or family yet, we wanted his home to have a firm foundation and direction. As we released our son to begin a life separate from our daily oversight, we wanted him to keep a right focus. Many distractions and temptations bombard us daily.

Each one of us, young and old, has to make those decisions daily. Who are you going to serve? We live in an instant culture. We are encouraged to want immediate gratification for selfish purposes. However, as Christians, we must remember to keep our eyes on God and eternity. Your steadfastness is not just for yourself, but for the sake of your spouse, family, and all those in your circle of influence.

Who do you choose to serve today? How strong is your foundation? Are you equipping and encouraging one another (your "household") to serve the Lord?

NOVEMBER 14

A Gentle Spirit

A gentle answer turns away wrath, but a harsh word stirs up anger. (Proverbs 15:1)

Think of a time when you were all worked up over a situation and started fuming and grumbling to someone else. When that person responded in a calm manner of explanation, what did that do to your demeanour? Oops! Perhaps you didn't have all the facts. Or perhaps you can recall a time when someone else stormed into your presence and you were able to calmly respond. Did you notice the positive change in their reaction? As you share these experiences with your spouse, you may even be able to laugh at them.

Now, think of a time when you were joyfully getting on with your day when someone raged at you. At first, you might not even have been able to sort out what they thought you had done wrong. What was your reaction? Our defences tend to set in. Even witnessing things such as someone berating a store employee, or road rage that doesn't directly involve you, can have a negative effect on your mood.

Which people do you prefer to be around—the calm and joyful, or the raging and angry? What does that tell you about what type of person you should strive to be? It's not as simple as deciding to be gentle at all times and then doing it. That would be like deciding to be a dentist and then opening an office. Preparation and training are involved.

As you spend time with the Lord, ask Him to fill you with a gentle spirit. When you practice being filled with the love of Jesus, you will be able to access that peace more readily. Where there is the love and peace of Jesus, anger and unforgiveness cannot exist. Peace to you.

NOVEMBER 15

The Ultimate Relationship

But the man who loves God is known by God.
(1 Corinthians 8:3)

I once visited a new friend. She offered to drive me around her beautiful community and show me the sites. It was a small community and most people knew all the other residents. This new friend worked at the local golf course and had the opportunity to get to know her clients on a first-name basis. As we drove along, she said we were on the street where a famous person lived. I am fond of this particular celebrity, and my friend offered to drop in on the way past, introducing me to her. I wasn't sure of my own emotions at this prospect, but I knew I wouldn't know what to say to this celebrity in person. In the end, the celebrity wasn't home (she was probably out running a mundane errand or off playing golf).

Perhaps you have the fortune of knowing someone famous or important. Perhaps you have them over for dinner or just coffee all the time. Perhaps you've been to their house a number of times. It must be interesting to watch the reactions of other people when they find out how well you know this celebrity. In fact, I've known people who love to "name drop" famous people who might not even remember meeting them.

There is nobody more important or well-known than Jesus! Many people, even those who don't believe in Him as God, know who we are referring to when we mention His name. How exciting it is to know Him intimately! We are even on a first-name basis. He not only drops by our house for a visit; He's with us all the time. To know Jesus is to love Him. I can confidently say that I am "known by God." When it is my turn to meet Him face to face, He will recognize me and remember my name. How familiar are you with Him?

NOVEMBER 16

Quarrels Are Not Effective

Starting a quarrel is like breaching a dam; so drop the matter before a dispute breaks out.
(Proverbs 17:14)

God has created each of us uniquely. We each have our own set of experiences and personalities. Some of us have been very blessed to find a person who fits well with us. We have chosen to travel through this life together as we seek to mature and develop into all that God would have us be. In the process of developing, we are continuously fine-tuning and smoothing out our rough spots. Different opinions, viewpoints, and ways of doing things will occur, but these should lead to growth, not anger.

The dictionary defines "quarrel" as "an angry dispute, argument, or disagreement… a breach of friendship" or "to find fault."[12] A quarrel is more than a difference of opinion. A quarrel is born out of anger or fault-finding. A quarrel is not an attempt to compromise or find a peaceful solution. It is a breach of friendship! It is very unlikely that either person will leave a quarrel feeling good. It may even cost you a friendship. That alone is damaging, but it will even affect your relationship with God! The Bible tells us to be forgiving, and that if we are not, it will affect our relationship with God.

Especially with your spouse, but in every relationship, your goal should be to use your differences to compliment, teach, and learn from each other. Don't allow those differences to evolve into anger. The dispute may erupt into more than can be repaired. *"It is to a man's honor to avoid strife, but every fool is quick to quarrel"* (Proverbs 20:3). Don't make a fool of yourself!

It may help to consider whether or not the issue at hand is important in eternity. If it isn't, let it go. If it is, pray that God would intervene, and that He would give you the wisdom to know your role in the situation.

---

[12] *The Winston Dictionary of Canadian English* (Toronto, ON: Holt, Rinehart and Winston of Canada, 1969), 566.

NOVEMBER 17

Refreshing Spirits

By all this we are encouraged. In addition to our own encouragement, we were especially delighted to see how happy Titus was, because his spirit has been refreshed by all of you.
(2 Corinthians 7:13)

Not everyone has been called, or blessed with the opportunity, to go into the missions field. I have been so blessed. I'm not sure what it would have taken Titus, in this 2 Corinthian event, to make his trip, but I'm guessing it would not have been a simple matter. Titus was blessed by the very people he obediently went to serve. I, too, have received encouragement and my spirit been refreshed by the missions experiences I have been involved in.

On one trip in particular, I travelled by myself to another country where most of the people didn't speak English. One Sunday morning, I stood in a church service, taking part in a worship time. I was suddenly overwhelmed with the realization that I was joined together with another body of Christians halfway around the world. Although we couldn't hold a conversation, we were joined together in the act of worshipping the same one and only God. Over my time there, with the help of interpreters, I was able to work, pray, and visit with these fellow Christians. I returned home much encouraged.

We don't need to travel afar to encourage and refresh one another. Fellow Christians cross our paths all the time. We may not have a lot in common, or even know that those around us *are* Christians. However, we have many opportunities to offer that *"cup of water"* (Mark 9:41) in Jesus' name.

In what ways do you give encouragement to others to refresh their spirits? In what ways do you receive that encouragement and refreshment?

NOVEMBER 18

Finding Satisfaction

I know that there is nothing better for men than to be happy and do good while they live. That everyone may eat and drink, and find satisfaction in all his toil—this is the gift of God.
(Ecclesiastes 3:12–13)

We don't understand all that God has planned. We don't even know why certain things happen, whether it's God's plan, man's choices, or Satan's attack. What this verse tells us is that we should endeavour to *"do good while [we] live,"* enjoying the blessings God provides for us. Why? Ecclesiastes 3:14 tells us the reason is *"that men will revere [God]."*

Some people appear to have easy and fun jobs who seem discontent. Then there are people whose jobs are laborious and difficult, yet they still seem to find joy. Have you ever noticed labourers singing while they work? I remember one man whose job it was to drive those little carts around the airport, helping people who need to get from one gate to another. As I waited for my flight, I noticed him going back and forth, back and forth, time and again. He spent his whole shift in one little area of the airport. It wasn't necessarily a very exciting job, was it? This man, however, was happy. He would make a sound like an air horn, then keep a deadpan face. It was so much fun to watch people look around for where the sound was coming from. Once they figured it out, they would in turn watch the next group of people, and there was laughter for all.

This man was providing a service for others. He was doing it with a joyful heart. His appearance told me that he was receiving all he needed to *"eat and drink,"* although I'm sure he would not have been highly paid. I don't know what challenges he may have been facing in life, but he was enjoying his gifts from God.

No matter what your days involve, do you enjoy God's gifts?

NOVEMBER 19

Joyful Parents

The father of a righteous man has great joy; he who has a wise son delights in him. May your father and mother be glad; may she who gave you birth rejoice!
(Proverbs 23:24–25)

My husband and I were both blessed to have righteous parents. They made many sacrifices for us and raised us to the best of their abilities. They taught us right from wrong and gave us opportunities to learn about Jesus from a young age. We love them and honour them. We know they love us, and that they delight in us.

We also take great joy in seeing that our children have grown into mature young adults! They both have good moral values and have demonstrated success in their chosen fields. It is a delight to see that, although we are not experts, my husband and I were successful in raising our children in God's grace.

Whether you are a child or a parent, this verse is meant as an encouragement. Wisdom is not caught; it is taught. You should purpose to learn from righteous men and women in your life. You should also purpose to teach, guide, and encourage the next generation of men and women.

How do your choices affect your parents or older generation? Do you bring joy or stress? How do your choices affect the younger generation? Can you think of any way to support the next generation in making wise and righteous choices? One thing we have done is have "passing the baton" evenings. A few couples have joined together in an effort to encourage our young adult children. The older generation makes dinner for the younger generation. Then we gather around and ask each young adult what they would like us to pray about for them. At the next gathering, we ask for a prayer report and then repeat the offer to pray for new requests. Be creative, and be encouraging.

NOVEMBER 20

Are You Friends?

...he is altogether lovely. This is my lover, this my friend...
(Song of Solomon 5:16)

How do you describe your spouse to those who don't know them? Song of Solomon 5 contains a Shulammite woman's very positive description of her husband, Solomon. She sticks pretty much to a physical description, but ends with the statement that they are friends. Our clue that their misunderstanding will be resolved comes not from the fact that she finds Solomon attractive, but rather that they are friends.

I was recently at a wedding where the importance of friendship between couples was recognized. In the groom's speech, he recognized the special friendship his parents had, and declared his new bride to be his best friend. What a wonderful lesson and blessing his parents have passed down to their children!

This certainly doesn't mean they will never have conflicts or disagreements. Even best friends don't agree on everything.

John M. Gottman, a relationship expert, says the quality of friendship a couple shares will predict how successful they'll be in resolving their differences. Notice I said "resolving their differences," not just surviving them.[13]

How successful would you rate your ability to resolve your differences? How would you describe your friendship with your spouse? Discuss with your spouse what it is you do or say that promotes your friendship. What do you do to protect your friendship? What might you do to further develop your friendship?

---

[13] John M. Gottman and Nan Silver, *The Seven Principles for Making Marriage Work* (Toronto, ON: Random House, 1999).

NOVEMBER 21

Going to the House of God

Guard your steps when you go to the house of God. Go near to listen rather than to offer the sacrifice of fools, who do not know that they do wrong. (Ecclesiastes 5:1)

How do we *"go to the house of God"* today? Because Jesus Christ died for us, and sent us the Holy Spirit to live in us, we no longer have to go to some special place to worship and communicate with God. (I have addressed the value of attending a church in another devotion.) We have access to God any time, any place.

Today's verse speaks to me of our prayer lives. We are to *"guard [our] steps,"* or be careful of our attitude when going to God. All too often, we jump right in with our grocery list of what we want God to do for us. To make it easy, we often even tell Him how to do it. How foolish does that sound?! Ridiculous, isn't it? We don't mean to be arrogant; we just get caught up in our own thoughts and good intentions.

It's okay to talk to God about our concerns and needs. He is aware of all of them. The issue is when we continue to rattle on and tell Him how we want Him to resolve the problem. "God, please make *(fill-in-the-blank)* receive their salvation. God, please get *(fill-in-the-blank)* to the right doctor to heal them. God, miraculously heal *(fill-in-the-blank)*. God, give *(fill-in-the-blank)* such-and-such job. God, make *(fill-in-the-blank)* read my letter and then do such-and-such."

Instead, you might try taking the time to quiet yourself in anticipation of hearing God speak to you. Ask Him to help you put aside distractions so that you can just *be* with Him. After focusing on God and praising Him, express your concerns, then listen for what God is telling you or directing you to do. Remember, the whole point is to bring glory to His name, not yours.

God is in control. Let's try to be faithful to His will.

NOVEMBER 22

You Are Set Apart

But when God, who set me apart from birth and called me by his grace… (Galatians 1:15)

It is interesting that the Apostle Paul was set apart at birth to do such great work in Jesus' name. I don't know what Paul's childhood was like, or what kind of a specific family or circumstance he came from, but God knew exactly what family Paul was being born into. God knew what paths Paul would choose to follow. Paul grew to a position of authority. He used his power to persecute the followers of Jesus! He even hunted them down to kill them! Then, in the book of Acts, everything changed for Paul. He heard God's calling, and finally embraced it. Paul eventually chose to serve God at all costs.

Elsewhere in the Bible, we read about people who were set apart at birth for God's calling—Jeremiah in Jeremiah 1:5, Israel in Isaiah 49:1, and Jesus in John 10:36. In fact, each Christian is set apart at birth for His calling. Remember, God knew you from the very beginning. He also knew your whole life before it even began.

Each person takes different paths to arrive at their calling. For some, it seems natural. They may be born into a Christian family and receive their salvation in childhood. They may appear to follow Jesus from their very beginnings. For other people, it is absolutely amazing to see them reach a point of salvation and walk with God. Look at the Apostle Paul again! Do you think his childhood, or even young adult friends, would ever have predicted his calling?

As a Christian, you were set apart at birth. It may or may not have seemed obvious in your early life, but you were. Discuss what each of you think you have been called by God to do. Where do you think you are on that path? Where might your calling take you in the future?

NOVEMBER 23

Building Your House

By wisdom a house is built, and through understanding it is established; through knowledge its rooms are filled with rare and beautiful treasures. (Proverbs 24:3–4)

Some Christians and non-Christians alike appear to believe we are just passing through this life, and what will be, will be. They believe we have no control, and that the spiritual world manipulates every aspect of our lives. They believe that if God wants to reveal something to you, He just will. I am not one of those people.

Yes, there definitely is a spiritual realm. Yes, it affects us. However, we do have control. Jesus sent the Holy Spirit to give us that control. It is our choice what to do about it. We know God is greater and more powerful than Satan. We know we can call upon that power in the name of Jesus.

The house referred to in this verse is our family. True wisdom is the wisdom of God. Understanding of that wisdom comes from God's revelation. If we seek God's wisdom and understanding, He will give it to us. As a result, He will fill our lives with blessings beyond our imaginations.

Building a house is work. Is doesn't just happen. The size and strength of the house is based on exactly how much material is used, and the knowledge of construction you have. If you want to take a chance that there will be no storms, a lean-to might work. If you want your home (family) to stand and be secure, you need to put more into its construction. Remember, no matter how well-built a home is, it always needs maintenance.

Discuss in which ways you seek God's wisdom and understanding. How do you apply that wisdom and understanding to your daily lives? How do you guide your family to attain that wisdom and understanding? How do you encourage each other to defend yourselves from the enemy? How do you prevent the enemy from hiding God's wisdom from you or your family members?

NOVEMBER 24

Campfire or Bonfire?

Without wood a fire goes out; without gossip a quarrel dies down. (Proverbs 26:20)

I remember one camping trip we took when our family was young. Our friends joined us in the next campsite. In the evening, we decided that a campfire would be nice. The mothers were thinking of a cosy little setting with our families. We would sit around and talk together, and maybe even roast a few marshmallows.

The fathers willingly jumped at the chance to create the campfire for us. Keep in mind that we had three school-aged boys with us. The male members of our group seemed to be gripped by the old adage that "more is better." Before we knew it, we had a huge bonfire going! Suddenly, we all smelt something out of place. The soles of the shoes of one of our friends were actually melting because he was too close to the fire, which was way too big to roast marshmallows on! It was time to stop feeding the fire and begin to douse it.

Likewise, our conversations can get out of control and cause damage if we aren't careful. When a conversation escalates into a quarrel or turns to gossip, it is out of control. Sometimes just cutting off the fuel (more angry words or negative gossip) is enough. Other times, you may actually have to douse it. It may be time to self-correct and ask for forgiveness. It may be time to extend God's grace to others. It may be time to stand up and say to others who are still fuelling the situation that you would like them to stop. Whatever is required, do it in the love of Jesus and with God's grace.

Like our campfire, you may need to check back and make sure that it's completely extinguished. Our campfire was a lesson learned, and an opportunity to pass that lesson on to our children. This may be your opportunity to pass Jesus' love on to others in your circle of influence.

NOVEMBER 25

Forgiving Yourself

Why should you be beaten anymore? Why do you persist in rebellion? Your whole head is injured, your whole heart afflicted.
(Isaiah 1:5)

Picture a child throwing a tantrum. She thrashes around, banging her fists and bumping various parts of her body against the hard floor. It hurts, but she keeps thrashing away. Nearby, the parent watches and waits. When the child exhausts herself, she stops and looks up. The child notices the parent, who opens his arms, and the child runs to him to be comforted. The girl knows where her help comes from.

That is the picture of a person who realizes she has sinned, but continues to wallow in guilt and condemn herself. God is not going to pin her down or force her to come. He patiently waits until she turns to Him. Then He opens His arms and allows her to run to Him.

"Come now, let us reason together," says the Lord. "Though your sins are like scarlet, they shall be as white as snow; though they are red as crimson, they shall be like wool." (Isaiah 1:18)

Have you or anyone you know been in that position? Have you noticed how unhappy that person was? Have you seen how much more miserable and full of despair they got? Have you thought, or heard, the excuses for not turning to God? *"But if you resist and rebel, you will be devoured by the sword"* (Isaiah 1:20). As long as they hold on to the condemnation and refuse forgiveness, the sin will continue to eat away at their very beings.

There is no unrepented sin that is too great for God to handle. Jesus can wash all sin and guilt away. Jesus has brought atonement: *"Look, the Lamb of God, who takes away the sin of the world!"* (John 1:29)

If you are a parent, have you ever forgiven your child for something he did that you didn't approve of? Don't you think God is better able to forgive than you?

NOVEMBER 26

Family of God

Because you are sons, God sent the Spirit of his Son into our hearts, the Spirit who calls out, "'Abba', Father."
(Galatians 4:6)

Many people develop special friendships with those who are not legally their relatives. You hear, "She's like a second mother," "He's like a nephew," or "He's the big brother I never had." These people may even go so far as to invite such special friends to family celebrations. Occasionally, these friends are even written into wills. However, they are never truly related.

The family of God is different. When we believe in Jesus Christ as our Saviour, God sends His very Spirit to enter into our hearts, our very beings. We become one with Jesus. Jesus is a part of us, and His Father becomes our Father. We become children of God. It's not *like* being children of God, but actual children of God!

Amazing, isn't it? We actually become equal family members in God's eyes.

...for all of you who were baptized into Christ have clothed yourselves with Christ. There is neither Jew nor Greek, slave nor free, male nor female, for you are all one in Christ Jesus. (Galatians 3:27–28)

We get to call God "Abba" or "Daddy." He loves us. He knows us intimately. We don't have to wait for an appointment or go through a secretary to get to Him. He loves us, guides us, teaches us, and acknowledges us as His own. Can you envision Him smiling and saying, "This is *(your name)*, my son/daughter"?

There is no amount of money, no recognition or fame, nothing more valuable than being a child of God. There is nothing we can compare with the privilege of spending eternity with our heavenly Father... Daddy. We will ultimately inherit more than we can ever imagine.

You can always opt out of the privilege of being part of God's family, but why would you?

NOVEMBER 27

Who Is This Jesus?

For to us a child is born, to us a son is given, and the government will be on his shoulders. And he will be called Wonderful Counselor, Mighty God, Everlasting Father, Prince of Peace.
(Isaiah 9:6)

We know Jesus by many names. It is an interesting exercise to take note, highlighting or journaling, of all the names used in the Bible as you read through it. His various names are used to denote Jesus' various attributes. In today's verse, the prophet Isaiah references four of those names as he prophesies about the coming birth and reign of Jesus.

First, Isaiah refers to Jesus' title of *"Wonderful Counselor."* Jesus spent about three years teaching His followers before His crucifixion. He promised that the Father would send a counsellor.

> *But the Counselor, the Holy Spirit, whom the Father will send in my name, will teach you all things and will remind you of everything I have said to you.* (John 14:26)

Second, Jesus is our *"Mighty God."* There is none greater or stronger than He.

> *"The virgin will be with child and will give birth to a son, and they will call him Immanuel"—which means, "God with us."* (Matthew 1:23)

Next, Isaiah refers to the *"Everlasting Father."*

> *I and the Father are one.* (John 10:30)

We know that He was in the beginning, and will be for eternity.

Finally, Isaiah refers to Jesus' title *"Prince of Peace."* Jesus told His disciples,

> *Peace I leave with you; my peace I give you. I do not give to you as the world gives. Do not let your hearts be troubled and do not be afraid.* (John 14:27)

This peace can only be understood by those who know Jesus. This inner peace exists regardless of what the circumstances are.

In part, Jesus is your *"Wonderful Counselor, Mighty God, Everlasting Father, Prince of Peace."* What awe, strength, and peace we have in this knowledge!

NOVEMBER 28

Watch For Those Interceptions

You were running a good race. Who cut in on you and kept you from obeying the truth?
(Galatians 5:7)

Suppose a man decides he would like to build a cabinet, but he doesn't have any training or experience in carpentry. He begins by taking a course called "How to Build Your Own Cabinet." He gathers all the necessary materials and is given access to specialized tools in the workshop. He begins the project with great enthusiasm.

The first session ends before his project is finished. He gathers up his work, and after receiving some further instruction heads home to continue. As he works on the cabinet, he tries to remember and execute all the things the instructor told him. At one point, he realizes he doesn't have all the right tools, or perhaps he forgets a step. Then someone else happens by. After some discussion, the first person decides to follow the advice of the second person instead of going back to consult the expert, and continues on with the project. Imagine his surprise when he returns to class the following session and compares his work to that of the master, only to find his item sadly lacking. How discouraging!

That is a lot like Christians. We are full of good intentions and enthusiasm about doing the Father's work. We try our best to be obedient to God and be of good will. We believe in Jesus, confess that He is our Lord, and have been washed clean of our sins in His name. 2 Corinthians 5:17 tells us we have become a new creation. We are headed in the right direction!

Then we find ourselves ill-equipped. Now what? The choice is ours. Do we return to the master (God), or listen to those who are not the true master?

Don't let Satan sidetrack you from the good work you have begun. Watch out for those interceptions!

NOVEMBER 29

You Are God's Delight

The Lord your God is with you, he is mighty to save. He will take great delight in you, he will quiet you with his love, he will rejoice over you with singing.
(Zephaniah 3:17)

We all have times in our lives when we experience worry, concern, or other forms of stress. That is when we really need to hang on to the fact that our *"God is with [us], he is mighty to save."* He's got us covered. It doesn't matter what it may look like from our viewpoint; God knows what He is doing!

What is even more amazing is that God takes *"great delight"* in each of us. He doesn't just tolerate us. He is not frustrated, disgusted, or disappointed in any of His children. He doesn't just overlook our flaws. He may not condone some of the things we do or think, but He continues to love us with His unconditional love.

When everything around us is in turmoil, we can find peace through Jesus Christ as we relinquish our cares to Him. *"He will quiet [us] with his love,"* if we let Him. There is a peace that makes no worldly sense, but is experienced as we rest in Him.

God *"[rejoices] over [us] with singing,"* and will continue to do so. This is future tense. It does not say, "He used to take delight in you" or "He used to rejoice over you with singing before you blew it." He loves us so much that He celebrates us by singing! Thank God! How amazing is that?

Now, the question is, do you think your concern is more than God can handle? Do you believe and trust Him to take care of it? Have you really turned the concern over to Him and *let go of it*? Our human nature often tempts us to keep our hands on the issues we try to give God, or to even take it back. Trust Him! Quiet yourself and rest in His arms. Listen for His creative solution and be prepared to act and speak only when you feel His presence guiding you.

NOVEMBER 30

The Devil Did Not Make You Do It

No temptation has seized you except what is common to man. And God is faithful; he will not let you be tempted beyond what you can bear. But when you are tempted, he will also provide a way out so that you can stand up under it.
(1 Corinthians 10:13)

A few decades ago, there was a saying going around: "The devil made me do it." It was used as an excuse for every wrongdoing, from little issues to big ones. I think there might have even been bumper stickers with this saying. People thought it was funny. I even heard Christians laugh and use the saying!

The devil doesn't have any more power over us than we give him. As Christians, we have invited Jesus Christ into our lives and have chosen to give Him reign. The devil cannot overpower the Holy Spirit within us. 1 John 4:4 tells us that *"the one who is in you is greater than the one who is in the world."* If we give in to temptation, it is because we have chosen to follow the world, or the devil's way. God will not force us to follow Him.

Do we face temptations? You bet! Every human will. Even Jesus was taken into the desert and tempted after His baptism. However, we are promised that *"God is faithful; he will not let you be tempted beyond what you can bear."* We are never left alone. When you face those temptations, God has promised to *"provide a way out so that you can stand up under it."* I don't know exactly what that way will be, but I encourage you to look to God and not to things of this world for your way out.

"Yes," you may say, "but you don't know the temptation I'm facing." No, I don't, but God does. No matter what it is—even if it's addiction, greed, or lust—God is there to point you in the way you should go. He is the way to wholeness.

DECEMBER 1

Pride or Humility

When pride comes, then comes disgrace, but with humility comes wisdom. (Proverbs 11:2)

In the book of Esther, we read about Haman and Mordecai.

Haman boasted to them about his vast wealth, his many sons, and all the ways the king had honored him and how he had elevated him above the other nobles and officials. (Esther 5:11)

Haman was full of himself! He had wealth, a large family (a status symbol in his day), and a successful career. In fact, the king had given Haman his signet ring (Esther 3:10), essentially giving Haman the authority of the king. I'm not saying that one cannot be blessed, but Haman's boastful attitude was his downfall. In addition, Haman unfortunately chose poor advisors in his friends and his wife. Proverbs 12:26 says, *"A righteous man is cautious in friendship, but the way of the wicked leads them astray."* Haman's evil plots led to his own demise. He was humiliated and eventually killed in the manner he had planned for another.

Mordecai was a humble man of God. His faith was strong, and he refused to bow to evil Haman as a divine being. Mordecai took in his cousin Esther when she was orphaned. He raised her and gave her wise counsel. When Mordecai learned of a plot to assassinate the king, he quietly revealed the information. Mordecai never looked for a reward or recognition. His motive was righteousness. Mordecai, through Esther, saved the lives of all the innocent Jewish people Haman had plotted to annihilate.

The story ends with Mordecai replacing Haman as the king's right-hand man. Unlike Haman, who had commanded the people to honour him, *"Mordecai…[was] held in high esteem by his many fellow Jews, because he worked for the good of his people and spoke up for the welfare of all the Jews"* (Esther 10:3). Both men rose to great wealth, power, and success. Haman, however, ended in disgrace and death.

Where will your blessings take you?

DECEMBER 2

How Well Do You Know God's Word?

Now the Bereans were of more noble character than the Thessalonians, for they received the message with great eagerness and examined the Scriptures every day to see if what Paul said was true.
(Acts 17:11)

I am going to suggest something a little different today. Let's look at some common deceptions about well-known Bible stories.

What was the forbidden fruit that Adam and Eve ate? Did you say an apple? Then you should reread Genesis 3. What creature swallowed Jonah? Did you say a whale? Then you should review the book of Jonah; particularly the first chapter. How many stones did David gather up when preparing to confront Goliath? Consult 1 Samuel 17 to see if you are right.

These may be small details in the scope of God's whole message, but my point is to make you question your knowledge of God's word. How do you know when you meet a false prophet or teacher if you don't make yourselves aware of the truths in God's inspired word, the Bible? The Lord has provided us with many good Christian teachers. Each of them, however, is human. Understandings, interpretations, and communications will sometimes be flawed. Whether that misinformation is intentional or not, we must be diligent in verifying whether it is true according to the scriptures.

The best way to make yourselves more familiar with the scriptures is to read them regularly. Today's verse suggests that you make time *"every day."* You are not a failure if you miss a day; you are more successful every day that you do spend time in His word.

Happy reading! May you be filled more and more each day with the knowledge and wisdom of God!

DECEMBER 3

Understanding Scripture

Trust in the Lord with all your heart and lean not on your own understanding.
(Proverbs 3:5)

It is easy for most people in Canada to pick up a Bible and read it. They can read it, listen to it on CD, study it, and even memorize it. However, none of these methods in themselves will give them understanding of the scriptures. Understanding will only come by asking for and receiving it through Jesus Christ.

In Romans 15:21, we read *"Those who were not told about him will see, and those who have not heard will understand."* Clearly, understanding is not *just* in the hearing or reading of the word. The Bible refers to asking for "understanding" in a number of places.

Let me understand the teaching of your precepts; then I will meditate on your wonders… Give me understanding, and I will keep your law and obey it with all my heart. (Psalm 119:27, 34)

We also read that "understanding" is God-given.

But it is the spirit in a man, the breath of the Almighty, that gives him understanding. (Job 32:8)

Luke speaks of Jesus giving His followers understanding of the scriptures.

Then he opened their minds so they could understand the Scriptures. (Luke 24:45)

Also, when Jesus met the two disciples on the road to Emmaus, He taught them. When He left them,

They asked each other, "Were not our hearts burning within us while he talked with us on the road and opened the Scriptures to us?" (Luke 24:32)

So that's the secret! Ask God to give you understanding of the scriptures. As you *"meditate on [His] wonders"* and keep His law in your heart, *He* will grant you understanding. No matter whom you are, what your education level is, or how long you have been a Christian, only God will open your mind. Just ask.

DECEMBER 4

Praise God and Pass the Ammunition!

May the praise of God be in their mouths and a double-edged sword in their hands…
(Psalm 149:6)

A sword is a weapon of war. At first glance, today's verse may seem a bit confusing. We are encouraged to praise God, which is a very joyous attitude. Then it tells us to have a double-edged sword in our hands, which is a very deadly weapon. When you picture killing someone with a sword, joy is not the expected emotion!

The double-edged sword in this case refers spiritually to the word of God: *"Take the helmet of salvation, and the sword of the Spirit, which is the word of God"* (Ephesians 6:17). Yes, the sword is a weapon of offence. The sword of the spirit is an offensive weapon meant to fight in the spiritual realm. Fend off and defeat the attacks of the enemy in the power of the Lord! A physical sword can only kill the body, bringing separation of the body from soul and spirit. The spiritual sword separates only the soul and spirit. The use of a spiritual double-edged sword is done in love and mercy. It may hurt for a time, but the purpose is to bring healing and eternal life. Hebrews 4:12 declares,

For the word of God is living and active. Sharper than any double-edged sword, it penetrates even to dividing soul and spirit, joints and marrow; it judges the thoughts and attitudes of the heart.

If we now look at today's verse with an understanding of the *"double-edged sword,"* it makes great sense! Praise God right out loud! Rejoice! Let that praise flow straight from the attitude of your heart, and therefore your thoughts. Add to that the *word* of God. How do you do that? Build up your ammunition supply. Spend time with God. Read the Bible (God-inspired scripture), listen to what He is saying to your spirit, and invite the Holy Spirit to fill you anew.

Let the word of God separate your sinful nature from your spiritual being, and *praise God, always!*

DECEMBER 5

Freedom

Now the Lord is the Spirit, and where the Spirit of the Lord is, there is freedom.
(2 Corinthians 3:17)

Freedom! We all dream of freedom. We seek the freedom to do what we want when we want. There used to be a financial commercial that talked about freedom at a certain age. They were referring to retirement and freedom from the commitment of having to go to work. Lottery commercials bombard us with suggestions of financial freedom, dreams of having more money than we could possibly ever spend. But what is true freedom?

True freedom is found in Jesus Christ. He died a horrible death to set each of us free from the grip of eternal death. Instead we have eternal life. We can have freedom from the lies, deception, and bindings of the evil one if we ask Jesus. Although we have been set free by the blood of Jesus, we are cautioned, *"Live as free men, but do not use your freedom as a cover-up for evil; live as servants of God"* (1 Peter 2:16). Also, *"You, my brothers, were called to be free. But do not use your freedom to indulge the sinful nature; rather, serve one another in love"* (Galatians 5:13). In fact, if we misuse the freedom we've been given through Jesus, we give up our freedom for the bindings of Satan again.

There is evil in this world. We are constantly attacked by sin and the demons of the evil one. We may think we're walking in freedom and then suddenly realize that we have allowed the enemy to slip in and bind us up. Thankfully, each time this happens, we can turn back to Jesus and ask Him to free us once more. As we invite the Holy Spirit to fill us anew, we will return to true freedom. If we are filled with His spirit, there will be no room for any other.

DECEMBER 6

The Next Generation

...what we have heard and known, what our fathers have told us. We will not hide them from their children; we will tell the next generation the praiseworthy deeds of the Lord, his power, and the wonders he has done. (Psalm 78:3–4)

We just had another baby dedication at church. What a beautiful observance and exciting time that always is. Relatives of the family attend, sometimes coming from a distance. Everyone, especially the baby, is all dressed up. After the church service, many families have some sort of gathering or party to celebrate.

I'm grateful that the church I attend realizes it is more than a ceremonial tradition. We recognize the parents' public declaration of their partnership with God. However, our entire church is asked to join together in supporting the family in instilling the knowledge of God—Father, Son, and Holy Spirit. Psalm 78 calls all of us to invest in the lives of the children, including those not yet born. We are to take the things of the Lord that have been revealed to us, and share that knowledge with the generations to come.

What's it to you? You might not even know this family personally. You might not even have children of your own. Well, what if the generations before you had not made such an investment? You may or may not have been raised in a Christian home. If you were, what a blessing! Still, you don't even know all those who in some way contributed to your coming to know Jesus. Thank the Lord for all those other people who chose to invest in your life even though you might not have been family.

Why? Psalm 79 ends this way:

Then we your people, the sheep of your pasture, will praise you forever; from generation to generation we will recount your praise. (Psalm 79:13)

DECEMBER 7

Christ-Like Relationships

Submit to one another out of reverence for Christ.
(Ephesians 5:21)

There's the word "submit" again! You will recall from a previous devotion that submit is defined as "to refer or present for criticism, judgment, or decision."[14] This, then, points to a respectful team attitude. The Apostle Paul is teaching that proper Christian personal relationships are mutually submissive based on *"reverence for Christ."*

I have a very people-orientated personality. I enjoy working in team environments where everyone has an invested interest. I believe in the old adage that "two heads are better than one." I have experienced over and over again how one person's idea is expanded and perfected by including the experience and knowledge of others. Nobody is an expert in everything! In a loving relationship, I can trust that the other person is concerned about me as much as I'm concerned for them. Sometimes, I also need to recognize that the other person may have more wisdom in a situation, or on a particular topic, than I do.

In our Christian personal relationships, it is expected that we have a mutual interest for the wellbeing of each other. Any decision or judgement should be made in light of each person's involvement. Our marriage relationship, of course, is the most crucial. Beyond the relationship in question is that with our children, other family members, friends, our church body, or our coworkers.

Why should you have mutual interest? *"Out of reverence for Christ."* You should be submissive because that's the way Christ wants you to be. Do you trust that God knows what is best? Do you believe that *"in all things God works for the good of those who love him, who have been called according to his purpose"* (Romans 8:28)?

To have a Christ-like relationship, you must be willing to be submissive.

---

[14] *The Winston Dictionary of Canadian English* (Toronto, ON: Holt, Rinehart and Winston of Canada, 1969), 714.

DECEMBER 8

Love Your Wife

May your fountain be blessed, and may you rejoice in the wife of your youth.
(Proverbs 5:18)

The book of Proverbs is known to be a collection of God-inspired wisdom. Proverbs 5 is devoted to instructing husbands in the wisdom of being faithful to their wives.

Being faithful in one's marriage appears to be a rather obvious virtue. The wisdom given in Proverbs 5, however, is about avoiding adultery. Those who enter into loving Christian marriages never intend to be unfaithful. It's not like one day a man wakes up from a perfect, loving relationship and decides, "Gee, I think today I'll go looking for someone else." Subtle, unchecked temptations permit the sin and poor choices to multiply. The author of Proverbs acknowledges the temptation that may rear its head, but encourages men to avoid enticing opportunities: *"Keep to a path far from her, do not go near the door of her house"* (Proverbs 5:8). Don't go there!

Instead, the author encourages husbands to focus on the blessing of their own wives. *"Drink water from your own cistern"* (Proverbs 5:15) and *"Let them be yours alone, never to be shared with strangers"* (Proverbs 5:17). The author goes on to counsel the enjoyment of a healthy sexual relationship only in marriage.

My husband and I have been blessed with over thirty years of marriage, and we still want to be married to one another! Neither of us has taken our marriage for granted. This year, we have witnessed a few couples we know celebrate their sixtieth anniversaries together. What an encouragement!

May you be blessed to have a mutually pure, loving relationship with your spouse. Protect the blessing of that relationship. Avoid temptations and situations that would distract you from your marriage relationship. Rejoice in the spouse you have taken!

DECEMBER 9

He Is Listening

Hear my prayer, O Lord; let my cry for help come to you.
(Psalm 102:1)

I have recently heard someone say, "I tried talking to God, but He isn't listening." I know the feeling. I've gone through difficult times when it seemed like God just wasn't listening to me. It's not true! I was the one not listening. I was unable to hear or see His response at the time.

When you cry out to the Lord, He is *always* there and will *always* hear you. Psalm 145:18 tells us, *"The Lord is near to all who call on him, to all who call on him in truth."*

Then why doesn't He seem to answer? That's a question each of us needs to ask in each situation. Some possibilities might be:

1. I'm too busy doing all the talking.
2. I'm telling Him how I think He should deal with the problem. In His wisdom, He knows it is not the best solution. In other words, "No."
3. He is answering, but I'm just not listening to what He's saying, or I don't like the answer so I'm ignoring it.
4. I'm too distracted by focusing on my issue.
5. I'm holding on to a sin. *"If I had cherished sin in my heart, the Lord would not have listened"* (Psalm 66:18).

What are we to do? *"Let us then approach the throne of grace with confidence, so that we may receive mercy and find grace to help us in our time of need"* (Hebrews 4:16). Be assured that He is listening! *"Before they call I will answer; while they are still speaking I will hear"* (Isaiah 65:24).

It is good to talk to the Lord. He does care. It is good to present your situation to Him. Then prepare your heart to hear, and as Samuel did in 1 Samuel 3:10, say, *"Speak, for your servant is listening."* Then, *"Be still, and know that [He is] God"* (Psalm 46:10).

Trust Him to know what is best. He sees the whole picture. Be willing to be the listener.

DECEMBER 10

Go and Tell It Everywhere

Come and listen, all you who fear God; let me tell you what he has done for me.
(Psalm 66:16)

In the moment, we think we will always remember and treasure special moments. Before long, it becomes, "Remember when What's-His-Name said something about…?" Or, "It was around such-and-such year, I think." I'm finding as I get older and busier, my memory fails me more and more often.

Remember the Israelites? God brought them out of slavery in Egypt to the Promised Land! He performed numerous miracles along the way. The Lord directed them to create certain reminders along the way and to tell their children what He had done. Why? Do you think God needed the ego boast? No! It was so that the Israelites wouldn't forget. Who would forget things like the parting of the Red Sea, you ask? Apparently the Israelites did. Again and again, they became disgruntled and questioned whether or not God knew what He was doing.

God instructs us to tell others about what He has done for us.

> *Go home to your family and tell them how much the Lord has done for you, and how he has had mercy on you.* (Mark 5:19)

> *Tell it to your children, and let your children tell it to their children, and their children to the next generation.* (Joel 1:3)

We need to tell others about the things God has done for us, not for God's bragging rights, but so that *we* remember, and as a witness to others. There's something about verbalizing what God has spoken to us, or done for us, that helps it sink into the core of our beings. It encourages us to trust in His will for future things. It creates confidence in Him. As the song goes, "Go tell it on the mountain. Go and tell it everywhere." It should be our joy and pleasure to share how awesome our God is! Ultimately, in sharing our blessings, we will bring glory to God!

DECEMBER 11

Prayer Changes Things

So Peter was kept in prison, but the church was earnestly praying to God for him.
(Acts 12:5)

If you have ever wondered if prayer really makes a difference, I would encourage you to read Acts 12. King Herod was out to persecute the followers of Jesus. In verse 2, we read that he had already killed James. Then, in verse 3, Herod had Peter arrested with the intent of having a public trial. The trail was, of course, meant as an attention-seeking event for the king himself, with the purpose of making a show of executing Peter for the people's approval.

However, today's verse indicates a very important intervention. We read that *"the church was earnestly praying to God for [Peter]."* What was the result? Peter was miraculously freed by *"an angel of the Lord"* (Acts 12:7). Peter not only survived, he went on to witness and teach others, building up the church of God.

I want you to notice a couple of things. First, the church prayed for Peter. The church is not a building! The church is each member of that particular group of believers. They were united in their intercession for Peter. Peter didn't have to do it all on his own. Secondly, Peter had to respond to what the angel of the Lord said. It wasn't enough to pray and then carry on doing things just as he had been. Peter had to do things as the Lord directed him. He had to listen and then take action.

Your prayers do matter. They matter when you talk to the Lord on your own behalf, and when you pray intercessory prayers for others. When Christians pray in unity about anything that is of the will of God, their prayers are answered. Listen carefully! It is important that when you pray, you are willing to hear what God says. Don't be tempted to tell God how you want things done. His ways are good. Be prepared to respond to what He tells you.

DECEMBER 12

Pure and Clean

The voice spoke to him a second time, "Do not call anything impure that God has made clean."
(Acts 10:15)

The Law of Moses prohibited the eating of certain foods. Eating any of those foods would make the person eating it "unclean." In Acts 10, the Lord offered Peter those foods to freely eat. Peter was shocked!

"Surely not, Lord!" Peter replied. "I have never eaten anything impure or unclean."
[The Lord] spoke to him a second time, "Do not call anything impure that God has made clean." (Acts 10:14–15).

As we read on, we find that God was teaching Peter a lesson about people. Jesus died for *everyone*, and will cleanse each person from their sins if they choose to believe in Him. Who are we to question Him?

Peter witnessed to the Gentiles and they were baptized by the Holy Spirit. We know that today Jesus continues to desire to reach *all* men and women, no matter who they are or what they have done in the past. He will wash each one clean.

That means you, too! If you have accepted Jesus Christ as your Lord and Saviour, confessed and repented of your sins, and asked Him into your life, you have been forgiven and cleansed. Who are you to call yourself *"impure or unclean"*? Don't you believe Jesus did a good enough job? Did He miss something? Of course not! Then don't remind Him again and again of the things you have confessed and repented of. They are done! God has forgotten about them. His forgiveness is sufficient! The only reason you need to even remember those sins is so that you don't repeat them. Learn from your mistakes and move on.

If you are ready, pray something like this: "Thank You, Jesus, for all You have done for me. Thank You for Your great mercy and forgiveness. Thank You for cleansing me and setting me free. Help me, Lord, to treasure and protect the purity You have given me. In the name of Jesus, Amen."

DECEMBER 13

Lessons from Barnabas

He was a good man, full of the Holy Spirit and faith, and a great number of people were brought to the Lord.
(Acts 11:24)

We can learn some important lessons from the life of Barnabas. According to Luke,

1. He was a good man.
2. He was full of the Holy Spirit and faith.
3. He fulfilled his purpose of leading others to the Lord.

It reminds me of the acronym KISS: "Keep It Simple, Stupid."

Barnabas *"was a good man."* He purposed to be the man the Lord wanted him to be. The evidence of his righteous living was visible to others. He was also *"full of the Holy Spirit."* How did he manage that? In faith, he would have asked for the Holy Spirit and received it. Jesus promised to send the Holy Spirit to be our counsellor and friend. Barnabas believed in that promise. Finally, *"a great number of people were brought to the Lord"* because of Barnabas. Barnabas fulfilled his God-given purpose.

What can we learn from Barnabas? We are to live righteous lives. People will be able to see the goodness in us and be drawn to want what we have. We are to invite the Holy Spirit into our lives and have the faith to believe He will come. Then we are to listen to the will of God through the Holy Spirit and walk in the ways the Holy Spirit directs us. That's it! God will do the rest.

Why do we humans complicate such an easy process? Why do we think God is going to make it hard for us to figure out? Why are we tempted to think that we need to help God perfect His work? Have faith that He knows what He's doing.

Keep it simple, and let God do the rest.

DECEMBER 14

Helping Hand

If one falls down, his friend can help him up. But pity the man who falls and has no one to help him up!
(Ecclesiastes 4:10)

Even Jesus received help. We read in John 19:17, *"Carrying his own cross, [Jesus] went out to the place of the Skull."* In the other three Gospels, we read that Simon from Cyrene was forced to carry the cross for Jesus. After reading the account of all the torture Jesus was put through, we can gather that Jesus began to carry His own cross but found it very difficult to do it alone. He accepted help.

It is not a sin to need help. There are times in life when one may feel bruised and weak from the many battles. God created us as social beings. He created Eve to be Adam's companion. He meant for us to be interdependent. There are many Biblical references to God's instruction to help the weak.

Blessed is he who has regard for the weak. (Psalm 41:1)

We who are strong ought to bear with the failings of the weak… (Romans 15:1)

…encourage the timid, help the weak, be patient with everyone. (1 Thessalonians 5:14)

When we are weak, God can do His work in us.

God chose the weak things of the world to shame the strong. (1 Corinthians 1:27)

…the Spirit helps us in our weakness. (Romans 8:26)

God will defend us in our weakness.

Defend the cause of the weak… (Psalm 82:3)

Thank God for the friend you have in your spouse. I would encourage you to turn to one another in times of weakness. It's okay to ask for help. One of the best ways to help one another in any situation is to pray together and utilize that third strand of strength you have in God. Remember that God uses moments of weaknesses to do His work in you. That's why the Apostle Paul spoke of being glad for his weaknesses.

None of us can compare to Jesus, yet even He accepted help.

DECEMBER 15

Blessings

May the Lord make your love increase and overflow for each other and for everyone else, just as ours does for you.
(1 Thessalonians 3:12)

1 Thessalonians is the Apostle Paul's letter of thankfulness, encouragement, and instruction to the Thessalonica church. He tells them how he prays to God in thankfulness, for *"your work produced by faith, your labor prompted by love, and your endurance inspired by hope in our Lord Jesus Christ"* (1 Thessalonians 1:3). Paul then blesses them with the verse above. One would have felt much support and love under Paul's leadership. This church went on to receive further instruction from Paul, given in such a loving way.

What can we learn from the Apostle Paul? Are we thankful for our spouses, and others in our lives? Do you let them know? Do you actually take time to thank God for each other regularly? Are your actions towards each other produced by faith, prompted by love, and your endurance inspired by hope? Are you able to receive and give instruction for and correction from one another, being confident that you are both striving for these attributes?

Do you purpose to bless one another? It doesn't have to be big or heavy. Simply saying "Have a good day" as you part ways in the morning is a blessing. Let your spouse know that you thank God for them and pray blessings on their lives. As you pour blessings on one another, can you see the fruit of those blessings overflowing into the lives of others around you and your spouse?

My prayer for each couple reading this devotion is this: may the Lord make your love increase and overflow for each other and for everyone else.

DECEMBER 16

Trust in the Lord

Do not let your hearts be troubled. Trust in God; trust also in me. (John 14:1)

God has blessed us with emotions, both good and bad. If we could not feel, we would not have the opportunities to experience joy, love, excitement, or compassion. However, we could not truly know those emotions without knowing sadness, worry, and anger.

Jesus spoke today's words to the disciples when He was preparing them for His departure from earth. Separation from Jesus! Now that would be distressing! Jesus admonished them not to *let* their hearts be troubled. That would indicate a conscious choice on the behalf of the disciples. Notice that Jesus didn't say He wouldn't *permit* or *allow* them to be troubled. Jesus was directing them to put their trust in God. The disciples were to take hope and comfort in knowing that God is in control.

Try to imagine a figure-skating couple. The male partner says, "Go ahead, jump! Trust me. I'll catch you." The female partner now has a choice. She might think about what will happen if her partner doesn't catch her. If he misses, she might get hurt. There is nothing she can do about it if he's not in the right place at the right time, or if he's not strong enough to hold her. On the other hand, she might know him well and from past experience know that he is strong and grabs her at the right time and in the right way. Together, they may perform a great routine! Even if she has had a good history with this partner, there is still the chance that this human may miss this time. What does she choose to do? Does she trust him?

Fortunately, our God doesn't miss. He is always there when we choose to go to Him. He knows exactly what to do. How well do you know Him? How much do you trust Him? Jesus has promised us, *"Peace I leave with you; my peace I give you"* (John 14:27). Receive it.

DECEMBER 17

Keeping the "Christ" in Christmas

This is how the birth of Jesus Christ came about...
(Matthew 1:18)

When I was still a very young woman, my dear grandmother expressed her distress at seeing "Xmas" written in place of "Christmas." To her, it meant taking the "Christ" out of Christmas. I took that to heart and I have never used "Xmas" again. It only takes a few more keystrokes or a bit more movement of the pen to write "Christmas" in full.

Since that time, I have learned that the letter "X" is the first letter of Christ in Greek and Roman. Therefore "Xmas" was actually meant as an abbreviation for "Christmas." If this is the intention, then using "Xmas" is not much different than using other common abbreviations, such as Mr. or Mrs.

However, I have noticed that our schools often have "winter concerts" (I've never heard of a school having a "summer concert.") Signs and cards wish us "Happy Holidays" or "Seasons Greetings." Do they mean "holidays" as in vacations? I suppose some people may be taking their vacation at this time of year. But "Seasons Greetings"? Do they mean "Winter Greetings"?

No, there is no harm in wishing others well at this time of year. I am certainly one of those people who loves to see the beauty of snow and will joyfully join into winter songs such as "Jingle Bells" or "Winter Wonderland." However, I do not do so to the exclusion of celebrating the wondrous miracle of Christmas.

Give your use of "Xmas" careful consideration. What does it represent to you? What might it convey to those you write to? Wintery songs, well wishes, and joyful gatherings are all fun, but let's keep the focus on Christ.

DECEMBER 18

The Candy Cane

...who Himself bore our sins in His own body on the tree, that we, having died to sins, might live for righteousness—by whose stripes you were healed. (1 Peter 2:24, NKJV)

Why do we have candy canes at Christmas? Legend has it that many years ago a candy maker in Indiana designed the candy cane to tell the true story of Christmas.

The shape of the candy cane resembles a shepherd's crook. Jesus Christ is often referred to as a shepherd in the Bible, and the Christians His sheep. The shepherd uses the crook to keep His sheep from wandering away and getting lost or hurt. Some people also believe the candy cane represents an upside down "J" for Jesus.

Although today's candy makers are getting more creative and secular, the original candy cane was white. The colour white represents purity. Jesus is pure and He has offered to wash all our sins away and make us "white," or pure in Him. Again, the candy makers of today have taken some liberty with the flavour of the candy cane, but the original one was peppermint. Peppermint is similar to "hyssop." In Old Testament times, hyssop was used for purification and sacrifice. This also signifies Jesus' purity and sacrifice for us.

Finally, let's look at the stripes referred to in today's verse. A candy cane's red stripes represent the stripes of blood on the body of Jesus Christ when He was whipped. He suffered such punishment and died on the cross for all who would believe in Him, that we might be washed clean of sin and have eternal life.

So, the next time you see or enjoy the taste of a candy cane, thank God. Thank God for sending His son Jesus to shepherd us and show us the way. Thank Jesus for His protection and sacrifice. Thank Him for His mercy.

Thank You, Jesus, that You are my shepherd and intercessor. Help me not to stray.

DECEMBER 19

The Christmas Tree

But the angel said to them, "Do not be afraid. I bring you good news of great joy that will be for all the people. Today in the town of David a Savior has been born to you; he is Christ the Lord."
(Luke 2:10–11)

I love Christmas and all the beauty of the season! To many people, the Christmas tree is the centre of their decorations for this very special celebration. But why a tree?

Martin Luther is credited with the initiation of this tradition. It is told that he brought a fir tree home one night to his family. They brought it inside and attached candles to the branches and lit them.

Many symbols are attributed to the tree. The fir tree is a symbol of fire or the spirit, as are burning candles. For safety and convenience, most people have now converted to light bulbs as representations of the candles. Jesus is, of course, the light of the world. It is rare indeed to find a Christmas tree without some form of lights.

We now use various types of trees, but they are traditionally an evergreen, which represents the eternity of the spirit. Oftentimes, the tree will be topped with an angel or star. An angel at the top represents the angel who appeared from heaven to announce *"the good news of… a Savior"* being born (Luke 2:10–11). A star represents the unusual star that appeared in the sky to lead the wise men to where Jesus was.

What a beautiful way of expressing our joy in celebrating the birth of Jesus Christ! Hopefully your Christmas tree inspires you to remember this joyous time of Jesus' birth. Perhaps it will even provide you with opportunities to retell the true meaning of Christmas.

Happy birthday, Baby Jesus!

DECEMBER 20

The Poinsetta

Where is the one who has been born king of the Jews? We saw his star in the east and have come to worship him.
(Matthew 2:2)

The poinsettia's original connection to Christmas came from Mexico. Legend has it that a poor child who wanted a gift for the baby Jesus collected weeds from the side of the road and placed them at the church altar on Christmas Eve. The story goes that the congregation witnessed the weeds, then known as "painted leaf" or "Mexican fire plant," turn into brilliant red and green flowers. The red colour was seen as a symbol of deep love for Jesus. The colour red symbolizes Jesus' blood in His sacrifice for us.

The ancient Aztecs considered this plant to be a symbol of purity. It is a representation of Jesus, who is the purest of all. The foliage pattern of the plant has been connected with the star of Bethlehem, which shone brightly in the sky the night of Jesus' birth.

It was years later, in 1826, when Joel Roberts Poinsett, a botanist and member of the South Carolina and U.S. House of Representatives, brought the plant back to the United States. The plant was then renamed "poinsettia." However, this beautiful plant's connection to Christmas remains to this day.

As we gaze upon its beauty, may we remember the heart of the child who desired to bless Jesus the best way he could. Like the little drummer boy in the Christmas song, this child did not look to what he did not have, but gave from his heart his love for Jesus.

How do you express your love to Jesus, not just at Christmas, but at all times?

DECEMBER 21

The Wise Men

…Magi from the east came to Jerusalem and asked, "Where is the one who has been born king of the Jews? We saw his star in the east and have come to worship him."
(Matthew 2:1–2)

How many wise men were there? Did you say three? Well, I'm sure you are not alone, but we really don't know how many there were. The Christmas story is often told with three wise men (or three kings), probably because that is the number of gifts mentioned in the Bible. Actually, these men were called "Magi." They were experts in the study of stars. They were obviously educated men, and hence were referred to as "wise men." It is only tradition that refers to them as kings.

The Magi brought gifts that would have been considered worthy to give to a king. The three different gifts mentioned are gold, frankincense, and myrrh. The gold is symbolic of Christ's deity, or His kingship. The frankincense represents the incense a priest would use to make an offering to the Lord. Therefore, it symbolizes Jesus' purity and priesthood. Finally, the myrrh would have been used as anointing and embalming oil. The embalming oil was a sign of Jesus' death and the critical role it is to the salvation of man.

The concept of the gifts and their significance is very interesting to contemplate. However, the gifts were not the focus of the Magi. The very first thing the Magi did upon finding Jesus was bow down and worship Him. Only then did they bring out their gifts to honour and bless Him.

Afterward, the Bible tells us they received a warning in a dream. They recognized the dream as being no random, ordinary dream, but insight from God. They got up and obeyed. Thank You, Lord, for the wisdom and obedience of the Magi. I pray that each of us would keep our focus on You as we continue to worship You and study Your word.

DECEMBER 22

Wreaths

Then they will go away to eternal punishment, but the righteous to eternal life.
(Matthew 25:46)

Christmas wreaths come decorated in a variety of beautiful ways. The one constant is the shape. A wreath is circular. Some believe this to symbolize the never-ending eternal love we have from our God. The evergreen that is usually used also represents everlasting life. No matter how the wreath is decorated, its beauty is only a shadow of the true love of Jesus.

Some people celebrate Christmas with an advent wreath. The word "advent" is defined as "the seasonal arrival of a person or thing."[15] As Christians, we are awaiting the arrival of the second coming of Jesus. The advent wreath has five candles on it—usually three purple ones, a pink one, and a white one in the centre. Starting four Sundays before Christmas, one candle is lit each Sunday in connection with a Bible reading and prayer. Then, on Christmas Day, the last candle is lit.

The purple candles represent the *hope* of Jesus' second coming; *peace*, or the Bethlehem candle (Jesus' birth place); and *love*, or the shepherds' candle. Purple is also considered the colour of royalty. The pink candle stands for the angel's proclamation of the *joy* of Jesus Christ's birth. Finally, the white candle symbolizes *Jesus Christ* in His complete purity.

- Hope: *"If only for this life we have hope in Christ, we are to be pitied more than all men."* (1 Corinthians 15:19)
- Peace: *"…resting on the hope of eternal life, which God, who does not lie, promised before the beginning of time…"* (Titus 1:2)
- Love: *"Greater love has no one than this, that he lay down his life for his friends."* (John 15:13–14)
- Joy: *"Rejoice in that day and leap for joy, because great is your reward in heaven."* (Luke 6:23)

May you receive the hope, peace, love, and joy of the season.

[15] Ibid., 9.

DECEMBER 23

Angels

But the angel said to them, "Do not be afraid. I bring you good news of great joy that will be for all the people."
(Luke 2:10)

Angels are one of the main symbols of a Christian Christmas. They are the messengers from God to man. It was, of course, an angel (Gabriel) who first spoke to Mary to tell her that God had chosen her to give birth to the Son of God. An angel also reassured Joseph that Mary had conceived by the Holy Spirit and that Joseph was still to marry her. It was also an angel that appeared to the shepherds to announce the good news. Then other angels joined in, praising God before returning to heaven (Luke 2:13–15).

The topic of angels would require a huge study on its own. It's easy to get caught up in things such as what they might look like, what different types there might be, whether we each have our own "guardian angel," and so on. What we read in the Bible about the Christmas story clearly indicates that angels are messengers from God. In Luke, we read that they can come to earth and return to heaven. We also read about how they join together and praise God.

Yes, it is nice to have cute or beautiful pictures of angels on cards, angel ornaments and tree tops, and little children dressed up as angels in plays. However, let us remember the angels' roles as messengers and worshipers of God. Let us follow their example, and with *"great joy"* tell the good news of the birth of our Saviour, who is the provider of salvation to *"all the people."* Let us join together to give thanks to Jesus Christ and worship the Lord our God.

DECEMBER 24

Santa Claus

On coming to the house, they saw the child with his mother Mary, and they bowed down and worshiped him. Then they opened their treasures and presented him with gifts of gold and of incense and of myrrh. (Matthew 2:11)

We have many different names and costumes to represent this symbol of Christmas. There is Santa Claus, Saint Nicholas, Kris Kringle, and Father Christmas. They each have a different costume, but they are all believed to come at some point in December and leave gifts for children.

Some Christians don't agree with acknowledging these Christmas symbols, as they believe it distracts from the true meaning of Christmas. Others object to the commercialism—or at the very least, that it is a lie.

Many Christians do not see any harm in this joyous tradition. For these people, it is a matter of the focus. Firstly, it is our responsibility as Christians to spread the good news of the true meaning of Christmas always, even if we don't have children. What an opportunity this season provides! Secondly, it is also up to us to teach and model responsible spending and thoughtful giving in expressing our love and blessings to others. Try to emphasize the giving aspect—be it material, talent, or time—and bless others in Jesus' name. Thirdly, as I have mentioned previously, I don't believe it is wrong to not be completely truthful when it is our purpose to surprise or bless another.

The wise men came to worship Jesus. Let us not miss out on that very crucial part of the story. Then they offered gifts to the child as a way of honouring and blessing Him. As we give this season, let it be with love and a desire to bless others, not begrudgingly or out of guilt.

May you receive the peace, joy, and love of the season!

DECEMBER 25

Don't Forget the Baby

Today in the town of David a Savior has been born to you; he is Christ the Lord.
(Luke 2:11)

This is what Christmas is really about. Hope. This is the remembrance of the day God sent His son Jesus to earth. His very being! Jesus Christ was born in the flesh. He was fully man and fully God. Jesus was born into our world and grew up like any other human. He was tempted in all the same ways each of us are. Yet Jesus was, and is, without sin.

Jesus' time on earth as a man enables us to wrap our mind around the fact that He can relate to our individual situations. He understands our human struggles. He has promised to intercede between us and our Father God. *"Therefore he is able to save completely those who come to God through him, because he always lives to intercede for them"* (Hebrews 7:25). Read that verse again, substituting your name for "those" and "them." Yes, it is personal!

Imagine Jesus Christ making such a great sacrifice just for you! Being sinless, He took upon Himself all of your sins and infirmities and died on the cross. Then He was raised from the dead and returned to heaven—all so that you and I, although we are undeserving, could have eternal life.

The exact date of Jesus Christ's birth can be debated, but the event cannot. This is indeed a great day to celebrate!

Merry Christmas!

DECEMBER 26

The Three of You

Again, I tell you that if two of you on earth agree about anything you ask for, it will be done for you by my Father in heaven. For where two or three come together in my name, there am I with them.
(Matthew 18:19–20)

You and your spouse make two. Therefore, today's verse tells us that when you pray together, Jesus is right there with you! You don't have to wait for Sunday morning, or the scheduled prayer meeting. Any and every time you join together with your spouse in prayer, Jesus is with you.

Does that mean you can ask for all your selfish desires and Jesus will grant your wishes like a fairy godfather? No! Jesus also said, *"And I will do whatever you ask in my name, so that the Son may bring glory to the Father"* (John 14:13). What is the purpose of your prayer? Is it all about you, or is it about glorifying the Father?

Hmm. Does that mean you are not to pray about any of your own needs? No. The point is that praying to win millions of dollars in the lottery so you can fulfill all your lustful, selfish needs, isn't what Jesus came to promise. It might be more in line to pray that He would help you find the right job to help support you and your family's needs, permitting you to bless others through your finances and possessions.

The important part of this verse is that Jesus is there with you. Don't forget to allow Jesus to contribute to your prayer time and requests. Are you seeking His will? Are you allowing Jesus to influence your heart's desires? Are you and your spouse in agreement? Remember, you are *"to come together in [Jesus'] name."*

Anything all three of you agree on, our Father in heaven will do. Pray wisely and in agreement.

DECEMBER 27

Powerful Christians

I tell you the truth, whatever you bind on earth will be bound in heaven, and whatever you loose on earth will be loosed in heaven.
(Matthew 18:18)

As Christians, we are blessed in knowing that we will have eternal life with Jesus. He has told us that we will actually rule with Him when He returns to earth in the second coming. In Matthew 18 Jesus, instructed His disciples in how they (and now all Christians) are to judge one another. This judgement is not meant to be a justification for being opinionated or throwing around the power He has given us. This judgement is to help us lovingly support one another to remain in the ways of the Lord and not be misled by the evil one.

In today's verse, Jesus has empowered us to bind up the work of Satan and free our fellow man from any bondage Satan has imposed on them. Although Satan has been given the world, we have been given authority over his works through the power given us through Jesus Christ! Wow!

With this blessing also comes a great responsibility. Satan would entice us to throw that power around. Do you curse or bind someone simply because they annoy you? Do you judge anyone simply because they have a different opinion or interpretation than you? Do you judge others based on appearance or gossip?

That power is very real! Before invoking judgement, seek God's wisdom and discernment. Ask Him to reveal the truth and how you should pray. Then, in the name of Jesus, go boldly forth and take control over the enemy! Don't let Satan win because of your apathy!

Jesus' intent was that we would be watchful over His sheep. Our motives are to be to guard His kingdom. God is to be glorified, not us! May His will be done.

DECEMBER 28

Knowing God

All that belongs to the Father is mine. That is why I said the Spirit will take from what is mine and make it known to you.
(John 16:15)

Jesus spoke these words to His disciples as He was preparing them for His imminent departure back to heaven. Jesus had told them that when He left, He would send the Holy Spirit to them to be their counsellor. This verse assured them that Jesus was one with Father God. Therefore, anything Jesus sent to them through the Spirit would be of the Father as well. Even though Jesus would not be with them in flesh anymore, the Holy Spirit would be able to continue to teach the apostles the truth. In so doing, the apostles were able to write down the teachings of Jesus, ultimately creating the New Testament. His word would be available to benefit generations to come.

Thank God for His precious word! By reading His word, we can learn what our purpose is. By reading His word, we know how to invite Jesus into our lives so that we, too, may receive the Holy Spirit as our counsellor. Yes, God has risen up some very good teachers of His word. We can learn much from those who have gone before us and who are blessed with the ability to instruct others. However, we are warned that *"there will be false teachers among you"* (2 Peter 2:1). The onus is on each of us to check what we are being taught against what God's word tells us—in the Bible and directly through the Holy Spirit.

If you aren't already doing so, I would encourage you to set aside time each day to read the Bible. Become familiar with the direct teaching of Jesus. I always find it amazing how God speaks to specific moments in my life through His word. Each time you read, invite the Holy Spirit to help you understand the truth of what God is saying to you.

DECEMBER 29

God's Arm is Not Too Short

In his distress he sought the favor of the Lord his God and humbled himself greatly before the God of his fathers. And when he prayed to him, the Lord was moved by his entreaty and listened to his plea; so he brought him back to Jerusalem and to his kingdom. Then Manasseh knew that the Lord is God.
(2 Chronicles 33:12–13)

Manasseh really blew it! Manasseh set up idols and worshiped many other gods.

He sacrificed his sons in the fire in the Valley of Ben Hinnom, practiced sorcery, divination and witchcraft, and consulted mediums and spiritists. He did much evil in the eyes of the Lord, provoking him to anger. (2 Chronicles 33:6)

As king, he also influenced his people into these horrific practices. This is much more serious than a child who is being disobedient to a human parent! The anger of a parent is distressing enough, but to anger God?

As a result, Manasseh was taken into captivity. He was bound and treated poorly. Finally, Manasseh realized the error of his ways. Today's verse was Manasseh's entreaty to God and God's response. Our God is a loving god, full of grace and mercy! Keep in mind that God knows our true hearts. There is no fooling or manipulating God. It's not like a child who says sorry because his parent told him to, but really he just wants to get out of the current trouble.

Be encouraged if loved ones have strayed from the ways of God. Continue to pray for recognition of God and His righteousness. Pray that God would soften their hearts and allow the Holy Spirit to enter their lives anew. When they humble themselves and repent, God will be there no matter how far they have strayed or what they have done.

God's arm is not too short. Trust in Him!

DECEMBER 30

Be Joyful!

Shout for joy to the Lord, all the earth.
(Psalm 100:1)

Praise the Lord!

Sometimes we have difficulty *feeling* like being joyful. At times in our lives, "joy" is definitely not the first word to come to mind when someone asks, "How are you doing?" No matter what your current response to that question is, I would encourage you to endeavour to *"shout for joy to the Lord."*

Why? Because our God is amazing! He is the one true God, a mighty God! He is omnipotent and omnipresent! Our God is merciful, gracious, forgiving, loving, our protector, our provider, our comforter, our strength, our creator, and the list goes on! Our joy is in the Lord, not in our circumstances.

Thankfully, God is always with us. He will never leave us or forsake us. When there is a separation, it is on the part of man. As we focus on the Lord and not on ourselves, we can't help but be joyful. Will that make our not-so-joyful circumstance disappear? Probably not. However, as we turn our eyes towards God, we receive His great blessings. He will meet all our needs, whether material, emotional, physical, or spiritual. Not only that, He will provide what He knows is best for us in His eternal view, not through our limited human view.

Go ahead and rejoice! Let the world see your joy and gladness. May the people in your circle of influence see that joy and seek what you have. Joy, like laughter, is contagious. Most of all; be joyful because we have great reason in our God!

For the Lord is good and his love endures forever; his faithfulness continues through all generations. (Psalm 100:5)

DECEMBER 31

Reflections

The Lord bless you and keep you; the Lord make his face shine upon you and be gracious to you; the Lord turn his face toward you and give you peace.
(Numbers 6:24–26)

On this last day of our calendar year, we often turn to reflections. We reminisce about the major, and not-so-major, events of this past year and perhaps the years before. I ask you this: what was the most memorable event of this past year for you? What is your first thought? How did that event affect your life? Did it encourage you, enlighten you, or perhaps mark a turning point for you?

I would encourage you to pause and take time to really think about this question and your response. Talk about it with your spouse. Consider the ramifications.

Now, I ask another question: God willing, what are your plans for the coming year? Take time to discuss what you might want to accomplish as individuals, and as a couple. Try to set some measureable goals where possible. For example, it is well-intended to say, "I want to make a difference for Jesus," but consider how that might look. Perhaps your goal could be, "I want to participate in supporting the homeless by working in the food bank once a month." I would also encourage you to consider some personal goals to help further develop your relationship with Jesus.

Please understand that I'm not asking you to make New Year's resolutions. This is not about fresh starts or unrealistic short-term goals. I'm suggesting life changes and development. You have permission to make mistakes without being a complete failure. When things don't go the way you planned, re-evaluate at any point, not necessarily on December 31. Make adjustments and strive forward again in the name of Jesus.

God knows your heart's intent. May He bless you greatly in your future as you work out your path for His glory.

VERSES AND DATES BY TOPIC

- **Anxiety/Fear:** Philippians 4:6–7 January 26; Luke 10:41 May 6; 1 Kings 17:16 June 25; 2 Kings 6:17 July 5; Proverbs 18:10 July 21; July 26; 3 Timothy 1:7 July 29; 2 Kings 5:20 August 18; Philippians 2:5 August 19; Acts 5:2 August 25
- **Attitude:** Acts 21:38 January 23; James 5:12 January 30; Hebrews 10:24 February 13; Ephesians 4:29 February 21; Matthew 13:44 February 22; Philippians 4:8 January 25 & September 12; Matthew 25:29 April 5; Matthew 23:27 April 7; Deuteronomy 25:15–16 April 12; Deuteronomy 17:14 April 13; Deuteronomy 8:17–18 April 17; Luke 6:45 April 19; Mark 2:21 June 12; 1 John 2:11 May 24; Psalm 19:14 May 25; 1 Peter 2:1 May 29; Psalm 139:24 July 14; Hebrews 13:15 July 15 & August 16; Psalm 26:2 July 23; Proverbs 18:21 August 3; 2 Chronicles 19:7 August 10; Psalm 100:1 December 30; Ephesians 5:21 March 15 & December 7;; Acts 15:8 September 5; Romans 12:2 September 11; Acts 19:32 September 19; Psalm 45:7 October 1; Psalm 90:12 October 6; Romans 6:13 October 14; 1 Corinthians 10:23 November 6; Psalm 15:1 November 14; Proverbs 15:1 September 27; Ecclesiastes 3:12–13 November 18
- **Blessings:** 1 Thessalonians 5:11 May 28; 2 Samuel 22:20 June 10; Ecclesiastes 3:13 October 10; Psalm 6:8 September 9; Psalm 90:17 September 14; 1 Corinthians 8:3 November 15; Galatians 4:6 November 26
- **Children:** Psalm 127:3 January 6; Matthew 19:14 July 3; Deuteronomy 6:7 April 8; Leviticus 20:1 May 3; Judges 13:8 June 3; 2 Kings 22:1–2 July 12; Psalm 33:6 August 2; Psalm 78:3–4 December 6; Acts 20:32 September 22; Psalm 78:4 October 15; Genesis 24:7 October 18
- **Christmas:** Matthew 1:18 December 17; 1 Peter 2:24 December 18; Luke 2:10–11 December 19 & 23; Matthew 2:2 December 20; Matthew 2:1–2 December 21; Matthew 25:46 December 22; Matthew 2:11 December 24; Luke 2:11 December 25
- **Comfort/Encouragement:** Deuteronomy 31:8 April 10; Zephaniah 3:17 April 23; Isaiah 43:2 April 25; Psalm 18:19 April 14; 1 Samuel 1:10 May 8; John 3:17 June 24; Zec 3:1–2 July 26; 2 Chronicles 33:12–13 December 29; Psalm 23:2 August 15; Psalm 23:6 September 24; 2 Chronicles 32:8 August 12; Acts 4:31 August 24; Jeremiah 24:7 August 28; John 10:29 August 31; Acts 17:11 December 2; Hebrews 3:13 September 4; Psalm 19:7 September 20; Acts 20:28 September 21; Psalm 24:1 September 23; Joshua 1:5 October 17; Psalm 121:7–8 March 28; 2 Corinthians 7:13 November 17
- **Companionship:** Genesis 2:18 February 1; Proverbs 19:13 September 1; Exodus 17:12 March 27; Ruth 1:16 May 7; Proverbs 27:17 August 5; Proverbs 17:9 August 21; Acts 17:23 October 13; 1 Corinthians 11:11–12 November 7; Song of Solomon 5:16 November 20
- **Difficult Times:** Matthew 7:24–25 January 3; Proverbs 22:6 February 5; Matthew 28:20 January 9; John 14:27 February 6; Hebrews 12:3 February 24; Genesis 50:19 March 18; Is 40:4 March 19; Exodus 18:17 March 30; Deuteronomy 8:2 April 16; Ruth 1:16 May 7; Psalm 109:22 June 4; Luke 21:15 June 5; 2 Samuel 22:7 June 9;

- **Tithes:** Luke 6:38 February 2; Leviticus 27:30 February 3; Matthew 6:21 February 4; 1 Samuel 30:23 May 22; Acts 5:2 August 25
- **Trust:** Genesis 17:21 February 26; 1 Corinthians 2:9 July 6; Psalm 33:6 August 2; John 14:1 December 16; Psalm 19:7 September 20; Psalm 127:1 October 28
- **Unity:** 3 Timothy 2:23 October 2; Luke 9:52 August 1; Mark 14:22–23 January 13; Hebrews 10:25 February 15; Luke 9:50 May 4; 1 Corinthians 12:18 May 15; Romans 15:5–6 May 18 & June 8; 1 Corinthians 12:18 May 19; Ephesians 4:15 June 17; 2 Corinthians 5:18–19 July 7; Romans 5:11 October 11
- **Wives/Women:** Proverbs 31:11–12 May 2; Ephesians 5:22 July 1; Proverbs 31:26–28 April 2; Ephesians 5:21 March 15 & December 7; Proverbs 12:4 May 20; Galatians 3:28 July 27; 1 Corinthians 7:4–5 October 8; 1Pe 3:3–4 November 10; Proverbs 14:1 November 12

To contact the author or send your comments,
please email Sheryl Sanderson at:
sanderson.publishing@gmail.com